Hendrik Visser, MD

Healing
For Your
Hurts

Essence
PUBLISHING

Belleville, Ontario, Canada

Healing for Your Hurts

Copyright © 2001, Hendrik Visser, MD

All Scripture quotations, unless otherwise specified, are from *The Holy Bible, New International Version*. Copyright © 1973, 1978, 1984 International Bible Society. Used by permission of Zondervan Publishing House. All rights reserved.

Scripture quotations marked (KJV) are from *The Holy Bible, King James Version*. Copyright © 1977, 1984, Thomas Nelson Inc., Publishers.

ISBN: 1-55306-233-7

First Printing, March 2001
Second Printing, August 2001

Essence Publishing is a Christian Book Publisher dedicated to further-ing the work of Christ through the written word. For more information, contact: 44 Moira Street West, Belleville, Ontario, Canada K8P 1S3. Phone: 1-800-238-6376. Fax: (613) 962-3055. E-mail: info@essencegroup.com Internet: www.essencegroup.com

Printed in Canada
by

Essence
PUBLISHING

To my wife, Cathy,
and my sons,
Andrew and Nathan.

Table of Contents

My Deepest Appreciation to... 11
Foreword 13
Introduction 15

PART I: WHY AM I SICK? 19

Chapter 1: What Do Today's Thinkers Say? 21

WHAT DO SCIENTISTS SAY? 24
    What is science? 25
    What does science say about why I am sick? 28
    Darwinian medicine 33

WHAT DO ALTERNATIVE HEALERS SAY? 36
    Why is Alternative Medicine becoming so popular? . . 37

CAM disease theory 40

CAM practitioners and holistic medicine 42

Chapter 2: What Does God Say? 43

THE BIBLE ON ORIGINS 44

Paradise lost 47

Is the biblical source of evil plausible? 48

RELATIONSHIP OF SIN AND SICKNESS 50

Spiritual health promotes physical health 50

God's punishment of sin. 51

Sickness and the work of the demonic realm. 51

Sickness and individual sin. 52

Chapter 3: Toward a Proper Worldview 55

DOES A SPIRITUAL REALM EXIST? 57

EVIDENCE THAT THE SPIRITUAL REALM EXISTS 57

1. The need for a "Master Designer"
to explain the cosmos. 57

2. Third-World experiences 60

3. The historical/archaeological evidence
that the Bible is true. 61

4. The experience of believers throughout
the years 67

TOWARD A CORRECT WORLDVIEW 69

Chapter 4: Why Am I Sick Now? 75

Is this a wake-up call? 77

Is my sickness the direct result of personal sin? 78

Is the demonic realm influencing me? 79

Is there a generational curse? 81

Am I being disciplined by God?. 82
Am I being tested by God?. 83
Have I abused the Lord's Supper? 84
Is there unresolved emotional baggage? 86
Are there unresolved relationships? 87
Is there secondary gain to my illness?. 89
Am I sick because of humanity's fallen state?. 90
Am I sick that God's work may be displayed? 91

PART II: HOW CAN I BE WELL?. 93

Chapter 5: What Can Your Healers Offer?. 95
WHAT DOES SCIENCE OFFER? 96
The role of science in medicine 97
Is there anything science cannot do? 101
WHAT DOES ALTERNATIVE MEDICINE OFFER? 102
Diagnostic techniques. 103
Therapeutic modalities. 107

Chapter 6: What Does God Offer?. 117
THE HEALING MINISTRY OF JESUS 118
Jesus granted eternal life. 119
Jesus exerted lordship over the created order 119
Jesus healed relationships 120
Jesus healed the sick and raised the dead 121
THE KINGDOM OF GOD. 123
THE HEALING MINISTRY OF THE CHURCH. 132
The Church as a healing community today. 133
The Community of the King. 135
The Church as the agent of the Kingdom 146

Chapter 7: Choose Your Healers Wisely 157

  Should I trust God for healing? 158

  What is the practitioner's worldview? 160

  Are there methods denounced by Scripture? 162

  Does science validate the healing discipline? 165

  Is the practitioner a "mixer?" 166

  What is the role of financial gain? 166

  Is there doctor bashing? 168

  Is there unethical promotion or advertising? 170

  What about healing crusades? 171

"BE HOLY" 174

PART III: YOUR PERSONAL JOURNEY
        TOWARD WHOLENESS 179

Chapter 8: Finding Your Place in the Cosmos 181

KNOW GOD 182

  Be a worshiper 183

  An undivided heart 188

  Know your enemy 190

KNOW YOURSELF 192

  Not an animal 193

  In Christ, I am 195

  Be filled with the Holy Spirit 200

  My body—a temple of the Holy Spirit 204

Chapter 9: Living Well—By the Manual 211

"SIX DAYS YOU SHALL LABOUR" 213

  Sabbath rest 215

"PHYSICAL TRAINING IS OF SOME VALUE" 219

"FOOD DOES NOT BRING US NEAR TO GOD". 221
    Balancing spirituality and science. 225
    What about pesticides and genetic modification? . . . 226
    What about vitamins and supplements?. 228
"MARRIAGE SHOULD BE HONOURED BY ALL" 231
"DO NOT GET DRUNK WITH WINE" 234

Chapter 10: Healing past wounds. 237
THE WOUNDS THAT FESTER 239
    Sources of wounding 239
    How our past affects our present 241
    Evidence of wounding 244
FINDING HEALING. 247
    Keys to freedom 249

Chapter 11: Aging with Grace 255
WHAT HAPPENS WHEN WE AGE 257
    Use it or lose it 259
PLANNING FOR ELDERCARE. 261
    Your own eldercare 262
    Your parent's eldercare 264
    Health-care directives 265

Chapter 12: Facing loss with dignity 269
UNDERSTANDING LOSSES 271
    Turning to God in our losses 275
    When God does not heal now 278
    You *are* healed—in Christ 278
DEATH—FRIEND OR FOE?. 280
    Death—the doorway to heaven 281

   Toward a Christian view of death. 282
   How to prepare for death 284
GRIEVING YOUR LOSS 284

Epilogue 287

Appendix A:
   FINDING PEACE WITH GOD 289

Appendix B:
   ASSESSING HEALING ARTS. 293

Appendix C:
   PRAYER FOR PERSONAL HEALING 303
   RELAXATION & MEDITATION PRAYER 305
   WARFARE PRAYER 307
   PRAYER FOR THE CHURCH TO BE HEALING
      FOR THE NATIONS. 309

Appendix D:
   ACCOUNTABILITY QUESTIONS FOR MEN 311

Endnotes 313
Order Information. 319

My Deepest Appreciation to...

My wife, Cathy, who is my most cherished friend on earth. I am so grateful that God joined us together. Your support and perseverance as a prayer warrior are constant sources of strength and inspiration. You are truly a blessing to me.

My sons, Andrew and Nathan, for your help around the home and in our clinic so this project could be completed. You boys are a joy to my heart and I love you both. God bless you as you start your life's journey.

My pastor, Dwight Ingersoll, for encouragement and prayer, and for helpful suggestions. Special thanks to Dr. H.C. Wilson for kindly writing the forward, for your helpful comments, and for your desire to see the Church move ahead as a healing community.

My adult Sunday school class at Island Wesleyan Church, for allowing me to try out some of these ideas. I pray that we may increasingly become a therapeutic community where we can be our best for God.

My brother, John, for the challenge and encouragement to proceed with this project. And to David, and the folks at Essence, for putting it all into a beautiful book.

My colleagues in medicine. A special thanks to Dr. Marvin Clark for "taking me under your wing" when we returned from Africa, and helping us get established. You were like a dad to me.

Above all, to God, for the inspiration to put these thoughts on paper. To Him be all the glory.

Foreword

It has been a perpetual quest. Sometimes pursued with extreme passion. Sometimes following after teachers and methods that could only be fairly described as "quackery." Sometimes immersed in superstition. Sometimes as a "guinea pig" for some new drug regimen. Sometimes with the investment of huge sums of money. Sometimes undergoing treatment or ingesting potions at great personal risk. Why is this elusive prize so highly valued: wellness, wholeness—even immortality?

As you read and ponder the content of this book, you will recognize early and often that Dr. Visser has approached this ancient quest from a studied and Christ-centred perspective. While consistently warning against aberrant teaching and practices that falsely promise wellness and wholeness, he thoughtfully and clearly directs us to the true source of wellness, wholeness, and even immortality.

The author is uniquely equipped to address this issue. He is a medical doctor. His career has seen expression through resident practice both in North America and in Africa. He has not only been a consistent and sensitive provider of medical treatment and counsel but has also been a consistent and sensitive Christian. You will sense repeatedly the gentle blending of the scientific and the divine. You will sense repeatedly the tactful exposure of error and the clear primacy of God's Word.

You will find both thoughtful explanation and practical application in the pages that follow. As you enter this journey of discovery, it is my prayer that the only true source of wellness, wholeness, and immortality will be a powerful reality in your own life.

It is my privilege to commend this book to you. Any serious study of unfamiliar terrain—like the topic under consideration—often produces appropriately searching questions. It is often through such mental and spiritual stimuli that new discoveries are realized. Read on with a searching spirit and an open mind. Enjoy the journey.

H.C. Wilson
District Superintendent
Atlantic District of the Wesleyan Church

Introduction

Everyone longs for the most out of life. We all want wholeness—physical health, emotional happiness, deep loving relationships, and peace and meaning in life. But can it be found?

Elaine was one such person. She had just moved to rural Prince Edward Island from Toronto, hoping the slower pace of life and cleaner air would help the chronic pain of her fibromyalgia. She came to my clinic in the hopes that I would be her family physician. On her first visit, we delved into her life story.

Elaine's childhood was unhappy and she had been sexually violated by a close relative at the age of thirteen. Her adult life was marked by depression and frequent visits to her family doctor for fatigue and numerous pains. She had been prescribed an antidepressant on several occasions. Her marriage had ended in a bitter custody battle which left her broken and bitter. Over the next several years she saw a number of specialists about her chronic pain and had many investigations which included x-rays, ultrasounds, CAT scans, MRI's, and endoscopies. Her medical file grew fat and heavy, but no one seemed to be able to help her. Her daily pain and fatigue intensified.

About a year before she moved to Prince Edward Island, a friend encouraged her to see a naturopathic doctor. He took the time to listen to her story and seemed very compassionate. Over several visits he embarked on a treatment regimen for her that included homeopathic medicine, acupuncture, dietary modification and vitamins. He encouraged her to meditate and visualize a healthier future.

Elaine started to experience marked improvement in her symptoms. Her depression lifted. At this point her company was downsized and she was given the opportunity for early retirement. She remembered vacations on P.E.I. as a child and dreamt of retiring here. She bought a beautiful property by the water and built a dream home. Shortly her unhappiness came back, however, and intense loneliness set in. She started to experience severe headaches and the fatigue returned. She slept poorly and spent most of the night worrying about cancer. That's when I met her.

Like Elaine, many search for wholeness, but most never achieve the level of satisfaction in life that they dream or hope for. With the frailties of the human body and emotions which are wounded ever so easily, suffering seems universal to the human experience. From the day of our birth we are all on a one-way journey toward our own mortality. Add to that the threat of environmental collapse due to climate change or pollution, and overpopulation, and our future seems bleak and dismal.

In the midst of this human condition, many dangle carrots of hope for solutions to our problems. Medical scientists have frantically mapped our genetic blueprint in the hopes of extending our lives, maybe indefinitely. Alternative healers point out the failure of medical science to arrest the onslaught of chronic diseases such as arthritis, and they peddle their goods through network marketers and the Internet. Religious healers of various stripes, from psychic healers to healing evangelists tell us we can be healed miraculously through mind-over-matter, or by the power of God.

In this modern milieu of medicine, alternatives and religion, can we begin to find true wholeness? It is the premise of this book that we *can* by carefully integrating scientific and alternative medicine with a spiritual worldview that rationally explains the existence of the cosmos and the problem of suffering. By embarking on a personal journey toward wholeness we can receive true healing for our hurts.

In this book, wholeness refers to physical, mental, social, and spiritual wellness. Brokenness refers to suffering in one's physical body, one's emotional health, one's relationships with others, or in one's spiritual well-being.

Having practiced medicine in the African setting under a primary health-care model, as well as a family practice in North America, and having a life-long interest in holistic medicine, I have developed the philosophical framework outlined in this book through extensive reading and research. It is written with the patient in mind, but it may be valuable to healing practitioners or religious leaders.

Part I examines why the human race is plagued by sickness, aging, and death. In order to understand wholeness, we need to know why we are broken. Starting with science, we explore explanations such as genetics, micro-organisms, the environment and evolutionary theory. We then look at the contribution that various religions have made to this question. We will see how our worldview affects the way we understand our origins and the cause of illness, so we will examine the most common worldviews of our day. Having decided which view of reality accords the best explanation for the cosmos, we will then be able to look at ourselves and our particular brokenness.

Part II examines the human quest for health and immortality. From the dawn of human history, records tell of practitioners who have responded to the human condition with their healing arts. Their progress is briefly chronicled. Guidelines for choosing safely from among the many healers today are offered.

Part III is the practical application of how I believe we can move toward wellness and wholeness in this millennium. We will see how, using principles penned many centuries ago, we can stay healthy, live victoriously and face death with dignity and peace.

For the reader without medical or scientific background, sections in Parts I and II that are more technical in nature can be skimmed or skipped without losing the overall message of the book. Concentrate on the practical chapters on choosing your healers, and Part III.

The appendices contain additional practical information to help those who seriously wish to proceed in their journey to wholeness.

The medical stories which I have shared are mostly gleaned from my own practice. Some of them are composite. Names and identifying details have been changed to protect confidentiality. I am deeply grateful for those who have allowed their stories to be told.

If your quest for wholeness has brought you to this book, I trust that you will find new hope for a better tomorrow. While filled with practical advice on better living, it is not meant to replace quality care from your health practitioners. But I do hope that it will help you choose your healers carefully.

Hank Visser
Crapaud, Prince Edward Island

PART I:

Why Am I Sick?

Since the dawn of history, humankind has struggled against sickness, aging, and death. They continue to be staunch enemies. Always, there is the question "Why?" Whom you ask will determine the answer you are likely to receive. The scientific healer will base her answer on what she has learned from science. She is likely to talk about things like micro-organisms, genetics, and evolution. The alternative healer may say there is an imbalance in yin and yang or too much sugar in your diet. The theologian may say that we fail to live in harmony with the spirit world or that we fail to live up to a certain moral standard.

Which is true? Is there some truth in all? Can we be sure?

If we want to be whole, we need to know why we are broken. And the answer to why we are broken will also determine where we should look for healing.

What Do Today's Thinkers Say?

1

Times are just now changing in fundamental ways. Much of what used to be unknowable is now knowable... It is time for religion to evolve, metastasize as it were, from its old forms into a new and more inclusive humanism.

C.S. Coon
www.progressivehumanism.com

It is a uniquely human endowment to ask the question, "Why?" Beginning in early childhood, the inquisitive toddler repeats that question over and over again to a sometimes frazzled parent who is often stumped for the right answer. Give one answer and the child just comes back with another *why?*

It is, of course, because of humankind's persistent yearning for answers to the *whys* of life that we have made such great strides in our understanding of the causes of illness. When faced with a new illness, researchers immediately set out to discover why the person is ill.

This is exactly what happened in Nigeria on January 19,

1969[1] when a missionary nurse, Laura Wine, working in a small mission station in Lassa, a town in northeastern Nigeria, developed severe pain in her back along with an unremitting fever. She had been prevented from becoming a medical missionary for years because of tuberculosis. In her sixties, the dream was at last fulfilled in Africa. She loved her work and was fearless in a compassionate pursuit of caring for the countless ill of sub-Saharan Africa. With only one doctor at the mission hospital, Laura did much more than her American training had prepared her for—she delivered babies, prescribed medicines, sutured wounds and set bones. She became adept at diagnosing such tropical diseases as typhoid, malaria and schistosomiasis.

But now Laura was ill. She attributed her back pain to arthritis, but that did not explain her fever. The following morning she woke with a sore throat, not a common complaint in the tropics. She mentioned it to Esther, her colleague, Dr. John Hamer's wife. Esther insisted that her husband examine Laura immediately. John found little of note other than fever and sore muscles. He insisted that she rest and take aspirin. With little laboratory support, he followed the dictum that all fevers were malaria unless proven otherwise, so he prescribed the usual chloroquin pills.

Laura did not improve. Thinking now it might be a strep throat, Dr. Hamer prescribed penicillin, again with no effect. By now Laura was becoming dehydrated, she had developed yellowish ulcers in her throat and her urine output had dropped markedly. Desperate, Dr. Hamer decided it was time to move her to the larger missionary hospital in Jos where better laboratory services might be able to confirm a diagnosis. The long trek by Land Rover to the airstrip was difficult, with a now comatose and convulsing Laura bouncing in the back, while Esther tried to attend her as best she could. The plane from the Sudan United Mission, piloted by Ray Browneye, was on time to carry Laura to Jos.

At the Bingham Hospital in Jos, Dr. Jeanette Troupe was the only full-time doctor. By the time Laura arrived she was clearly in congestive heart failure and it appeared she might be near death. Blood tests were drawn, and Dr. Troupe placed a tube of her blood in the freezer, a big help for investigators later. Laura's white blood count was extremely high and her bleeding time was noted to be prolonged, indicating that she had a bleeding disorder. Round the clock nurses were ordered and every available therapy was tried for Laura.

The evening nurse was Charlotte Shaw. Before coming on duty, while working in her flower garden, she had punctured her finger with a thorn. When Laura's mouth filled with secretions, she took gauze, wrapped it over her finger and swabbed the phlegm in Laura's mouth. She felt a little sting at the puncture site and immediately cleansed her finger with alcohol, but told no one. That evening Laura convulsed again and her urine output ceased entirely. She died by 9:30 p.m. An autopsy later failed to reveal the cause of death, so Dr. Troupe would have to depend on word from the Center for Disease Control in Atlanta, Georgia for a final diagnosis. After a painful funeral for all the mission staff, life at the missions in Jos and Lassa began to return to normal.

That is, until eight days later when Charlotte Shaw, the nurse who had punctured her finger, became ill. After an almost identical course as Laura's, Charlotte died on the eleventh day of her illness. With her death, began a saga of scientific investigation on both sides of the Atlantic—in Nigeria and at the Center for Disease Control in Atlanta, Georgia, that resulted in several more deaths before the question of Laura's death was answered. The best science of the late 60s was enlisted.

It was dubbed *Lassa Fever* after the town where Laura contracted her illness. Scientists at the Center for Disease Control recognized the cause of the unrelenting febrile illness to be a virus normally found in rodents, but which had found its way into the human population. I was thankful for the medical science that clearly described this illness when I encountered it during my five years of medical work in Mkar, Nigeria.

The discovery of the virus causing Lassa Fever illustrates the scientific quest for the explanation of disease. When doctors come across a new illness, the first question they ask is, "Why is this person sick?" They want to know what the cause of the illness is and how the patient acquired it. Only then are they able to offer treatment and cure.

Chances are that when you are sick, you also want to know why. You would like to know why your back hurts. Or why you have developed that itchy rash. Or why your joints seem to be wearing out. Let's explore some of the reasons offered by scientists, philosophers and theologians

WHAT DO SCIENTISTS SAY?

In the bygone, pre-scientific era, most illness was thought to have spiritual causes and most doctors used magic and witchcraft to heal their patients. They were mainly tribal priests whose job it was to pacify the angry gods or drive out evil spirits. Although their treatments were primarily ritualistic, and probably herbal, there is archeological evidence that they even used surgical techniques, such as boring a hole in the skull to release evils spirits or maybe to treat headaches.

Today however, we look to modern science to explain the cause for much of what ails us. Beginning with Hippocrates who showed that diseases had natural as opposed to supernatural causes, through Leeuwenhoek who first saw bacteria under his primitive microscope, to Watson and Crick who discovered DNA, medical scientists have determined the cause of a vast number of diseases. They are even beginning to understand the genetics of aging—why we appear to have a maximum life expectancy of about 120 years. The scientific explanation for the cause of sickness has contributed immensely to effective healing and to our ability to prevent disease. Especially during the twentieth century, great gains have been made in life expectancy. There are even some who now claim that science may be able to counter aging so as to extend our lives, possibly into immortality.

What is science?

Science is the study of the natural realm, that which we can observe and measure through our senses or with instruments that extend our senses. The word *science* comes from the Latin word *scientia*, which means *knowledge*. Scientists use systematic methods of study to make observations and collect facts which are then added to a body of knowledge that is verifiable and reproducible according to the fundamental laws and principles of nature.

Science can be divided into four major branches: (1) mathematics and logic, (2) physical sciences such as chemistry, physics, and astronomy, (3) life sciences such as biology and medicine, and (4) the social sciences such as psychology and sociology. It has been through the life sciences like anatomy, physiology and genetics that most of our understanding of the human body has been gained.

The realm with which science is not concerned is the spiritual realm. Theology and religion deal with that area and we will examine these and their contribution to our understanding later. We might call that realm *extra-dimensional*, as it is outside the known dimensions of time and space.

For our purposes, we do not include the study of the paranormal in our definition of science. Parapsychology is a growing field of study of phenomena that defy the laws of nature, such as extrasensory perception (ESP), telepathy, clairvoyance, and telekinesis. It would be reasonable to conclude that these are extra-dimensional and part of the spiritual realm.

Science, therefore, is inherently secular and excludes religion and religious considerations from its study. This is the official position of the Council of the U.S. National Academy of Sciences which decreed in 1981 that:

> Religion and science are separate and mutually exclusive realms of human thought whose presentation in the same context leads to misunderstanding of both scientific theory and religious belief.[2]

Historically, science has often been at odds with religion and continues to be in such discussions as creation versus evolution and the origin of humankind. There are many who hold the view that science has explained everything, or will eventually explain everything that was once explained by belief in a god or gods. In the area of medical science and the causes of illness, this is certainly the case. Where illness was once thought to be due to evil spirits or an angry god, medical scientists now believe there are physical, natural causes.

How did we get there?

It is only in recent centuries that science has shed its light on the cause of sickness. The journey from a primarily religious explanation for sickness back in prehistoric days to a scientific explanation accelerated immensely during a period of history known as the Enlightenment, starting in the late 17th century. During this time the laws against human dissection were relaxed and the scientific method was developed, with its emphasis on experimentation and careful observation. Table 1.1 heralds some of the major landmarks of this journey.

From Religion to Science

ERA	DISCOVERER	DISCOVERY	IMPLICATIONS
Iron Age 1200–600 BC	King David	Sickness is a result of God's punishment	Health is achieved by a right relationship to God
400 BC	Hippocrates	Illness is rooted in natural causes rather than spiritual causes	Illness could be treated according to the workings of nature
100 AD	Galen	Performed experiments with animals	Medical theories became based on scientific experiments
Renaissance 1500s	Leonardo da Vinci Andreas Vesalius	Laws against human dissection relaxed	Greater understanding of human anatomy and first anatomy textbook published
Enlightenment 1600–1700s	Copernicus Galileo	Earth is not the centre of the universe	Displaced the view that man was the centre of the universe
1755	Immanuel Kant	Mechanistic model for the evolution of the universe	A non-theist explanation for the existence of the universe

Table 1.1 (cont'd on next page)

From Religion to Science (cont'd)			
ERA	DISCOVERER	DISCOVERY	IMPLICATIONS
1859	Charles Darwin	Theory of evolution of species through natural selection	A non-theist explanation for the existence of life
late 1800s	Louis Pasteur	Bacteria caused specific illness	A greater understanding on how to prevent disease
1900	Sigmund Freud	Ego, id and super-ego	Human character not shaped by a conscience or religious wisdom, but by innate lust and rage
1916	Albert Einstein	Theory of relativity	Matter and energy are one and the same
1929	Edwin Hubble	The universe is expanding	The *Big Bang* theory and a scientific explanation for the origins of the universe

Table 1.1

What does science say about why I am sick?

Using the tools of the scientific era, medical scientists now have categorized the things that can go wrong in the body to cause aging, sickness and death:

- *Trauma.* From our early history, the human race has been subject to the ill effects of trauma. The effects of war, natural disasters, animal attacks and falls are evident in the human fossil record which shows healed fractures, missing limbs and embedded weapons. More recently, sports injuries, plane crashes and motor vehicle accidents have added to the burden of sickness in our species. The human propensity to invent and use tools has made us prone to mishaps using them and the discovery of fire led to the risk of burns. Every technological advance brought new threats to our health and ironically the very technologies that helped extend our lives also threatened to shorten them.

- *Genetics.* Genetic diseases fall into one of three categories: genetic accidents such as Down's syndrome due to an extra chromosome, inherited disorders which follow the Mendelian rules of inheritance such as cystic fibrosis or Huntington's disease, and defects in genetic expression such as congenital heart disease or cleft palate. Scientists have concluded that who we are is at least 50 percent due to our genetic inheritance. Many diseases, such as high blood pressure or heart disease, have genetic predispositions which strongly interplay with the environment we live in. I have found in my own practice that longevity is largely determined by the longevity of a person's parents.

- *Degeneration.* The longer we live, the more likely our parts will wear out and we'll develop diseases like osteoarthritis, hearing loss and cataracts. The cartilage in our joints thins out and our brains shrink. Our skin loses its elasticity and starts to wrinkle. Our heart gets tired. Lenses thicken and are less pliable, resulting in far-sightedness and decreased vision. The ears lose their ability to hear high-pitched tones, and smell and taste grow dull. Muscles waste and bones become riddled with cavities, weakening them. Kidneys become less efficient in filtering and lungs lose their elasticity.

- **Infection.** Infections with viruses, bacteria, or fungi and infestations with parasites are still the leading cause of illness and death around the globe. In developed countries, at least one quarter of the people seeking medical attention do so for infections, and in developing countries this proportion is much higher. Epidemics of smallpox, tuberculosis, the plague, influenza, and now AIDS are fresh in our memory and have killed millions. Even conditions formerly thought to have other causes are now being discovered to be due to infectious agents, such as peptic ulcers now known to be caused by the bacteria *helicobacter pylori* and cancer of the cervix caused by the *human papilloma* virus. Some diseases are due to toxins released by bacteria and affect organs far removed from the infection. Research is ongoing for possible infectious causes for diseases such as juvenile diabetes, multiple sclerosis and chronic fatigue syndrome.

- **Altered immunity.** We have a wonderful defense mechanism against infection—our immune system—which seeks out and destroys infectious agents. However, this system can turn against us in two different ways. For some unknown reasons, our body can start developing antibodies against its own tissues. Mistaking certain cells in our bodies as foreign, our body errs in making antibodies to these cells thus rendering them subject to attack and destruction. The second way in which our immune system can become misdirected is in its role in allergies. Some people develop excessive reaction to the antibodies produced by exposure to inhaled substances such as pollens or house dust mites, swallowed foods such as peanuts, or contacted substances such as jewelry or clothing fabric. These excessive reactions manifest as itchy eyes, runny nose, asthma, or hives. They can, in fact, be fatal as they can cause anaphylactic shock.

• *Neoplasia.* This is the term medical scientists use to describe cells that start to reproduces uncontrollably, causing cancer or tumors, usually due to an alteration in the chromosome of the cells in a particular organ. Various factors, sometimes referred to as *carcinogens*, are thought to predispose cells to undergo this genetic mutation in their chromosomes: viruses, radiation, chemical toxins such as those in the environment, work place or in cigarette smoke, foods, drugs, ultraviolet radiation from sunlight or genetics. *Malignant neoplasia* refers to those tumors that endanger life through spread to other body areas. *Benign tumors* are neoplastic growths where they only affect local tissues, although, if left unchecked, in some cases can still cause death by pressing on vital areas or organs.

• *Psychological.* It has been postulated that up to 50 percent of visits to primary caregivers such as family doctors are for psychologically-caused illness! Obvious are the patients we see complaining of anxiety, depression, insomnia, marital problems or parenting problems, but less obvious are those with physical symptoms such as fatigue, headaches or abdominal pain. Scientists are increasingly discovering the close relationship of the mind to the body. Once thought to be separate, we now know they are inextricably linked—the body affects the mind as much as the mind affects the body. Emotional pain can cause physical pain, and physical pain will cause emotional pain. And emotional pain can run deep, originating from such painful memories as sexual abuse, major losses such as the death of a parent, spouse or child, rejection due to abandonment in childhood or marital strife and divorce. And not only do psychological factors affect illness, we also know that they affect our healing. The *placebo effect* is well documented with significant percentages of people taking a sugar pill (placebo) reporting improvement in their symptoms (in many drug-evaluation studies, up to 20 or 30 percent).

- *Nutritional.* There is an old saying—"You are what you eat." The discovery of vitamins revealed some of the truth of that, thereby justifying parents' age-old admonition to their children to eat their vegetables. Not only have medical scientists documented our minimal daily requirements of vitamins and their role in preventing disease, they also have catalogued the trace elements and minerals the body needs. In addition, research continues on the relation of dietary cholesterol to heart disease and the effects of diet on cancer. Scientists are also discovering that particular foods have disease-preventing properties, and of course we have known for centuries that many plants contain chemicals that are pharmacologically active in the body. Nutritional disorders may be due to deficiencies such as vitamin C deficiency that leads to scurvy. Other nutritional disorders may be due to dietary excess. Obesity is the obvious example and has become a major epidemic in North America. Too much sodium may contribute to high blood pressure while excessive dietary fat may contribute to hardening of the arteries which is known to cause heart attacks and strokes.

- *Environmental.* The Industrial Revolution has radically altered our environment. From our water supply, to the air we breath, to the radiation in the atmosphere, we are constantly being exposed to agents known to be harmful to our health. Environmental noise in the workplace, or the noise we generate ourselves by turning up our electronic gadgets, causes damage to our ears with subsequent hearing loss. The ozone layer is being destroyed with a threat of radiation to future generations. High-voltage power lines may have electromagnetic radiation around them which may cause blood cancers.

This list answers the question of *how* we get sick, or the pathways to sickness. But it doesn't answer the "bigger picture" question of *why*. Why are we prone to sickness and aging to begin with? Why is the human body so frail and prone to failure? Why do we age? To answer these questions, scientists are looking to a new branch of medical science called Darwinian Medicine.

Darwinian medicine

In *Why We Get Sick*, authors Randolph Nesse and George Williams suggest that natural selection is ultimately the cause of illness, aging, and death. They argue that, on the basis of Darwinian evolutionary theory, genes that increase lifetime reproduction will be selected even if they result in reduced longevity, while genes that reduce reproduction will be eliminated even if they increase the individual's survival. Consequently, they see the human body as a product of organic evolution that is a bundle of compromises, each which offers an advantage but often at the price of susceptibility to disease. They suggest five reasons why the human body is so unreliable:[3]

1. There are genes that make us vulnerable to disease. Some genes become defective because of mutations which are not eliminated because they cause no disadvantages until it is too late in life for them to affect reproduction. Others are actively maintained by selection because they have unappreciated benefits that outweigh their costs, particularly in their heterozygous (mixed) expression.

2. Disease results from exposure to novel factors that were not present in the environment in which we evolved. Given enough time the body would have adapted, but the time from the beginning of civilization is not nearly enough. For example, infectious agents evolve so fast that our defenses are always a step behind.

3. Disease results from design compromises, such as upright posture with its associated back problems. Autoimmune disease is the price of our remarkable ability to attack invaders. Cancer is the price of tissues that can repair themselves.

4. We are not the only species with adaptations produced and maintained by natural selection. It works just as hard on "bugs" trying to eat us and the organisms we want to eat. Bacteria develop resistance to antibiotics faster then we can produce them.

5. Disease results from unfortunate historical legacies, such as appendicitis or choking on a piece of meat (the swallowing pathway crosses our airway putting us at risk for choking). If the human body had been designed with the possibility of fresh starts and major changes, there would be better ways to preventing many diseases.

In a similar fashion, Dr. Leonard Hayflick in *How and Why We Age*, argues that aging is selected because maximum energy for reproduction occurs early in the reproductive years. Beyond the reproductive years, he suggests that longevity is no longer important.[4]

But is the evolutionary explanation tenable and satisfactory for all possible disease scenarios as we know them? Consider the following:

• Genetic disorders that do affect reproduction should be rapidly eliminated. Evolutionists use the example of sickle-cell anemia to counter this objection in that its heterozygous expression offers relative resistance to malaria and is therefore selected. Similarly, the heterozygous expression of cystic fibrosis is thought to offer protection against cholera. However, no advantage is known for the heterozygous expression of innumerable other genetic conditions including muscular dystrophy and hemophilia, both of which are expressed early and are likely to affect reproductive potential. And what about the homosexual gene, if such a gene exists? Since gays (those who are not bisexual) are much less likely to reproduce, their gene pool should be eliminated within a few generations.

- Why are lower life forms, such as reptiles (tortoises, crocodiles), virtually immortal (they don't age, continue to grow, and continue to reproduce), while mammals age relatively rapidly?

- The Darwinian model fails to account for the role of mental and emotional illness. How are mental illnesses which are at least partly genetically based, such as manic-depressive illness and schizophrenia, selected for? What are the reproductive advantages of these disorders?

- The Darwinian model does not take into account an extra-dimensional realm, which even the best science (relativity, quantum mechanics) demonstrates. (See Chapter 3 for evidence that such a realm exists.)

In conclusion then, most people in the mainstream scientific community view humans as the product of natural laws. Shaped by chance mutations which are perpetuated by natural selection, we are ultimately either destined to extinction or to evolve into some other life form. Within this model, disease and aging are evolutionary byproducts brought about by design compromise.

While many can accept a "chance" cosmos and human life as a happenstance of nature, many do not and look to religion for the origins of the universe and life and an explanation for illness. The seemingly empty explanation offered by secularists is partly the reason for the rise in *postmodernism*, the term used to describe renewed spiritual awareness. Within our society, many are returning to religious explanations to fulfill the yearning in the human heart for spiritual meaning. For some, this has led them to world religions, including those from the East.

WHAT DO ALTERNATIVE HEALERS SAY?

The rise in Alternative Medicine (AM) is evidenced by the increasing proportion of health-care dollars spent on alternative medicines and treatments and growing numbers of individuals and families patronizing their services. Also referred to as Complementary Medicine (CM), AM encompasses all those healing arts that are outside the scope of scientific or conventional medicine (*allopathy*). The term *alternative* is preferred by some, implying that these treatments are alternatives to scientific medicine. Others prefer *complementary* and see themselves as complementing or coming alongside scientific medicine. Many writers now refer to this field as *complementary and alternative medicine* and use the acronym CAM. Another phrase, when combining CAM with conventional medicine, is *integrative medicine*. Yet another phrase, and probably the oldest, is *wholistic medicine* (sometimes spelled *holistic*), implying an approach to health, sickness, and healing that encompasses the whole person—physical needs, social needs, psychological needs and spiritual needs. *New Age Medicine* is a term coined by some writers in this field because of the heavy emphasis on Eastern healing methods, such as those from China or India.

Alternative Medicine by Any Name

- Alternative Medicine (AM)
- Complementary Medicine (CM)
- Complementary and Alternative Medicine (CAM)
- Integrative Medicine
- Holistic Medicine
- New Age Medicine

Figure 1.1

Why is Alternative Medicine becoming so popular?

A 1997 CTV/Angus Reid poll in Canada revealed that 42 percent of Canadians use complementary and alternative medicines. The overall growth in CAM since 1992 has been 81 percent. Twenty-five percent of Canadians use chiropractors, 23 percent use herbs and 18 percent use homeopathic medicines. In 1997, 415 million dollars were spent on CAM. So why this rise in CAM?

One reason is that scientific medicine does not have all the answers. Doctors are not only having problems identifying the cause of such illnesses as fibromyalgia, chronic fatigue syndrome or multiple chemical sensitivities, scientific medicine is ineffective in treating many of these very conditions as well. Advanced malignancy defies such conventional treatments as surgery, chemotherapy and radiation. Many psychiatric illnesses are chronic, causing lifelong disability, only tempered at best by powerful drugs. Simple viruses that cause colds resist efforts to eradicate their troublesome sniffles and coughs, while their varied strains defy attempts at developing a vaccine. People with chronic pain syndromes simply develop tolerance to the pain-killing medicine that once seemed to be their saviour.

Many people seek out CAM practitioners when they have reached the end of the road with conventional medicine.

Another reason for the increase in CAM is that doctors have been seen primarily as curative rather than focusing on prevention and wellness. Many CAM practitioners are wellness oriented, stressing diet and preventative maintenance. The escalating costs of curative or maintenance treatments with surgery and pharmaceuticals are seen as strong reasons to embrace cheaper wellness care.

Many CAM therapies have spiritual or mystic roots, and being more wholistic they address spiritual needs, whereas in conventional medicine, spiritual needs are often relegated to clergy and religious professionals or not addressed at all. There is a resurgence of interest in the spiritual and in mysticism, so many people prefer the integrated approach of the CAM practitioner.

Many CAM therapies are seen as safer than conventional medical therapies. Surgery and pharmaceuticals are seen as invasive and toxic, often doing more harm than good, while many CAM therapies use natural remedies often derived from plants and sometimes diluted manyfold to seemingly benign concentrations.

Scientific medicine has lost favour in the eyes of many because of impersonal care, with many doctors working in walk-in clinics and seeing many patients every hour. The Marcus Welby image of a caring family doctor has been replaced the busy Emergency Room Physician, running from emergency to emergency. Institutional care in hospitals and nursing homes is seen as cold and uncaring. CAM practitioners however, are often known for spending time with their clients and offering more personalized care.

A new consumerism amongst wellness seekers, spurred by effective marketing, is another reason for the rising interest in CAM. People are used to choices in the marketplace and they take the time to educate themselves about these alternatives, making highly informed decisions which they perceive suit them best. They demand the same for their health care with a growing trend toward self-medication and self-care. This is particularly true of baby boomers who don't have the commitments and allegiances that their parents had to brands, politics, or religion. Many CAM products are distributed by network marketing with non-professionals selling out of their homes to friends and acquaintances. It can no longer be assumed that the primary health-care provider for an individual or a family is the family doctor.

The "green movement" has raised the interest in herbalism and natural therapies, with a parallel backlash against science and technology. Conventional medicine with its connections to multinational pharmaceutical corporations and big business are seen as environmentally unfriendly.

Recent media attention with most major magazines running cover stories on CAM has raised the credibility of alternative treatments, lifting many of them out of presumed "quackery." Many CAM treatments are now being subjected to scientific analysis and study. Several reputable journals have come up with articles reviewing CAM philosophies and treatments. Many books on health and healing, such as those by Dr. Andrew Weil and Dr. Deepak Chopra, are best sellers and some authors have their own syndicated television shows with a faithful following. With media affirmation of these therapies, there is increased pressure on governments to regulate and fund CAM.

Finally, many CAM therapies are perceived to have stood the test of time, often predating the scientific revolution and therefore considered safer and better. There is a renewal in folklore with many people searching out their roots. As they do, they may discover North American native, Eastern, or African roots and feel a connection to the traditional healers and therapies of their ancestors.

Given the rising interest in CAM, what can we learn from these philosophies about the causes of sickness, aging, and death?

CAM disease theory

CAM practitioners often view the causes of sickness differently than MDs. For them, disease is evidence of what they call a *loss of homeostasis*, or balance. They believe that health is maintained by a balance within the body and mind of either internal or external energies, substances, or structures. Generally, they theorize a loss of homeostasis in either the spiritual, biochemical or structural arenas. Therapies are then directed toward re-establishing homeostasis in the area of presumed imbalance.

The first arena for loss of homeostasis is the spiritual one. Several CAM healing disciplines postulate an imbalance in "energy" which the healer then attempts to restore through therapeutic intervention. This theory is found in the disciplines of Traditional Chinese Medicine (TCM), Ayurveda, and Therapeutic Touch (TT). The "energy" is called *qi* (sometimes spelled *chi*) in TCM, *prana* in Ayurveda (Indian), and *bioenergetic fields* in TT, and presupposes an invisible, extra-dimensional force of life that pervades the universe and affects the health of individuals in positive or negative ways. This has been called the theory of *vitalism* and can be shown to be based on the Eastern worldview of *pantheism*. Eastern religions, such as Hinduism (on which *prana* is based) and Taoism (on which *qi* is based) believe the divine permeates the universe and is one with it. This is similar to the "Force" of the Star Wars trilogy and is incompatible with monotheistic religions such as Christianity, Judaism, and Islam in which God is seen as transcendent, above and separate from His created order. Each of these healing arts has its own theory as to what affects this energy. In Ayurveda, it is influenced by the balance of *doshas* and is centred in the seven *chakras*, while in TCM it is influenced by a balance of *yin* and *yang* and travels along *meridians*. Healing disciplines that attempt to manipulate this energy are called "energy based" and are described in Chapter 5 as well as the table in Appendix B.

The second arena in which loss of homeostasis is felt to cause loss of well-being is in the biochemical arena. Here deficient or excessive nutrients, intolerances to foods or the environment, or excessive toxins are postulated to affect the body's ability to resist disease. This is not the sole domain of alternative practitioners, as medical scientists have researched nutrition and toxicology extensively. However, CAM practitioners often take these concepts further and advise dietary restrictions or supplements, or detoxification well beyond mainstream medicine.

Putrefaction, a theory of yesteryear which postulated that toxins released by decaying stool in the colon caused illness, has seen a resurgence among naturopaths and other CAM practitioners. Some may be old enough to remember the dreaded enema administered as "punishment" for having gotten ill. Autointoxication is today's buzzword which describes the toxins released from the colon due to constipation, parasites or incomplete emptying. Conventional doctors discredited the putrefaction theory shortly after the turn of the century.

The third area is structural imbalance such as the chiropractic theory of disease. Chiropractic was founded in 1895 by D.D. Palmer who reasoned that improper alignment of the spine presses on nerves that leave the spinal column, thereby influencing the organ systems supplied by the nerves. He postulated that problems in joints, particularly in the spinal column, called subluxations, could interfere with proper function of the nervous system and might therefore cause disease. In the 1930s, this theory was slightly modified by Belgian chiropractor Henri Gillet. He developed a theory of intervertebral motion and fixation, in which he asserted that it was loss of normal spinal joint movement, rather than misalignment, that was the underlying explanation for the vertebral subluxation. Later work by researchers verified the complex role of the "vertebral motor unit," consisting of bones, muscles, ligaments, blood vessels and nerves. This model is now widely accepted by chiropractors. Osteopathy and massage therapy address similar theories of structural imbalance.

CAM practitioners and holistic medicine

Biomedicine (MDs) is often criticized by CAM practitioners for being disease focused—treating symptoms without getting at the cause of illness. We are accused of following symptoms and physical signs toward a diagnosis, confirming it with tests and then treating the illness rather than the whole person. CAM practitioners, on the other hand, see themselves as being *holistic* in their approach—treating the whole person.

Conversely, CAM disease theorists often find themselves at odds with scientific medicine on the one hand, and Christianity on the other. As we will see later, with energy-based healing arts clearly based on an Eastern worldview, they are considered incompatible with both the secular naturalist worldview and the Christian worldview. CAM practitioners who use these theories as the basis for treatment, however, point to the test of time and their anecdotal success stories as proof that these assumptions are true and valid. Many satisfied clients would echo these sentiments and endorse the principles as evidenced by their rising popularity.

Given the Eastern spiritual underpinnings of so much of Alternative Medicine, let's now examine the spiritual underpinnings of the Judeo-Christian tradition. For that we turn to the Bible and its interpretation of reality.

2 | What Does God Say?

In the form in which men have posed it, the Riddle of the Universe requires a theological answer. Suffering and enjoying, men want to know why they enjoy and to what end they suffer. They see good things and evil things, beautiful things and ugly, and they want to find a reason—a final and absolute reason—why these things should be as they are.

Aldous Huxley

The famed Hubble Space Telescope, despite all its flaws and blunders, orbits high above the distorting atmosphere of our planet, probing far into the seemingly endless expanse of the universe. It is named after Edwin Hubble, the astronomer who, in 1929, while peering through a much smaller telescope on Mount Wilson in Southern California, discovered that the universe was expanding and, therefore, finite in both time and space. His discovery elated Albert Einstein, whose theory of relativity predicted either an expanding or contracting universe, but who had been convinced by the astronomers of his day that it was infinite and therefore static. Against his better judgement, he had dirtied his beautiful equations with what he later called "his greatest blunder." Now he could remove this adulteration and, in 1931, he personally traveled to the top of Mount Wilson to see the telescope and thank Hubble personally for "delivering him from folly."[5]

What was this folly? The notion of an infinite universe without beginning and end.

The creation of the universe has now become a virtually scientifically-proven event, with greater than 99 percent probability.[6] Cosmologist James Trefil explains: "The simple fact of universal expansion compels us to conclude that the universe had a beginning in time."[7] And if there was a beginning, it begs the question, "*Why* the beginning?"

> Many people believe that if something comes into existence, it must do so in response to the actions of some rational being. Because of that belief, astronomers, even though they hate to get involved in theological discussion, find themselves in one when they posit the Big Bang universe. It puts them squarely in the middle of the age-old debate about the existence of God.[8]

Science may try to explain *how* the universe began, but will it ever explain *why*? Why the big bang? Why with just the energy to sustain life? Why organization from disorganization contrary to the second law of thermodynamics? Why life from inert chemicals? And why do humans have a consciousness to even ask the question, "Why?"

While scientists grapple with the *how* questions, it is philosophers and theologians who grapple with the *why* questions. Ultimately, every human being must wrestle with the question of a creator who lit the fuse of the big bang, a "master designer" who brought order out of chaos and life out of the inert.

Likewise, knowing why life begins will help us to understand why life ends. And, since sickness and aging are forerunners of death, this will help us to understand why we become ill and age. And so, our quest to the answer of why we are ill takes us to the biggest question of all: "Is there a God?" Is there an unseen spiritual realm beyond the seen natural realm, the four known dimensions of height, width, depth, and time? What is the probability that such an extra-dimensional realm exists?

For those who seriously doubt the existence of such a realm, I would ask you to look ahead at the evidence outlined in Chapter 3. From that information, it is very logical to conclude that the existence of God is the only rational explanation for the universe as we know it.

THE BIBLE ON ORIGINS

Three world religions (Christianity, Islam, and Judaism) hold the Genesis account as the divine authority on the origins of the cosmos. God crowned his creation with human life, *in his image.* Then God said,

> *...let us make man in our image, in our likeness... So God created man in his own image, in the image of God he created him; male and female he created them* (Gen. 1:26,27).

Being image bearers of God meant we had the unique endowments of self-awareness, imagination, conscience and independent will, set apart from all other animals in creation. What made humans so different from all other creatures? God "breathed" into them the *breath of life* (Genesis 2:7). This godly life force made man a spiritual being, with not only an external body and an inner soul (mind, emotions and will), but with a spirit activated to communicate with the Creator. Figure 2.1 illustrates the biblical concept of humankind as a tripartite (three part) being.[9]

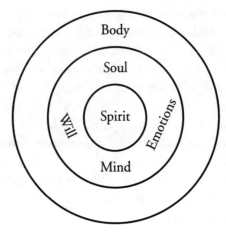

Figure 2.1
Tripartite humanity

With their spirits activated by God's life, Adam and Eve were created to live in absolute harmony with their environment and they were perfect—they were without fault. *"God saw all that he had made, and it was very good"* (Gen. 1:31).

As God's image bearers, humankind was destined to:

- Experience eternal fellowship with God;
- Rule over the created order;
- Experience healthy interpersonal relationships;
- Experience physical/emotional health and immortality.

God clearly stated that humankind's state of blessing, perfection and authority over the created order was dependent on his obedience and submission.

> *And the LORD God commanded the man, "You are free to eat from any tree in the garden; but you must not eat from the tree of the knowledge of good and evil, for when you eat of it you will surely die"* (Gen. 2:16,17).

Disobedience would mean loss of immortality and rulership.

Paradise lost

Where Genesis 2 ends in bliss and harmony in the Garden of Eden, Genesis 3 introduces us to a third spiritual being (besides God and humans), the devil, also called Satan. We know from later Scriptures that Satan was an angel of high rank who rebelled against God sometime before the last day of creation and took about one third of all the angels with him in defiance of God's authority. Angels are spiritual beings created by God that are part of the extra-dimensional, spiritual realm. Those angels which rebelled were expelled from God's presence in heaven and made their residence in the atmospheric realm of the proto-earth. A picture is painted of that in Isaiah 14:12:

> *How you have fallen from heaven, O morning star, son of the dawn! You have been cast down to the earth, you who once laid low the nations!*

Fallen angels are also referred to biblically as evil spirits, or demons. Satan, disguised as a snake, showed up in the Garden of Eden and tempted Eve to disobey God by eating the forbidden fruit. He used the same lie that caused his fall: *For God knows that when you eat of it your eyes will be opened, and you will be like God, knowing good and evil* (Gen. 3:5). This is the same lie that we see today in New Age thinking and the old age religions upon which it is based—all is one, therefore all is divine.

When Adam and Eve disobeyed God, they plunged themselves and all their descendants into what the Bible calls sin. In Genesis 3 we see what the consequences of sin are.

- Loss of eternal fellowship with God: *So the Lord God banished him from the Garden of Eden* (v.23). Also known as spiritual death, this leads to eternal separation from God. The spirit of man loses its ability to communicate with the Creator.

- Loss of lordship over the created order: *Cursed is the ground because of you; through painful toil you will eat of it all the days of your life. It will produce thorns and thistles for you and you will eat the plants of the field. By the sweat of your brow you will eat your food...* (v.17-19). Creation also lost its state of perfection and humankind would struggle against weather, natural disasters and the laws of nature.

- Loss of healthy interpersonal relationships: *"To the woman he said, "...Your desire will be for your husband, and he will rule over you"* (v.16). The struggle between the sexes started here, as well as hatred and strife.

- Loss of health and immortality: *You (will) return to the ground, since from it you were taken; for dust you are and to dust you will return* (v.19). Aging, sickness, and physical death are all results of sin.

Here then, we see God's explanation for the problem of evil and suffering in the world—sin, also called the fall of mankind. Later Scripture writers reiterate this as the ultimate cause of death: *For since death came through a man ... in Adam all die* (1 Cor. 15:9).

Many non-theists stumble over this reason, failing to understand how a good and loving God could allow the creatures He created to pursue evil and reap its consequences. They prefer a chance universe with evil, suffering, and death being the consequence of evolutionary processes, particularly the survival of the fittest.

Is the biblical source of evil plausible?

Is the biblical explanation for evil, suffering and death plausible? Humanists argue that aggression and sexual oppression are biological impulses which have worked in our favour through evolutionary forces. Under this philosophy, murder is excusable and rape, good for the human race. But what about mass murder and genocide? What about the killing of our unborn children? Are these the results of evolution? There is hardly a chance for natural selection to be at work here—extermination of potentially the fittest. No, rather this is evil, and the biblical explanation of the struggle of good against evil is far more plausible than the evolutionary one. Dr. Hugh Ross in *Beyond the Cosmos* agrees:

> Many who argue that the existence of evil and suffering proves the nonexistence of an all-powerful, all-loving Creator have no idea that it proves just the opposite. Naturalistic materialism, the notion that the natural world accounts for itself and needs no outside explanation, cannot account for the evil and cruelty we see among humans. Survival of the fittest does not result in the behavior humans exhibit all over the planet toward the land itself and toward plants, animals, and fellow humans.[10]

It would seem to me that a critical examination of the facts, with objectivity and openness, would render a view that evil is the result of an outside force, apart from God, which has set itself up in opposition to all that is good. Again quoting from Hugh Ross:

> Though the words sound shocking, we can reasonably say that the quantity of evil expressed on earth exceeds by far what atheistic evolutionary explanations can account for. Only the real existence of God and his adversary, Satan, and the biblical account of God's purpose for this life, make sense of evil and suffering.[11]

We often hear God's critics say that if they were God, they would design a world in which there would be no opportunity given to evil and suffering. What would such a world look like? Would it not closely resemble the Garden of Eden, that place of perfect unity with nature and absolute safety? That's exactly what God had in mind, but it was human will that thwarted His plan, throwing humanity into sin and its consequences.

RELATIONSHIP OF SIN AND SICKNESS

With an understanding of the notion that sickness, aging and death are the result of sin, let's explore this relationship further. Is this concept advanced in other parts of the Bible? Did Jesus teach this principle? And if Satan ultimately caused sin, does he also cause sickness? Let's explore some Scriptures.

Spiritual health promotes physical health

Do not be wise in your own eyes; fear the LORD and shun evil. This will bring health to your body and nourishment to your bones (Prov. 3:7,8).

To fear the Lord means to recognize there is Someone greater than ourselves who deserves our respect, obedience, and worship and that it is His authority we are ultimately to submit to. Shunning evil means avoiding sin and reciprocally avoiding its consequences.

If you pay attention to these laws and are careful to follow them...the LORD will keep you free from every disease. He will not inflict on you the horrible diseases you knew in Egypt, but he will inflict them on all who hate you (Deut. 7:12,15).

God made a covenant with his Old Testament people and promised that if they were obedient and kept his laws, there would be a consequence of health. By implication, disobedience would produce sickness.

See, I set before you today life and prosperity, death and destruction. For I command you today to love the LORD your God, to walk in his ways, and to keep his commands, decrees and laws; then you will live and increase, and the LORD your

God will bless you in the land you are entering to possess... This day I call heaven and earth as witnesses against you that I have set before you life and death, blessings and curses. Now choose life, so that you and your children may live and that you may love the LORD your God, listen to his voice, and hold fast to him. For the LORD is your life (Deut 30:15,16,19,20).

God's punishment of sin

Because of your wrath there is no health in my body; my bones have no soundness because of my sin. My guilt has over-whelmed me like a burden too heavy to bear (Ps. 38:3,4).

The psalm writer (King David) sees a connection between his sickness and God's punishment on his disobedience.

For anyone who eats and drinks without recognizing the body of the Lord eats and drinks judgment on himself. That is why many among you are weak and sick, and a number of you have fallen asleep. But if we judged ourselves, we would not come under judgment (1 Cor. 11:29-31).

In this passage, the Apostle Paul tells the believers in Corinth that their disrespect and mockery of the Lord's Supper (communion) caused some of them to be sick and some of them to die prematurely.

Sickness and the work of the demonic realm

Then the LORD said to Satan, "Have you considered my servant Job? There is no one on earth like him; he is blameless and upright, a man who fears God and shuns evil..." Skin for skin!" Satan replied. "A man will give all he has for his own life. But stretch out your hand and strike his flesh and bones, and he will surely curse you to your face." The LORD said to Satan, "Very well, then, he is in your hands; but you must spare his life." So Satan went out from the presence of the LORD and afflicted Job with painful sores from the soles of his feet to the top of his head (Job 2:3-7).

Here we see sickness as the direct result of the activity of Satan and his realm. Although God allowed it, it was Satan who caused the sickness.

> *A man in the crowd called out, "Teacher, I beg you to look at my son, for he is my only child. A spirit seizes him and he suddenly screams; it throws him into convulsions so that he foams at the mouth. It scarcely ever leaves him and is destroying him... Even while the boy was coming, the demon threw him to the ground in a convulsion* (Luke 9:38,39,42).

This is the story of a boy who obviously has what today we call epilepsy. His healing involved deliverance from an evil spirit which appeared to be the root cause.

Sickness and individual sin

While sin is the biblical cause of sickness in the human race, Jesus taught that individually, there is not always specific sin at the root of a particular illness. This was illustrated in the story of the blind man:

> *As he went along, he saw a man blind from birth. His disciples asked him, "Rabbi, who sinned, this man or his parents, that he was born blind?" "Neither this man nor his parents sinned," said Jesus, "but this happened so that the work of God might be displayed in his life"* (John 9:1-3).

The disciples wanted to connect individual sin, or generational sin, to a specific illness. Jesus clearly refutes their mistaken notion.

In summary then, we see that the problem of humanity's sickness in the Bible is seen as an extension of the effects of sin. This relationship is clear from the beginning of the Bible to the end. It was emphasized in the Old Testament dealing of God with his people and Jesus taught it. The New Testament people of God, the Church, are also subject to this relationship. And in the redemption motif throughout the Bible, the restoration of people in right relationship with God through Jesus, as we will see in Chapter 6, leads to health and ultimate immortality.

In light of what we know scientifically, is this view plausible today? Is coming full circle reasonable? Because of the overwhelming evidence of the existence of a spiritual realm, we must consider this probable and that, ultimately, life only makes sense with consideration of the spiritual. The spiritual craving of humankind bears this out.

So which disease theory do you adhere to? Can they all be a little true? Or is one true and the others false? How we answer that will ultimately be determined by our *worldview*, our next topic for exploration.

Toward a Proper Worldview

3

> We believe... that traditional dogmatic or author-
> itarian religions that place revelation, God, ritu-
> al, or creed above human needs and experience do
> a disservice to the human species... We find
> insufficient evidence for belief in the existence of a
> supernatural.

Humanist Manifesto II, 1973

Henry Morgentaler, MD, is one of the Canada's signatories of the *Humanist Manifesto 2000*, drafted by the International Academy of Humanism. It was created on the heels of *Humanist Manifesto I* published by the American Humanist Association (AHA) in 1933 and *Humanist Manifesto II* of 1973. All three manifestoes openly state the non-theistic position of humanists. The 2000 Manifesto puts it this way:

Neither the standard modern cosmology nor the evolutionary process provides sufficient evidence for intelli-
gent design, which is a leap of faith beyond the empirical evidence. We think it time for humanity to embrace

its own adulthood—to leave behind the magical thinking and mythmaking that are substitutes for tested knowledge of nature.[12]

Humanists view the world through atheistic eyes and draw conclusions based on that *worldview*. Thus, for Dr. Morgentaler, the morality of abortion is not an issue as his atheistic worldview leads to a conclusion that there are no absolute rights or wrongs.

A worldview is a way of looking at all of reality and explaining, to our own satisfaction, how and why things are as they appear. It is our view, or the glasses through which we look at the world around us. If I am wearing clear glasses, to me the sky is blue and the grass is green. However, suppose you have red-coloured glasses on and, while looking at the same scene, you strongly disagree with me and insist that the sky is red and the grass is black. Our perception of reality is coloured by which glasses we have on. Similarly, our worldview will determine what we understand when we consider the origins of the universe, our perception of an ultimate being such as God (either His existence or non-existence), our sense of why we are here, and what happens to us when we die. What is important is that our glasses are clear and we view reality properly, because we can't all be right—either the sky is blue or red. Only one worldview can be correct as they are all mutually exclusive by definition.

As North American readers, we are likely to find ourselves in one of three worldviews. The one we hold to will largely determine what we look for in the area of health and healing, because it will determine what we believe about why we age and become sick. To find out which worldview you adhere to, the first question to ask is whether you believe in a spiritual realm outside the observable cosmos. The humanist worldview promoted in the Manifestoes denies such an existence, while the other two affirm it.

DOES A SPIRITUAL REALM EXIST?

A period in history known as the Enlightenment has carried us into the modern era of naturalism, or modernism, the primary secular worldview held by the majority of academics and scientists and clearly articulated by the humanists of the International Academy of Humanism. Naturalists believe that scientific laws are adequate to explain all observable phenomena and any unknown questions will one day be answerable through science.

Is this the best explanation for all of reality? In the Enlightenment era, rational thought essentially crossed out the possibility for the existence of a spiritual realm based on the postulation that the universe was infinite in time and in space. But cosmologists now know, for example, that the universe is expanding and finite in both time and space, and that, therefore, a moment of creation exists. So the issue of a Creator is raised in the minds of all serious cosmologists. How else could one explain the existence of evil in such regimes as Pol Pot's in Cambodia or Hitler's Nazi Germany? How else could one explain spontaneous organization out of the chaos of the Big Bang which goes contrary to the second law of thermodynamics? And why are we genetically programmed to age and die with a theoretical life expectancy of 120 years?

Let's take a serious look at the evidence for an invisible, extra-dimensional realm.

EVIDENCE THAT THE SPIRITUAL REALM EXISTS

1. The need for a "Master Designer" to explain the cosmos

The Big Bang theory has several problems which are easily reconciled by a "Supreme Being," but when left to chance alone face inexplicable and very unlikely odds.

a. The energy of the big bang

Scientists agree that the energy of the big bang was crucial. A fraction less energy and the universe would simply have imploded without any possibility of supporting life. Likewise, a fraction more energy and the universe would expand at a rate which could not support life. Just the right energy was required to support life—no more, no less. The odds for just the right amount of energy are one in ten[55] (one in ten followed by fifty-five zeros).[13] Typically, odds in cosmology and evolution were accounted for by infinite time and infinite chances. But now knowing that the universe is finite, for the big bang there was only one chance and only one chance for just the right amount of energy.

A Creator with a design plan would orchestrate the moment of creation with just the energy to support the life He wanted to establish within the cosmos. It seems illogical to argue against the existence of God when there is only a one in ten[55] chance that He doesn't exist!

b. Organization from disorganization

Cosmologists concede that there are problems explaining the hierarchical organization of the universe (stars grouped in galaxies, galaxies in clusters, and clusters in superclusters). In his chapter entitled *Five Reasons Why Galaxies Can't Exist*, Trefil expresses the frustration this causes scientists:

> The problem of explaining the existence of galaxies has proved to be one of the thorniest in cosmology. By all rights, they just shouldn't be there, yet there they sit. It's hard to convey the depth of the frustration that this simple fact induces among scientists.[14]

He goes on to list the five problems in explaining organization from disorganization. This problem is not new to parents and homeowners! Every parent knows that a child's room becomes increasingly disorganized unless regular clean-up and organization is scheduled. Likewise, homeowners know that without regular maintenance a house will eventually cave in. These are illustrations of the second law of thermodynamics which states that the direction of spontaneous change in isolated systems is toward maximum disorder. This is called *entropy*, the measure of the amount of disorder or randomness in a system. Because there are many more random ways of arranging a group of things than there are organized ways, disorder is much more probable. For example, shuffling a deck of cards always leads to a jumbled distribution of cards, not to an ordered sequence.

Contrary to the second law of thermodynamics, the Big Bang theory postulates a universe of increased randomness spontaneously giving rise to a universe of increased order. Disorganized clouds of atoms coalesce to form galaxies, galaxies form planetary systems, planets form life and ultimately this evolves to human life.

Again, the infinitesimally small odds of all this happening spontaneously begs a theistic explanation for the universe and for life. Only a Master Designer with a design plan could shape the universe and orchestrate the conditions to support human life.

c. The anthropic principle

Human existence is possible in the universe because planet earth is such a fit habitat. And to be fit, a great number of factors, or parameters, such as the energy of the creation event mentioned above, need to fall within highly restricted ranges.[15] The fact that these parameters are all fine-tuned to support life, has lead cosmologists to coin the term *anthropic principle*. It proposes that the whole of creation was designed expressly to lead to the existence of humankind. This incredible design points to a God beyond the limits of time and space who personally shaped the universe in preparation for humankind. The incredibly minuscule chance of this happening spontaneously can be likened to the chance of an explosion in a Boeing factory producing a perfect, ready-to-fly 747 jet or a monkey with a typewriter producing the entire works of Shakespeare.

d. The age of the universe

One of the problems with non-theistic evolutionary theory is the complexity of the human genome (all the genes that make us what we are) and the relatively young age of the universe as estimated by scientists. For a complex organism such as a human being to develop from chance mutations and natural selection in the length of time possible, is again highly improbable. It is estimated that the universe is in the order of magnitude of ten billion times too young for life to have assembled itself by natural processes.[16]

2. Third World experiences

Many people from the West who have traveled or worked in countries like Haiti, Costa Rica, or black Africa have little doubt about the reality of a spiritual realm because they have seen manifestations of it firsthand. We hear of things like psychic surgery or the effects of Voodoo spells, but unless we experience them firsthand we are left with skepticism.

One person with first-hand experience in this area is a personal acquaintance from Prince Edward Island who lived in Costa Rica for twenty years. Disillusioned as a young person, Sharon ran, ending up living on a beach in Costa Rica with what appeared to be a good life of tropical beaches and endless peace. Unfortunately, she found herself next to a neighbour who was a Voodoo practitioner and Sharon became the object of her witchcraft. As the spells increased, so did the physical manifestations—expressions of the metaphysical, the paranormal. On one particular day, as the intensity of what appeared to Sharon to be a death curse escalated, she found herself levitating, suspended in midair. Known as *telekinesis* in parapsychology, it obviously invoked intense fear and dread in Sharon. Although not a Christian at the time, she recalls yelling out the name of Jesus in desperation, and she came crashing to the floor. Although not the end of her struggle against the curses placed upon her, it was the turning point in her life, and she subsequently converted to Christianity.

I have no reason to doubt Sharon's account of her encounter with the power of Voodoo. Telekinesis is clearly extra-dimensional, outside the physical laws of the universe, in this case defying the law of gravity. It exemplifies clearly that a spiritual realm with real power exists, and that, within that realm, there are forces of good and of evil.

Someone who has extensively researched this territory around the globe is George Otis Jr. In his book, *The Twilight Labyrinth,* he shares what he learned during his seven-year odyssey as he "listened to the stories of Tibetan Buddhist lamas, Native American medicine men and leading theorists of the New Age movement"[17] in order to comprehend the dark spiritual realm which he calls the "Otherworld." His conclusion—this realm really exists and it can hold sway over people, communities and even regions. But he has also seen and documented, in an award-winning video, communities that have been freed from these dark powers through the power of faith in Jesus Christ and united, fervent prayer.[18]

3. The historical/archaeological evidence that the Bible is true

The Bible claims a spiritual realm exists. It teaches about a transcendent, infinite God, about heaven and hell, about angels and demons and about the power of prayer. And there is the claim by Jesus that He was divine, the Son of God.

How can we know that the Bible is true and not merely

the product of humankind's spiritual yearnings? Let's look at the objective evidence.

a. Archaeologic evidence

In the last 150 years, biblical archaeology has become an exacting science and increasingly, discoveries are being made to verify the accuracy of Scripture. From the time of King Solomon, the biblical record has been confirmed through artifacts and relics found in archaeological digs. More and more discoveries are being made from earlier dates. For example, in 1990, Frank Yurco, an Egyptologist, used hieroglyphic clues from a monolith to identify figures in a wall relief dated to 1207 BC as ancient Israelites, confirming that the Israelites were a distinct people more than 3000 years ago and not just because the Bible tells us so.[19] In 1993, Avraham Biran, a Jewish archaeologist, announced that he had found an inscription, dated to the 9th century BC bearing the phrases "House of David" and "King of Israel," thereby refuting the skeptics' claim that David was a fictional character.[20] In 1986, lumps of figured clay called *bullae*, were found which bore the seals of Jeremiah's scribes, confirming that the Old Testament Jeremiah existed.[21]

One of the best-known biblical archaeologists is William Albright from John Hopkins University. He describes how archaeological findings confirm the Bible's historical accuracy.

> The excessive skepticism shown toward the Bible by important schools of the eighteenth and nineteenth centuries, certain phases of which still appear periodically, has been progressively discredited. Discovery after discovery has established the accuracy of innumerable details, and has brought increased recognition to the value of the Bible as a source of history.[22]

> Nelson Glueck, a renowned Jewish archaeologist, claimed that "no archaeological discovery has ever controverted a biblical reference."[23]

b. The evidence of New Testament reliability

The testing of ancient documents for authenticity is a common practice among literary scholars. Essentially, the more texts we have and the smaller the time between the original and the first copies, the less doubt there is about authenticity. When we compare the New Testament to many other classical works, such as the *Iliad* by Homer, we see a greater reliability because there are far more copies and a much shorter time period between the original and the copies. The following table compares the New Testament to several other classical works:[24]

Work	When written	Earliest copy	Time span yrs.	No. of copies
Herodotus	488–428 BC	900 AD	1300	8
Thucydides	460–400 BC	900 AD	1300	8
Tacitus	100 AD	1100 AD	1000	20
Caesar's Gallic War	58–50 BC	900 AD	950	9–10
Livy's Roman History	59 BC– 17 AD	900 AD	900	20
New Testament	40–100 AD	130 AD (Full manuscripts 350 AD)	300	5000+ Greek, 10,000 Latin, 9300 others

Table 3.1

Sir Frederic Kenyon, who was the director and principal librarian of the British Museum and an authority on ancient literature, said this about the reliability of the New Testament:

> The interval then between the dates of original composition and the earliest extant (not destroyed or lost) evidence becomes so small as to be in fact negligible, and the last foundation for any doubt that the Scriptures have come down to us substantially as they were written has now been removed. Both the authenticity and the general integrity of the books of the New Testament may be regarded as finally established.[25]

So we have little doubt about the reliability of the historical text that chronicles the life of Jesus Christ. Not many question His existence, but what about His claim to be the Son of God?

c. Jesus claimed to be God

In the Gospel of Mark, the following conversation between Caiaphas, the Jewish High Priest, and Jesus is recorded:

> *Again the high priest asked him, "Are you the Christ, the Son of the Blessed One?" "I am," said Jesus. "And you will see the Son of Man sitting at the right hand of the Mighty One and coming on the clouds of heaven"* (Mark 16:61,62).

What is the evidence that Jesus was who He said He was? Table 3.2 summarizes why we believe in the deity of Jesus Christ.

Evidence to Support Christ's Claims of Divinity	
His teaching	Christ's teaching is widely acknowledged to be the greatest teaching that has ever fallen from anyone's lips. It is the foundation of our entire civilization in the West, including many of our laws.
His works	Throughout His life He healed the sick, raised the dead, fed the thousands, stilled the storms, walked on water, cast out demons and forgave sins. *Do not believe me unless I do what my Father does. But if I do it, even though you do not believe me, believe the miracles, that you may know and understand that the Father is in me, and I in the Father* (John 10:37,38).
His character	Jesus exemplified supreme unselfishness but never self-pity; humility but not weakness; joy but never at another's expense; kindness but not indulgence. His enemies could find no fault with Him other than His claim to be divine.
Fulfillment of Old Testament prophecy	Jesus fulfilled over 300 prophecies recorded by different prophets over 500 years. The place of His birth, the manner of His death and the place of His burial were all foretold.
His resurrection	The greatest evidence of all was Jesus' victory over death. The empty tomb is a fact of history which many have tried to explain away. His post-resurrection appearances to the disciples changed their lives and they, in turn, the world.

Table 3.2

Christ was either divine as He said He was, or an intentional deceiver, or psychiatrically ill with delusions of grandeur. C. S. Lewis, the great British thinker and writer who was himself a skeptic for years, put it this way:

A man who was merely a man and said the sort of things Jesus said would not be a great moral teacher. He would either be a lunatic, on a level with the man who says he is a poached egg, or else he would be the Devil of Hell. You must make your choice. Either this man was, and is, the Son of God; or else a madman or something worse ... but let us not come up with any patronized nonsense about His being a great human teacher. He has not left that open to use. He did not intend to.[26]

If Jesus intentionally deceived generations of followers, He was the greatest con man to ever live but also the kindest and the most selfless. If He was schizophrenic with delusions of grandeur, the rest of His behavior certainly didn't show it. On the other hand, if He was God, He deserves our allegiance.

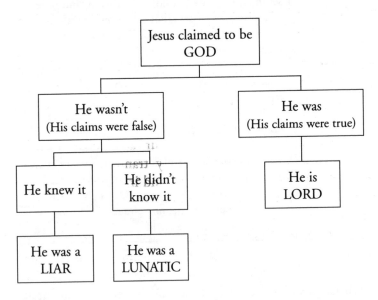

Figure 3.1 Jesus
Liar, Lunatic or Lord

What about other world religions? Christianity is the only religion which claims that God incarnated (took on human form) as a man. Eastern religions such as Hinduism and Buddhism maintain that God is infinite but not a personal being—rather, all is God and God is all. The Western gods of the Greeks were personal beings, but they were not infinite. Of the three religions that teach that God is both infinite Creator and a personal being, Judaism and Islam exist on the basis of God revealing Himself to certain prophets, while Christianity rests on the foundation of God becoming a man. And Christianity's validity is bolstered by being the only religion with an empty tomb.

4. The experience of believers throughout the years

It's hard to argue that the teachings of Jesus represent everything good in humanity. Although His followers have their share of blunders—the conflict in Ireland between Catholics and Protestants, the Crusades, Apartheid in South Africa, fallen TV evangelists—it must be noted that Christ taught peaceful conflict resolution and loving enemies. True followers of Christ were influential in the abolition of slavery; they help feed the poor, treat the sick, encourage literacy and education, help abolish child labour and reduce crime. Christian revivals in history literally transformed cultures, such as the Wesleyan revival in England in the 18th century. Social conditions in England improved dramatically with reductions in alcoholism, family breakdown and crime as the result of John Wesley's work. The Great Awakening in North America, under George Whitefield, had similar effects. More recently, the culture in Colombia, South America, is being transformed from drug-trade driven to Christian as the result of Christian revival in that country. No other movement in history has had the civilizing force of Christianity, including the new-found religions of humanism or New Age. Herein lies, I believe, one of the strongest evidences for the validity of Christianity.

And ask any of the millions around the world who profess a personal relationship with Jesus Christ and you will hear stories of peace, healed relationships, forgiveness, and purpose for living. You will hear stories of strength in the midst of difficulty and answered prayer. And you will hear stories of courage and commitment beyond measure—such as Mother Theresa in her compassion for the poor in Calcutta, such as a teenager looking down the barrel of a gun in Columbine High School.

Finally, look at the evidence of genuinely transformed lives. An encounter with Jesus Christ is the best antidote for repeated crimes, imprisonments, and drug addiction. Nicky Cruz was a gang leader and street fighter in the worst slums of New York City, ready to kill at a moment's notice. After his conversion through David Wilkerson's outreach, he has become a respected member of his community, a loving husband and devoted father, a speaker and writer, and an evangelist committed to reaching the very people that almost brought him to ruin.[27] Many, many more identify with such conversion stories, literally seeing their lives transformed from hopelessness to genuine purpose.

Is there evidence for extra-dimensionality, a spiritual realm beyond the observable four-dimensional universe? Theists and non-theists will still disagree, but I believe that the objective evidence above points overwhelmingly to a God who is not dead and an unseen spiritual realm. In actual fact, this argument is bolstered by recent advances in cosmology, particularly in string theory, that point to a ten-dimensional creation event. Although exploration of this concept is beyond the scope of this book, a scientific discussion can be found in Dr. Hugh Ross's book, *Beyond the Cosmos*.[28]

TOWARD A CORRECT WORLDVIEW

Given the fact that there is objective evidence, when the best science bears down to the smallest particles of matter and to the farthest reaches of the universe, or when relativity is taken to infinity, an extra-dimensional, spiritual realm exists. We need now correct our vision by properly balancing our synthesis, or blending, of science and theology—the created and the Creator. Only then will we satisfy the human yearning for ultimate truth and meaning in life.

The Creator has manifested Himself through the created, as well a through written revelation. The imbalance of these two has lead to errors in the past and continues to fuel the conflict between science and theology today.

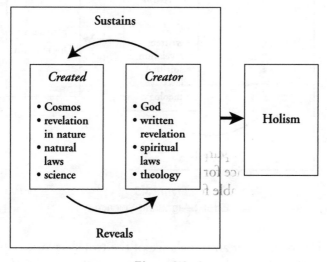

Figure 3.2
Biblical Worldview

Figure 3.2 is a view of reality, or a paradigm, which merges what we know from science with what we know from written revelation. The Creator is infinite and transcendent, self-existent and self-sufficient. Out of His omnipotence (all-power-fulness) He brought something (the cosmos) out of nothing-ness (creation) and now sustains it until its inevitable end. The created, the universe as we know it, operates by natural laws such as gravity and relativity which science can observe, ana-lyze, and prove. The circle is completed when what we learn from science reveals the hand of the Creator. Both aspects of this paradigm are essential to perceive reality accurately, which leads to genuine holism.

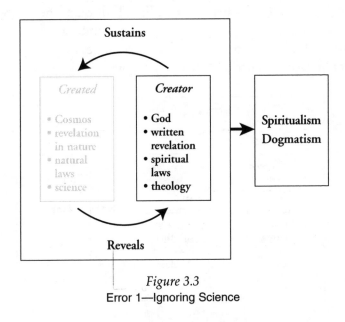

Figure 3.3
Error 1—Ignoring Science

Errors occur in an imbalance of the two sides of our para-digm, or in their fusion. In the first instance (Figure 3.3 above), an error occurs when theology and religion are emphasized and science is ignored. Here we see the errors of spiritualism and dogmatism. This error caused Galileo to be imprisoned by the church of his day because he supported the Copernican theory that the sun was the centre of the solar system rather than the earth. And flat-earth proponents based their arguments on several biblical references that included the words, "the four corners of the earth."

Spiritualism is the view that spirit is the prime element of reality. (The alternative definition of spiritualism—communicating with the spirits of the dead—is not intended here). Dogmatism occurs when people are instructed to think that black is white if religious leaders declare it to be white, despite empirical evidence that it is black. These are building blocks for cults and the extremes of fundamentalism.

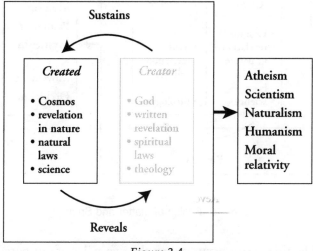

Figure 3.4
Error 2—Ignoring the Creator

The second error occurs when the Creator is ignored, and science is emphasized (Figure 3.4 above). This leads to the errors of atheism, scientism, naturalism, humanism, and moral relativity. These, of course, have advanced the dominant, secular, humanistic worldview of today. Atheism denies the existence of any god and the spiritual realm. Scientism is an exaggerated trust in science and the application of it to all areas of study. In essence, it becomes god and the only source of knowledge. Naturalism is the doctrine that natural, scientific laws are adequate to account for all phenomena. Humanism is the belief that humankind is not accountable to any deity but is the master of its own destiny. Moral relativity occurs when there are no absolute rights or wrongs.

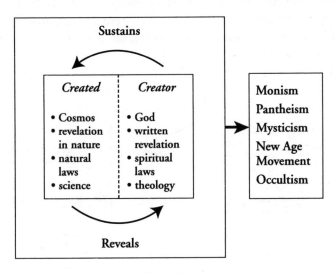

Figure 3.5
Error 3—Fusion of Matter and Spirit

The third error occurs when the two poles of our paradigm are fused into one (Figure 3.5 above). Now matter and spirit are viewed as one. Monism is the belief in the unity of all things—one is all and all is one. This leads to pantheism, the view which equates God with the matter and energy of the entire cosmos, and animism, the attributing of spiritual power to nature and natural objects. Pantheists and animists see their god in nature, in astrology, and in themselves. In essence, they say, "We are all gods." This is the basis for the New Age Movement, a mixture of Eastern mysticism from such religions as Hinduism and Taoism with latent occultism and Western materialism.

All three errors miss reality. Holism can only be found in the balanced cycle of our wholeness paradigm (Figure 3.2). This healthy balance is achieved when scientific analysis of the natural universe is used to discover the character of the Creator and when written revelation is used to guide the ethics of further scientific research and the development of new technology.

In the area of health and healing, this balance is essential. True holism requires this. Imbalance leads to the errors of New Age Medicine in the use of mysticism and the occult to heal, as well as the use of scientifically-unverified treatments. Imbalance leads to Christian spiritual healers who advise their followers to ignore medical science and avoid conventional medicine. Just as significant are the errors which occur when medical scientists ignore the spiritual realm and place all their hope for immortality in science.

Now that we have proper glasses to see through, we can sharpen our focus and examine the specifics of why we are sick.

4 Why Am I Sick Now?

*That is why many among you are weak and sick,
and a number of you have fallen asleep.*

Paul, 55 AD

aving examined the larger question of why we
age, become ill, and die, we now need to consider the possible reasons for our present illness. We will see in Part III that living well in
obedience to biblical principles will improve our health
vastly, but we will continue to be mortal this side of eternity because of humanity's fallen state. One hundred percent of us will face death if the Lord tarries—the ultimate
statistic. *Man is destined to die once*, Scripture says (Heb.
9:27). Hence, our bodies will continue to age and eventually fail, so there may be seasons in our lives when we are
faced with sickness. In this chapter we want to look at some
possible specific reasons for present illness and how to
respond to these seasons. Should we immediately run to
doctors or other practitioners for help? Perhaps some have

chronic illnesses and all avenues to healing have failed. How do we deal with pain in our lives? What about those with terminal diagnoses?

In the second book of Chronicles we see one of the kings of Israel who, in his younger days, was devoted to God. Later in his reign, however, he lost his first love for God and became very self-sufficient. When illness struck, this was his response:

> *In the thirty-ninth year of his reign Asa was afflicted with a disease in his feet. Though his disease was severe, even in his illness he did not seek help from the LORD, but only from the physicians* (2 Chron. 16:12).

Like Asa, we may be faced with illness and our biggest mistake would be to fail to "seek help from the Lord, but only from the physicians." So before we run to our healing practitioners to seek healing and restoration, here are some questions we should prayerfully ask ourselves:

- Is this a wake-up call?
- Is my sickness the direct result of personal sin?
- Is the occult influencing me?
- Is there a generational curse?
- Am I being disciplined by God?
- Am I being tested by God?
- Have I abused the Lord's Supper?
- Am I carrying unresolved emotional baggage?
- Are there unresolved relationships?
- Is there secondary gain to my illness?
- Am I sick because of humanity's fallen state?
- Am I sick that God's work may be displayed?

As we prayerfully consider these questions, we may find there are times God allows sickness to draw us to Himself or to build character in our lives. Other times it may be a corrective measure. Sometimes sickness is evidence of spiritual warfare in our lives and we may need deliverance. There may be deep emotional roots causing unresolved illness. Or God may use us in our weakness as a testimony to others.

If you want to start on the road to wholeness, I encourage you to ask these questions. You may need to get the help of a spiritually mature friend, counselor, or pastor to help identify unresolved issues in your life—some may reach back far into childhood. Particularly helpful for you would be someone with the spiritual gift of knowledge.

Is this a wake-up call?

Many people go through life busily climbing the success ladder. Only later do they regretfully discover their ladder is leaning against the wrong wall. The ladder may be to become CEO of a company. It may be political fame, wealth, their sport's Hall of Fame, or simply pleasure. Many times God will allow a major sickness in such a person's life to help them realize this is not what life is about—that leaving a Christian legacy and preparing for eternity are much more important. It may be cancer, a heart attack, or a major motor vehicle accident. It may be a recreational accident.

One person who had such a wake-up call was Jack, who shared his story on CBC's *This Morning,* in a series entitled, "Real Life with Cancer." At the age of sixty-one he was diagnosed with an aggressive brain tumor and shared, in his discussion with two other cancer patients, how thankful he was to be blessed with the opportunity to "get his house in order" and how his "spiritual renewal" helped him prepare for what may lie ahead. It gave him the opportunity to make peace with his God.

People who may need such a wake-up call are often driven in their career or vocation. Often prone to workaholism, they may neglect family and relationships, and invariably there is little time to pursue spiritual disciplines. They may recall spiritual passion somewhere in their past, maybe in their youth, but, like Asa, God was long ago left to simmer on the back burner.

If you have received such a wake-up call, rejoice and confess your spiritual apathy and get your spiritual life on track. Start living for the Lord with the same zeal with which you climbed the wrong ladder. Make the rest of your life count—lean your ladder on the right wall. It is very likely that God will give you a second chance—He won't take you home until His plan for your life on earth is fulfilled.

Is my sickness the direct result of personal sin?

We have already seen the direct relationship of sinful living and sickness. Obesity, AIDS and other sexually transmitted diseases, lung cancer or emphysema from smoking, and Hepatitis C from shared needles are all examples of personal sin resulting directly in illness. As you seek healing and restoration from such illnesses, the following biblical principles should be applied:

- Recognize the behavior that caused your illness as sin—don't try to rationalize or justify it.

- Repent of your sin—acknowledge to God in prayer that you sincerely regret your sin and the damage it caused your body, and the Body of Christ.

- Confess your sin to others as appropriate. We read in James that you are *to confess your sins to each other and pray for each other so that you may be healed* (Jas. 5:16). This may be one person, especially if you sinned against that person (in such cases as adultery), or it may be your small group in church, or possibly the whole church if you feel God requires that.

- Find the emotional root cause of what triggers the sinful behavior in your life. Get inner healing of this root. Chapter 10 has more detail on how to do this.

- Once you are healed of the emotional root you will easily turn from the sinful behavior, whether it is overeating, a chemical addiction, or immorality.

- Pray for physical healing—only after the sin is dealt with are you in a position to believe God for supernatural healing of your illness.

There are times when God does not remove the consequences of sinful behavior this side of eternity. Rest assured though, from an eternal perspective, your salvation is complete. Chapter 12 has more insights in facing such losses with dignity.

Is the demonic realm influencing me?

We have seen in our study on worldviews in Chapter 3, that a balanced view of reality needs to account for a spiritual realm where good and evil are rivals in a battle known as spiritual warfare. The question before us now is whether the dark side of that realm can influence our minds or bodies and have a detrimental effect on our health.

Most Christians believe this realm is real with power to cause illness as well as to heal. There are people today who call on these powers either recreationally, vocationally, or sometimes with evil intent. Since Scripture clearly relates the work of the demonic realm with illness, we need to prayerfully consider that possibility when faced with our own illness. Consider this particularly when faced with an illness for which no medical or scientific explanation exists, although this need not always be the case. Demonically-caused illness may, in fact, be due to a virus or a chemical imbalance which is the host factor that is altered by the spiritual realm.

There are some who feel that Christians can't be "demonized." While it is true that a true believer cannot be "demon possessed," it is possible for Christians to be influenced or harassed by the demonic realm. This is particularly true where demons have gained entrance prior to regeneration through occultic activities or childhood trauma such as incest or abuse. Prayerfully consider the following:

- Consider the demonic realm when faced with a chronic illness, particularly if it keeps you from worship or pursuing your spiritual disciplines (e.g. allergies that keep you away from church).

- Consider the demonic realm with recurring illness, particularly at times of spiritual significance (e.g. you are asked to share your testimony at an evangelistic meeting).

- Consider the demonic realm if you are beset with fear, chronic anxiety, phobias or obsessions.

- Consider the demonic realm if you have a history of sexual or physical abuse, near-death experiences or suicide attempts. Forgiveness is key if someone has seriously hurt you. (There is more on forgiveness in Chapter 10.)

- Examine your pre-Christian, as well as post-Christian exposure to non-Christian spiritual experiences, particularly occultic activities such as Ouija boards, seances, Dungeons and Dragons, fortune telling, palm reading, psychic fairs, or horoscopes.

- If there is any possibility of an occultic etiology, seek out a pastor, counselor, or Christian ministry with experience in inner healing and deliverance

- Pray for the Holy Spirit to fill the void. *Submit yourselves, then, to God. Resist the devil, and he will flee from you. Come near to God and he will come near to you* (Jas. 4:7,8). Chapter 8 contains details on how to be filled with the Holy Spirit.

Is there a generational curse?

There are times when lingering illness or recurring illness may be the result of a generational curse. Although science may increasingly attribute most of this to genetic heritage, we should not simply succumb to genetic fatalism without regard for spiritual principles. In many cases, illness is not caused solely by genes but also by multiple environmental factors as well as a host factor which may be spiritually influenced. Examples might be recurring accidents or recurring financial failures. There may be addiction tendencies and problems with spousal or child abuse.

What is a generational curse? It is a host-factor weakening mediated through spiritual forces that have legal rights to your body or soul because of ancestral sins or ancestral occultic involvement. This may go back three or four generations:

> *I, the LORD your God, am a jealous God, punishing the children for the sin of the fathers to the third and fourth generation of those who hate me* (Exod. 20:5).

- Consider a generational curse if there is a strong family history of a particular disease, especially if death or disability is premature.

- Consider a generational curse for recurring patterns in multiple generations, such as alcoholism, abuse, accidents, financial failures, marriage failures, homosexuality.

- The Holy Spirit can reveal generational sins or curses, frequently through someone with a spiritual gift of knowledge. Usually you do not need to dig deep into your past to expose family secrets, although there are times when it may be helpful for other family members to know what was uncovered. Pray about this and follow the counsel of a trusted, mature Christian. Sometimes whole families can be freed.

- If a curse is found, break it through the power of the blood of Christ back through each generation. Stop the curse at *your* generation so your children will be protected. You may need the help of a pastor, counselor, or mature friend. Appendix C has a spiritual-warfare prayer for additional help.

- Pray for the Holy Spirit to fill the void. Exercise your spiritual disciplines as outlined in Chapter 8.

Am I being disciplined by God?

Some illness may be allowed by God in order to discipline us, particularly to draw us back into His loving arms. Scripture puts it this way:

> *And you have forgotten that word of encouragement that addresses you as sons: "My son, do not make light of the Lord's discipline, and do not lose heart when he rebukes you, because the Lord disciplines those he loves, and he punishes everyone he accepts as a son." Endure hardship as discipline; God is treating you as sons. For what son is not disciplined by his father? If you are not disciplined (and everyone undergoes discipline), then you are illegitimate children and not true sons* (Heb. 12:5-8).

Sometimes our rebellion or disobedience requires the Lord's discipline. Our heart may have become divided, following after false gods of our own making. Maybe we are in rebellion to someone in authority over us—a teacher, a parent, a husband, a pastor, or a boss.

- Consider the Lord's discipline if the Holy Spirit reveals rebellion, disobedience, or idolatry in your heart.

- Confess the rebellion, disobedience or idolatry as sin, repent of it, and resolve with God's help to restore Him as your first love.

- Pray for healing only after the Holy Spirit prompts you to do so. Don't run to health practitioners without clear spiritual guidance.

A loving father will remove the hand of discipline once corrective action has been demonstrated. Disciplinary sickness is likely to be healed once you sincerely correct an erring way.

Am I being tested by God?

God may use sickness in order to strengthen us spiritually and to build character by testing our faith.

Consider it pure joy, my brothers, whenever you face trials of many kinds, because you know that the testing of your faith develops perseverance. Perseverance must finish its work so that you may be mature and complete, not lacking anything (Jas. 1:2-4).

God has our spiritual well-being in mind, and our value to Him as warriors for His Kingdom, far more than our physical comforts. As we will see in Chapter 12, men and women whom God has particularly called are sometimes the very ones thrown into complete reliance on God through such testing. Take the Apostle Paul, for example.

To keep me from becoming conceited because of these sur-passingly great revelations, there was given me a thorn in my flesh, a messenger of Satan, to torment me. Three times

I pleaded with the Lord to take it away from me. But he said to me, "My grace is sufficient for you, for my power is made perfect in weakness." Therefore I will boast all the more gladly about my weaknesses, so that Christ's power may rest on me. That is why, for Christ's sake, I delight in weaknesses, in insults, in hardships, in persecutions, in difficulties. For when I am weak, then I am strong (2 Cor. 12:7-10).

We don't know for sure what Paul's thorn was, but I heard an argument by the late Dr. Gurney, founder of the Red Sea Mission, which absolutely convinced me that it was trachoma, an eye disease that causes the eye lashes to turn inward, thereby causing the cornea to become opaque with resulting visual impairment. Dr. Luke probably went along on Paul's missionary journeys to help him by intermittently "plucking" these eye lashes from his eye lids.

Here are some scriptural guidelines:

- When faced with illness, particularly if you have been making great strides in spiritual maturity, pray whether it is a test.

- If you sense a test, thank the Lord for it and rejoice that He is shaping you more into Jesus' likeness and that He wants to build character in your life.

- Follow Paul's example—pray several times in faith for its removal. If you find that God does not remove it, pray for the strength to endure, so that your life and ministry are not hindered by the illness.

Have I abused the Lord's Supper?

In the passage of Scripture often read in communion services, known throughout Christendom as the institution of the Lord's Supper, there is a reference to eating and drinking in an unworthy manner which leads to weakness and sickness and possibly death:

> *Therefore, whoever eats the bread or drinks the cup of the Lord in an unworthy manner will be guilty of sinning against the body and blood of the Lord. A man ought to examine himself before he eats of the bread and drinks of the cup. For anyone who eats and drinks without recognizing the body of the Lord eats and drinks judgment on himself. That is why many among you are weak and sick, and a number of you have fallen asleep. But if we judged ourselves, we would not come under judgment. When we are judged by the Lord, we are being disciplined so that we will not be condemned with the world* (1 Cor. 11:27-32).

Traditionally, this is interpreted to mean that someone who is not a true believer, who then partakes of communion, puts himself in a judgement position. It is also possible for a believer to take communion carelessly, thereby sharing in the guilt of those responsible for the crucifixion rather than receiving by faith the benefits of Christ's sacrifice which include physical healing. It is for this reason, I believe, improper communion leads to divine chastisement expressed physically in illness. Verse 32 clearly indicated this is not eternal judgement.

- Hold communion (Mass, Eucharist, Lord's Supper) in high regard. It need not be mournful—it is not Christ's funeral. Rather it is a celebration of the salvation (spirit, soul and body) that is ours through Christ's finished work on the cross.

- When faced with illness, ask the Holy Spirit to reveal whether you have committed the sin of disregard for Christ's death. In particular, ask your pastor for help in discerning this.

- If God reveals a sin in this area, confess it and repent.

- This is not an unforgivable sin. Pray for healing after repentance.

Is there unresolved emotional baggage?

My home village of Crapaud is known in Prince Edward Island as the "Home of the PEI Tractor Pulls." Here, for two days every year, competitors use their tractors to pull a drag sled with a concrete weight that moves up the sled causing increased resistance of the drag on the ground. The further the driver moves down the track, the closer the weight moves to the front of the sled and heavier the drag becomes, until eventually the tractor stalls or spins out. The winner is the tractor who pulls the drag the furthest.

If we carry emotional baggage with us through life's journey, sooner or later it too will creep up on us until we crash—either emotionally or physically. The stress will be more than our bodies or minds were designed to carry. Many people can get to about mid-life although many will crash as early as adolescence. For many, the busyness of parenting and pursuing a career keeps us sailing along fairly smoothly, just like the first half of the tractor pull track. But when the nest is empty or there is a major loss, the weight becomes too much to bear. Frequently depression sets in, followed by physical illness.

What are some of these bags? It may be a spirit of rejection—perhaps from being given up for adoption. There may be guilt from an abortion or an illicit sexual encounter. It may be shame resulting from sexual violation in childhood. For some there may be intense fear of death or of cancer which may be rooted in the loss of a loved one in childhood.

How do you know if you are carrying unwanted baggage?

- You know of emotional or physical trauma in childhood that you haven't dealt with.

- You never received your parent's favour—you never

seemed to measure up and they never told you that they loved you and appreciated you for who you were.

• You were spiritually or physically abused by a pastor or priest, either early in life or even into adulthood.

It is my experience that many with chronic illnesses, particularly ones that defy medical treatment, are rooted in unresolved emotional baggage. Frequently, the bags being carried are also an entry point for demonic influences, thus intensifying the pain. In many cases, very skilled Christian counseling is required to achieve freedom in this area, although some can do it on their own. Many sincere Christians, who deeply love the Lord and want to serve Him, never get the healing they need in this area. Consequently, many churches are more needy than they are centres of healing for others.

But the good news is that you can be completely set free from this baggage through Christ. Get the inner healing you need. Chapter 10 is a place to begin but you will likely need help from a pastor or counselor.

The corollary of negative emotions causing ill health is that positive emotions, particularly the fruit of the spirit—love, joy peace, patience, kindness, goodness, gentleness, self-control—will lead to physical and emotional wholeness. Cultivate them. Be filled with the Holy Spirit. Exercise your spiritual disciplines.

Are there unresolved relationships?

Akin to unresolved emotional baggage is unresolved relational baggage. Unforgiveness and a spirit of offense are deadly tools of the enemy to destroy marriages, destroy churches and to destroy your body. Even secular writers and counselors recognize that reducing interpersonal stress will yield better physical health. In *Good Relationships are Good Medicine*, Barbara Powell argues that repairing shattered relationships is paramount for improving your physical health.[29]

I'll say it again. Unforgiveness and bitterness toward someone who hurt you are poisons to your body and soul. If you have a recurring and chronic illness, look deep within your relationship history for people whom you still hold a grudge against. Ask yourself the following questions:[30]

- Are you compelled to tell your side of the story?

- Do you fight thoughts of suspicion or distrust?

- Are you rehearsing past hurts?

- Have you lost hope because of what someone did to you?

- Do you find you are constantly justifying yourself?

If you uncover an unresolved relationship, follow these steps:

- Confess your unforgiveness to God.

- Pray that God will help you to forgive the person.

- Start praying specifically for God's blessing on the offending person's life. You need to sincerely desire God's best for him or her.

- If the person has died, or if you have lost contact with him or her, write a letter of forgiveness. Share it with a trusted friend, counselor, or pastor, and ceremoniously burn it.

- Ask in prayer whether you need to meet with the offending person to share your forgiveness. This meeting may be in person, however, in some instances, communicating by letter is appropriate.

If there is ongoing conflict that needs resolution, follow Jesus' recommendations in Matthew.

> *If your brother sins against you, go and show him his fault, just between the two of you. If he listens to you, you have*

won your brother over. But if he will not listen, take one or two others along, so that "every matter may be established by the testimony of two or three witnesses." If he refuses to listen to them, tell it to the church; and if he refuses to listen even to the church, treat him as you would a pagan or a tax collector (Matt. 18:15-17).

- If someone has hurt you or offended you, go to him or her in humility to seek reconciliation.

- If that fails to resolve the issue, find at least two people who are unbiased and mutually acceptable, and who have maturity and spiritual sensitivity, to help resolve the issue and to offer judgement on the matter.

- If that is unsuccessful, then it becomes a corporate issue for the church. If the matter is still unresolved, you are absolved of responsibility before God. You must still forgive the person in your heart and pray for God's blessing on him or her, otherwise it will become a root of bitterness. Allow no thoughts of personal vindication to overwhelm you.

Unresolved relational baggage between children and parents will invariably lead to major problems when the parents later require eldercare. This is fertile ground for elder abuse, as we will see in Chapter 11, "Aging with Grace."

Is there secondary gain to my illness?

It is no secret or surprise that some people take advantage of being sick—it may give them recognition, it may give them financial benefits, it may be an excuse for laziness. Some like the narcotics they can get, others the monthly pension cheque. Others may use their illness as an excuse to be a social recluse. Most will not genuinely be aware of any secondary gain issues.

Don't get me wrong. There are genuine illnesses with genuine disability claims. However, as physicians and insurers know, it is not easy to discern the genuine from the malingerer. Again, many people are completely unaware of secondary gain issues in their illness. Consider secondary gain in your illness by sincerely asking the following questions:

- Do you have a pension as the result of your illness?

- Would you rather be working?

- Do you enjoy special attention at public events because of special seating or other benefits?

- Do you enjoy discussing your illness with others, particularly to feel their empathy and care?

- Do you feel the society, insurer, employer, or perpetrator owes you because of your illness or injury?

- Are you using narcotics or other mood-altering drugs?

- Is there a ministry God called you to that you are not fulfilling because of your illness?

If God convicts you of secondary gain issues, confess this attitude as sin and seek out the help you need to be free from it. You will either be healed, or God will give you the strength to endure the illness with His grace. Stop talking about your illness or drawing attention to it.

Am I sick because of humanity's fallen state?

Some of you will genuinely ask all the above questions and answer, "No." And yet, that chronic disability, that wheelchair, that colostomy will be there. We acknowledge that God can heal whomever He wishes, but in reality, not everyone is healed. This side of the New Creation, there will be sickness and death. Natural disasters, accidents, war zones are no respecter of persons but symptoms of a fallen state. Jesus never promised this side of eternity that these would go away.

> *You will hear of wars and rumors of wars, but see to it that you are not alarmed. Such things must happen, but the end is still to come. Nation will rise against nation, and kingdom against kingdom. There will be famines and earthquakes in various places* (Matt. 24:7,8).

And there will be aging and its effects. Although our spirit and soul are fully redeemed here and now through faith in Jesus Christ, our body will not fully realize its redemption until its physical death and subsequent resurrection into a new, glorified body.

Am I sick that God's work may be displayed?

One final reason for sickness is illustrated in the story of the blind man in John 9.

> *As he went along, he saw a man blind from birth. His disciples asked him, "Rabbi, who sinned, this man or his parents, that he was born blind?" "Neither this man nor his parents sinned," said Jesus, "but this happened so that the work of God might be displayed in his life* (John 9:1-3).

Perhaps the best contemporary illustration of this is Joni Eareckson Tada. Paralyzed from the neck down by a diving accident as a teenager, she prayed fervently for healing. Rather than healing, God has used her mightily in her gifts of music, mouth art, and speaking to share God's redeeming love with millions of people. She is a living testimony of what someone with a major disability can do for God.

Having considered the possible reasons for your sickness, you are now in a position to consider to whom you might turn for help with your healing.

PART II:

How Can I Be Well?

The reality of sickness, aging, and death in the human race has perpetuated the healing arts since early recorded history. We have records of healing practitioners from the days of ancient Egypt (3000 BC) and the Shang dynasty in China (1700 BC). Modern medicine traces its roots back to Hippocrates in ancient Greece.

The human response to the problem of sickness has been a quest for healing and perpetual youth. Healing arts, from the spiritual medicine men of Africa and North American aboriginals to acupuncturists in China, have proliferated during the centuries. Today, beside modern scientific medicine (allopathy), there are over ninety alternative healing methods to choose from. All claim success and have their adherents.

Which do you choose for healing? How do you decide? Are all equal? Are all valid? Let's look at what is available to us.

What Can
5 | Your Healers
Offer?

Tact, sympathy and understanding are expected of the physician, for the patient is no mere collection of symptoms, signs, disordered functions, damaged organs, and disturbed emotions. He is human, fearful, and hopeful, seeking relief, help, and reassurance... The true physician has a Shakespearean breadth of interest in the wise and the foolish, the proud and the humble, the stoic hero and the whining rogue. He cares for people.

Harrison's Textbook of Medicine
1st Edition, 1954

Childbirth has obviously been part of the human experience from our very beginnings. A blend of pain and joy, every mother will remember it well. The African women in central Nigeria, where I served, had a particularly hard time with childbirth. An unusually narrow pelvis and a propensity to wail in labour, rather than relax and allow the muscles of the pelvis to stretch, contributed to the difficulty with which these women gave birth. And so the hospital midwives often called the doctor on call for help with especially difficult cases. Some of these were women who had laboured for days in their villages under the supervision of untrained native midwives.

One such case I was called to attend was that of a woman who was brought in from a remote village with what midwives and obstetricians call *shoulder dystocia* (a shoulder that won't deliver after the head has been delivered). The native midwives and healers had spent too much time with their arts, so it was already too late to save the baby—there was no fetal heartbeat. Our own midwives were unable to do the usual maneuver to deliver the stuck shoulder, and I too was unsuccessful. A senior Nigerian nurse, who was one of our anesthetists, suggested I might check for a second head—he remembered a similar case years ago. Sure enough, I could feel the second head, bent backwards where I expected to find the shoulder. So, it was not shoulder dystocia, it was really a severe case of Siamese twins— two heads, two spines but only 4 limbs in total.

What to do now? One head was out, so a Caesarean section was out of the question. You could never pull the head back, and besides, there would certainly be a high risk of infection for the mother. The only solution was to decapitate the second head, deliver the baby's body, then deliver the second head.

That's what I did with the best skill that training in scientific medicine had given me. It was not an easy task, as anyone who has ever tried this will know. Where traditional African medicine had failed this woman, we called upon a scientific approach to help her.

What can science do for you?

WHAT DOES SCIENCE OFFER?

Scientific medicine, or biomedicine, is the art of healing through the use of scientific thought and experimentation. We have already seen in Chapter 1 how scientific reason affects our understanding of the cause of illness. We look now at how science has helped us in the treatment of illness and disease.

Our survey will be brief, as most readers will have experienced biomedicine firsthand or know of family members or acquaintances who have encountered the health care system. I do not wish to chronicle the obvious. What I want to emphasize is the ideology behind the field of modern medicine which separates it from much of the alternative health movement.

The role of science in medicine

We have already seen that science is the study of the natural realm—the cosmos as we can perceive it through our senses and the technology that extends our senses to the minuscule and the distant. The hallmarks of scientific study are *objectivity* and *reproducibility*. By objectivity we mean that the observer views an event without a preconceived notion of it—he is unbiased. By reproducibility we mean that different observers viewing the same event report the same findings, thus drawing the same conclusions. Compare this to the humanities, where in the field of art, for example, two observers may reach two different interpretations based on their tastes and previous life experiences, while observing the same piece.

Practically, scientists do their work by using the following methods:

- *Observation.* Through the use of our senses and the instruments that extend our senses (such as the microscope or the telescope) the cosmos and the human body are examined and studied as to structure, composition, and function. The Human Genome project was the epitome of this, breaking the human chromosome down into ever smaller pieces for examination and classification, the next step.

- *Classifying data.* The results of careful observation are carefully classified, and reproducible relationships are observed. For example, a given gene is observed to produce a certain protein, establishing a relationship between the two.

- *Using logic.* The use of rational thought and logic are used to explain relationships between observed events. For example, if a certain bacteria is always present with a certain set of symptoms, it is logical to associate the cause of the symptoms with that bacteria.

- *Forming hypotheses.* To test the results of associations that logic predicts, hypotheses are developed. A researcher will thus hypothesize that the streptococcal bacteria is the cause of tonsillitis.

- *Conducting experiments.* To test a hypothesis, an experiment is designed in which the desired results can be measured objectively, without observer bias. The experiment is then repeated over and over to guarantee reproducibility. The experiment may involve animals or human volunteers. In medicine, the gold standard experiment is the double blind study. Two randomly selected groups of patients are given at least two different types of treatment—often one is a placebo—with neither the researches nor the patients knowing which group they are in. After a certain amount of time, the outcomes of the treatment groups are compared and the code is broken.

- *Expressing findings mathematically.* The data collected from controlled experiments are then analyzed and tested for statistical significance. If chance alone could account for differences, the results are discarded and the hypothesis is dismissed. The treatment would not become a standard of practise for physicians.

This is of course the scientific method, and we express our gratitude for the influence it has had on human society. We owe much of the technology that make our lives so much easier to it. While there are some who presume incompatibility of science and Christianity, this is not so. Here are some observations that Nicky Gumbel makes about this contention.[31]

- Christianity is monotheistic, and a belief in one God led people to expect a uniformity in nature, with the underlying laws of nature remaining the same in time and space.

- The Christian doctrine of creation by a rational God of order led scientists to expect a world that was both ordered and intelligible. C.S. Lewis put it this way: "Men became scientific because they expected Law in Nature, and they expected Law in Nature because they believed in a Legislator."

- The Christian belief in a transcendent God, separate from nature, meant that experimentation was justified. This is not the case under pantheistic belief systems.

- Historically, science and Christianity have been allies, not enemies.

We have seen in Chapter 3 that what is needed is a proper balance. When the Creator is ignored, science becomes a god unto itself and the hope for humanity's salvation. Not only that, when ethics are stripped by moral relativity, no boundaries of the descent are established. We can only speculate about where genetic engineering will lead us.

Let's look a some of the specific contributions science has had in medicine.

Diagnosis

Science and technology have vastly improved our ability to diagnose disease. Beginning with simple instruments like the stethoscope and the otoscope, our senses are extended to view and hear inside the body. In more recent years, fiberoptics has allowed us to peer inside virtually every organ of the body through natural orifices, or surgical ones, taking biopsies and doing surgical corrections as we go. X-rays have extended our vision since the day Wilhelm Roentgen discovered them in 1895, but have been vastly enhanced in recent years through computers giving us Computerized Axial Tomography (CAT) scanners. Newer imaging technologies are the MRI and PET scanners. Meanwhile, in the laboratory, ever more sensitive equipment measures every conceivable substance in our body, right down to our genetic material.

Along with the trend to more investigative technology has been the reduction in the art of diagnosis. Formerly, physicians depended almost entirely on their interview of the patient and what they could find on a physical examination. Now, we almost always wish to validate our clinical impression with objective investigations before we embark on the prescribed treatment. The medico-legal climate in North America virtually dictates this code of practise. As we will see later, many of the alternative healing arts do not operate on this premise.

Treatment

On the treatment side of medicine, science has given us the technology to do ever more complicated surgery and to prescribe more sophisticated, tailor-made drugs. Kidney stones can be smashed through sound waves, tumors can be removed through fiberoptic scopes, and arteries can be spread open through small balloons on the end of long catheters. Cancers may melt with powerful chemotherapy and radiation. Lasers can correct our eyesight, and genetic engineering has instructed bacteria to produce the exact replica of human insulin for patients with diabetes. There is now hope that genetic engineering will allow us to develop cells that will regenerate damaged or absent body parts.

Prevention

Much has been learned in disease prevention, and some diseases, such as smallpox, have been eradicated. Science has given us the tools which governments may use to promote the health of their people through immunization programs, supervision of the food supply and drinking water, and the careful isolation of individuals with infectious diseases. Risky behaviors have been identified, such as smoking, and public health policy can help promote abstinence.

Is there anything science cannot do?

Given the amazing progress of scientific medicine in recent decades, we may be led to believe that there is nothing which science cannot do or fix. In fact, there are some who believe this and place their hope in science to save our species and our planet. Charles Colson, in an excellent chapter on science as saviour from his book *How Now Shall We Live*, describes the fallacy in believing that science can save us. He points out that science and technology have always been used for good and evil, for improvement or corruption. He says that the faith that we can save ourselves through science can be sustained only if we shut our eyes to the human capacity for barbarism.[32]

Clearly, the issue of ethics surrounding genetic research and genetic engineering is a major threat to our future. The February 19, 2001 issue of *Time* headlines, "Human Cloning is Closer Than You Think." It is only a matter of time before someone attempts to produce a superhuman by tinkering with our genes.

Another major concern in scientific research is the role of big business in deciding where research funding is directed.

This is particularly an issue in medicine, where large pharmaceutical companies fund studies which they hope will prove their drug superior and thereby increase their bottom line.

There are some who recognize these problems and have written that we are likely to destroy ourselves before we evolve to a higher stage. For example, Stephen Hawking, author of *A Brief History of Time,* warns that evolution will not improve the human race quickly enough to temper our aggression and avoid extinction.[33] Colson goes on to show how the only hope for a people like this is to link up with beings elsewhere in the universe—a civilization of extraterrestrials who have themselves advanced beyond humanity and who might save us.[34] Hence, vast sums of money have been committed to groups such as the Search for Extra-Terrestrial Intelligence (SETI). And then there are still others, who, recognizing the false hopes of scientism and modernism, have turned to the East for answers.

WHAT DOES ALTERNATIVE MEDICINE OFFER?

We have already seen how the explanation for life offered by secular naturalists is the reason for the rise in postmodernism, with its renewed spiritual awareness that there must be more than the observable cosmos. Consequently, many are returning to religious explanations to fulfill the yearning of the human heart for meaning, and there is a renewed interest in many of the alternative healing arts, several of which are rooted in spirituality. Because of its religious roots, much of alternative medicine is different in its approach and ideology.

Where scientific medicine is based on an objective evaluation of the natural realm, much of alternative medicine is based upon ancient tradition or anecdotal evidence. However, in recent years, some healing arts are being evaluated by double blind studies. Let's look at the underpinnings of the diagnostic and therapeutic approach of CAM. Then, we will examine a few of the more popular healing arts as illustrations. (A more exhaustive list can be found in Appendix B.)

Diagnostic techniques

Where biomedicine works hard at confirming diagnoses through objective means, the approach taken by many alternative healers is quite different. Complementary diagnostic techniques are usually based on one or more of the following principles:

- *Examination of a body part said to represent the whole.* An eye, a foot, or a wrist is said to have intricate connections to all other organs and thereby reveals disease states of these distant organs.

- *Detection of alterations in "life energy."* Called *qi, prana,* or *bioenergetic fields*, alterations are detected by various means.

- *Extrasensory perception.* Clues about diagnosis are perceived remotely without previous knowledge of the practitioner.

Practitioners using such techniques claim that the conventional diagnostic techniques used by medical science do not detect the deficiencies or weaknesses leading to the loss of homeostasis as described in Chapter 1.

Let's look at some of these diagnostic techniques.

Pulse diagnosis

Conventional doctors check the radial pulse (the pulse at your wrist) to detect the rate and rhythm of the heart, as well as the volume of blood each heartbeat puts out. It is, therefore, an indication of cardiovascular health. Alternative healers, particularly traditional Chinese and Ayurvedic practitioners, check the pulse at each wrist to measure the flow of *qi* and *prana*, respectively. The TCM practitioner uses three fingers to check three pulse points and is said to be able to detect the flow of *qi* associated with diseases in various organs. Similarly, in Ayurveda, three pulse points on each wrist are used to analyze the condition of various organs by assessing the circulating *prana* through the *nadi* (channels similar to the meridians of TCM). As we saw previously, these "life energy" concepts are based on a pantheistic worldview.

Tongue diagnosis

The examination of the tongue to assess a person's health crosses most healing therapies. As doctors, we examine the tongue for signs of dehydration, vitamin deficiency, or yeast infection. Homeopaths check the tongue and may determine their therapies based on their findings, such as a red tip or a red tongue with coating. TCM practitioners believe the tongue is linked to all the organs of the body via meridians. They, therefore, examine the tongue with a view toward detecting the flow of *qi*, as well as the balance of *yin* and *yang*. Similarly, in Ayurveda, the tongue surface is felt to reflect disturbances in the three vital energies or *doshas*.

Iridology

Examination of the eye, the iris (the coloured part of the eye) in particular, to assess a person's health is called *iridology*. Its origins can be traced to a Hungarian doctor, Ignatz von Peczely, who as a child noticed a dark mark appearing in an owl's iris which changed colour as the bird's broken leg healed. He dedicated his career to charting patients' diseases from markings in the iris. Then, in 1950, a detailed map of the iris was constructed by an American, Bernard Jensen, which is used by iridologists today. They believe that the iris is connected to every organ and tissue through nerve endings, and that the colour of the iris changes to reflect disease states in these body parts. Careful examination of the eye, using instruments such as magnifiers and cameras, is used to document suspected disease and healing.

Scientists remain skeptical about the validity of iridology. Several studies reported in major medical journals failed to reveal a connection between iris appearance and diseased organs. It is akin to *reflexology*, where the feet are felt to be connected to various organ systems—hard skin, corns, bunions, or infections are interpreted by the practitioner as external manifestations of problems in corresponding areas of the body.

The reading of body parts for remote information is an ancient practice. In Ezekiel 21:21, we see the practice of *hepatoscopy*, the examination of the liver for guidance.

> *For the king of Babylon will stop at the fork in the road, at the junction of the two roads, to seek an omen: He will cast lots with arrows, he will consult his idols, he will examine the liver.*

Liver maps made of clay, similar to modern iridology maps, have been found in archeological digs in the Middle East. Of course, the practice continues to this day by psychics who read people's palms.

Medical intuition

The use of *clairvoyance* to make medical diagnoses has been renamed *medical intuition* and its practitioners, *medical intuitives*. Formerly known as psychic healing, the practice goes back as far as Hippocrates and Galen in ancient Greece. However, it was primarily pioneered by Edgar Cayce, who gave almost 15,000 readings while in trance, resulting in many accurate diagnoses and suggested treatments. Dr. Norman Shealy, founder of the American Holistic Medicine Association, studied the practice in detail in the 1970s and dedicated a chapter in *Miracles Do Happen* to the subject. He studied seventy-five medical intuitives in 1973 and proved them to be approximately 50 percent accurate (compared to expected accuracy of 5 to 10 percent by chance alone).[35] Later, he studied an internist, Dr. Robert Leichtman, whose accuracy in physical diagnosis was 80 percent and in psychological diagnosis was 96 percent, just by hearing the patient's name, birthdate, address or telephone number.[36] Another medical intuitive he studied is Caroline Myss, whom he found to be 93 percent accurate.[37] Caroline has co-authored *The Creation of Health* [38] with Norman Shealy and is the author of several of her own books on healing. Similarly, Dr. Larry Dossey, in his book *Reinventing Medicine*, talks about a new dimension in medicine which he calls Era III or *nonlocal medicine*, another euphemism for clairvoyance in medicine.[39]

Authors such as Dossey and Shealy take intuition seriously and request serious consideration from readers. Although their arguments arise from a pantheistic worldview, they appeal to the scientific mind through quantum physics. They suggest intuition works on the basis of people being able to tune in to a "morphogenic field" consisting of subtle electromagnetic background information.[40] Some authors call this "cosmic consciousness" or "anomalous cognition."[41] Myss makes a direct connection between intuition and Eastern pantheism:

> Much of my personal experience in working with intuitive diagnosis corresponds to the teachings of the Eastern spiritual traditions in terms of understanding the human body.[42]

Similarly, Dossey speaks of the unfulfilled spiritual yearning of post modern society:

> People everywhere are starved for meaning, purpose, and spiritual fulfillment in their lives. To lead healthy, full lives, we require a positive sense of meaning, just as we need food and water, for without meaning life withers. As we shall see, nonlocal mind is suffused with spiritual meaning and can help fill the inner void that has become such a painful feather of modern life.[43]

Our reaction to medical intuition will obviously depend on our worldview. For the naturalistic worldview holder, these anomalous phenomena will be viewed as chance hits by good guessers. In the Christian worldview, clairvoyance apart from the work of the Holy Spirit is viewed as occultic and mediated through the demonic spiritual realm.

Electrical diagnosis

Healees of complementary practitioners may encounter a variety of electronic gadgets used as diagnostic aids. Many of these incorporate principles of TCM with Western science, using sensitive electronic equipment to measure changes in electrical resistance at various points on the patient's body. Most are based on "energy" theories of disease, such as the *qi* in TCM.

One example of such a diagnostic device is the Omega AcuBase/B.E.S.T. system, a computerized device used to measure various energies emitted by the body in order to detect imbalances. A probe is placed on various points of the fingers and toes closely correlated to acupuncture meridians. The computer records the results, indicating food or chemical sensitivities, imbalances in vitamins or minerals, or diseased organ systems. A printout is produced and used by the practitioner to advise on treatment.

When faced with making a decision about subjecting yourself to some of these diagnostic modalities, please examine the principles in Chapter 7, "Choose Your Healers Wisely." Equally important is your consideration of these principles as you contemplate alternative treatments.

Therapeutic modalities

Based on the disease theories outlined in Chapter 1, CAM therapeutic modalities are generally in one of the following categories:

- *Manipulate energy.* By exerting control over *qi, prana,* or *bioenergetic fields,* the practitioner attempts to re-establish homeostasis or balance.

- *Replenish biochemical deficiencies.* Vitamins, herbs, or medications are used to replenish deficiencies felt to be the root of diseased states or to counteract imbalances.

- *Removal of toxins though detoxification.* Toxins produced by the body or as the result of disease are removed in order to aid healing.

- *Realignment of imbalanced body parts.* Chiropractic and osteopathy attempt to re-establish normal alignment of body parts which are not in proper place or balance.

- *Potentiate mind over body control.* The power of the mind over the body is well known, and these methods seek to intensify that power.

We will examine a few of the more common therapies that illustrate these principles. This is not nearly an exhaustive list, as there are at least 90 such therapies available. Appendix B contains a more complete list in table form.

Acupuncture

Acupuncture is at the heart of Traditional Chinese Medicine (TCM) and may date as far back as 3000 BC. Practitioners insert fine needles at various body points to treat various conditions, from asthma to pain. These needles are said to affect the flow of life energy (*qi*) along pathways (*meridians*) that connect the various body systems. As we saw in Chapter 1, disease is understood to be caused by an imbalance of *yin* or *yang* resulting in the altered flow of *qi*. Acupuncture is believed to re-establish the proper flow of *qi*. There are 365 acupoints along the meridians at which *qi* is concentrated and can enter and leave the body.

Here its flow is either suppressed or stimulated through needles.

Acupuncture made great news in the 1970s when western physicians traveled to China and observed major surgery being done with acupuncture anesthesia. Since then, it has been subjected to scientific research, and it has been found to be effective, particularly for pain control. However, attempts to quantify energy passing through meridian pathways has not been validated scientifically. It appears that acupuncture releases the neurotransmitter *endorphin,* which is a powerful alleviator of pain. Endorphin is the same neurotransmitter that gives a "runner's high" after exercise. This theory is supported by the fact that naloxone, a drug that blocks endorphins (and narcotics), blocks the affect of acupuncture in experimental animals.

A couple of variants on classical acupuncture are *acupressure* and *auricular acupuncture.* Acupressure is essentially acupuncture without needles; the practitioner stimulates acupoints with her fingers, thumbs, or even feet and knees. Auricular acupuncture is based on the theory that there are over 120 acupoints on each ear (representative of an inverted fetus) which correspond to specific parts of the body, similar to iridology and reflexology. These points are then stimulated with needles, laser treatment, or electrical currents. Practitioners of auricular acupuncture do an ear reading in order to reach a diagnosis.

Acupuncture is clearly grounded in Eastern pantheistic thought, particularly Taoism. Although effective through its ability to release endorphins, there are other ways, such as exercise, simple needling, and Christian prayer, to release them without the spiritual dangers of Taoism.

Ayurveda

Ayurveda is a system of healing based on Hinduism and brought to North America by Maharishi Mahesh Yogi and popularized by Dr. Deepak Chopra. Its underlying disease philosophy is an imbalance in *doshas* diagnosed through examination of the tongue, the pulse, and the abdomen. Imbalances in the *doshas* lead to a disruption or reduction of *prana*. *Prana* is the Hindu concept of "life energy," similar to the Chinese concept of *qi*, which is concentrated in the seven *chakras*, centres of ascending spiritual significance from the pelvis to the top of the head.

Ayurvedic treatments are all based on the principle of realigning the imbalances in *doshas*, thus allowing *prana* to increase. Ayurvedic treatments concentrate on diet and detoxification techniques designed to purge *ama*, toxic substances felt to negatively affect *prana* and cause disease. The detoxifying regime is called *panchakarma* and takes the form of enemas, laxatives, therapeutic vomiting, and washing out of the nasal passages. Other treatments include herbal remedies, postures, breathing exercises, meditation, and yoga.

Ayurveda has been researched extensively in India, and several of its herbal remedies have been shown to be effective in certain conditions. However, most medical scientists question the underlying principles on which the healing system is based, particularly the concept of *doshas* and *prana*. Because of its Hindu roots and its origins in Eastern pantheism, most Christians see the inherent danger of using these therapies.

Crystal therapy

From the Inuit in the Arctic to the Indians of the Amazon, animistic cultures throughout the world have valued precious and semiprecious gems for the magical and therapeutic qualities attributed to them. Crystals, particularly quartz crystals such as amethyst and rose quartz, are believed to possess healing "life energy." Many CAM practitioners have widely adopted these theories into their treatments for physical and emotional problems. In particular, Shirley MacLaine's books and lectures have actively endorsed the use of crystals.[44]

Crystal therapy is based on the principle that crystals adjust "energy" by concentrating or absorbing its flow. Practitioners who use crystal therapy frequently use them in conjunction with other treatment modalities such as acupuncture, Therapeutic Touch, yoga, or meditation. The connection of crystal therapy to frank occultism should be noted. Uma Sibley's *The Complete Crystal Guidebook* reveals this connection:

> You can meet (spirit) guides and beings from different dimensions and uncover ESP abilities.... A curious thing starts to happen as you work with crystals. You start becoming aware of an energy or force or a "potential" higher than yourself. You start becoming aware of and can begin to interact with something very powerful and wonderful.[45]

Clearly, crystal therapy is based on a pantheistic worldview, and practitioners clearly relate their experiences with spirit guides, which those within a biblical worldview would equate with demonic beings.

Herbalism

In the modern alternative health movement, herbs have found immense favour as a therapeutic modality. In addition to CAM practitioners who prescribe herbs, many people self-treat by purchasing herbs readily available in drugstores, in health food stores, and through network marketers. The therapeutic benefits of some plants are becoming common knowledge, and the resurgence of interest in their use has become big business for growers and suppliers of these plants.

Herbalism has roots in cultures near and far and was the basis for many original pharmaceuticals in western medicine, such as aspirin and the heart medication, digoxin. That plants have many medicinally active ingredients is quite obvious when you consider the effects of nicotinic acid of tobacco plants (a potent poison) and morphine derived from poppy plants (a potent narcotic). Traditional healers from many cultures have exploited these effects, and scientists continue to discover new effects of plants used by indigenous people groups for various purposes. The branch of science devoted to the study of the medicinal effects of plants is known as *pharmacognosy*. As a result of this research, many popular herbs, such as Echinacea, garlic, ginger, ginkgo, and St. John's wort, are being used to treat infections, hypercholesterolemia, nausea, circulation, and depression respectively. Scientists still warn us, however, that the long-term effects of these herbs are not known. For example, because Echinacea stimulates the immune system, some speculate that overuse may lead to autoimmune diseases, where the body produces antibodies against its own cells. Scientists also warn of the poor labeling, possible contamination with fungi or bacteria, lack of quality control and standards, and inconsistency in dosage recommendations. Some users are lured by the promise of remedies being "natural," as opposed to synthetic pharmaceuticals made in the lab. Some natural "herbs" are, of course, highly toxic—a fact that any parent of a child who has ingested poisonous mushrooms knows only too well.

Readers should also be warned, however, of the traditional association of herbalism with occultism on one hand and with New Age on the other. That mood-altering herbs are used for the initiation, development, and training of shamans in traditional cultures is well known. We saw this in Nigeria, and readers may be aware of this in North American native rituals as well. But, readers may not be aware of the subtle association of herbalism in New Age Medicine. For example, in *The Perelandra Garden Workbook: A Complete Guide to Gardening with Nature Intelligences*, the author explains how the spirit world can be contacted and used in gardening and herbalism.[46] Two other books similarly relate the use of plants for psychic communication or intuitive diagnosis: *The Secret Life of Plants* and *The Psychic Power of Plants*.[47] These works all assume the divine in the plant world, which we have seen is the pantheistic worldview.

Homeopathy

Dr. Samuel Hahnemann founded homeopathy in the late 1700s. Rejecting the barbaric medical practices of his day, he was determined to find a gentler way of curing disease. Noting that quinine, which was used to treat malaria, caused the symptoms of malaria in a healthy subject (himself), he developed the hypothesis that like cures like—if large amounts of a substance cause the symptoms of illness, small amounts of the same substance can cure that same illness. By routinely testing substances on healthy individuals, he catalogued enumerable substances which could be used to treat illness. He then diluted these substances, in ever increasing dilutions, and shook the mixtures vigorously, a process called *succussion.* Hahnemann noticed that the more diluted the solutions were, the more powerful they were in their ability to heal, a principle he called *potentization.*

Science has no rational explanation for how homeopathy works. Dilutions are such that not even a single molecule of the original substance remains in the medicine. The explanation offered by homeopaths is that the substance leaves an "imprint" in the medicine taken. They argue that some yet undiscovered law of quantum mechanics will one day explain this imprint. Hahnemann, on the other hand, suggested that *succussion* energized the medicine to activate the patient's "vital force."

Homeopathy has made a remarkable comeback after almost complete oblivion in the 1930s. It is now one of the most common alternative medicines, particularly in Europe. Many experts, including Dr. Andrew Weil, the American guru of alternative medicine, believe it is a form of spiritual healing, working through extra-dimensional methods.[48] This squarely puts homeopathy in the energy-based healing systems.

Hypnotherapy

Healing trances can be traced back to ancient Egyptians and Greeks, and tribal cultures in Africa and America have used the technique for centuries. Modern hypnotherapy is generally traced back to the work of Franz Mesmer, who, in the late 1700s, treated his patients by sending them into a "therapeutic crisis" of shaking, coughing, and convulsions, after which they reported feeling better. His techniques were modernized in the 1950s and 1960s by American psychotherapist Milton Erickson.

Hypnosis is a state in which the conscious, rational part of the brain is bypassed, making the subconscious mind very receptive to suggestion. No one knows how this works although some scientists believe that hypnosis causes the release of morphine-like neurotransmitters called endorphins and enkephalins. During such a trance, patients can be desensitized to fear, phobias, or pain. They can also be influenced to give up addictions such as an addiction to nicotine.

Hypnosis works and is attested to by stage hypnotists who do it for entertainment, drawing extraordinary physical feats from their subjects. Some published studies in the Lancet and British Medical Journal have shown benefits in treating irritable bowel syndrome and asthma as well as psychosomatic and neurotic illnesses.

Generally, hypnotherapy has gained respect in biomedicine. However, those with a Christian worldview regard hypnosis with caution due to the potential spiritual danger of allowing your mind to be influenced by others or the demonic realm.

Therapeutic Touch

Therapeutic Touch (TT) was founded by Deloris Krieger, a professor of nursing at New York University, in the late 1960s. It is based on the principle of "human energy fields" which are said to positively or negatively influence one's health. The practitioner initially does a diagnostic technique called *centering* which is meant to read the patient's energy field. Then, using the hands a distance from the body, the practitioner manipulates the patient's imbalanced energy.

TT has become very popular among nurses in established hospitals and they use it to supplement scientifically based treatments. Although medical scientists are skeptical about the existence of bioenergetic fields, the practice is becoming more popular.

Although TT may appear close to the Christian practice of laying on of hands, it is in fact based on a pantheistic world-view. In fact, Deloris Krieger learned these techniques from Dora Kunz, who was the president of the Theosophical Society. As we will see in Chapter 7, this technique is clearly prohibited in the Bible.

Yoga

Known primarily in the West as a gentle exercise program, yoga has its roots in India and is part of the Ayurvedic method of healing outlined above. It's spiritual roots are Hindu and it has been used for its physical, as well as spiritual, benefits. Yoga consists primarily of *asanas* (physical postures) and *pranayama* (breathing techniques) followed by meditation. The most popular yoga in the West is *hatha* yoga, which uses the *asanas* and *pranayama* to regulate *prana*, the Hindu concept of life energy described above.

While no one can argue the benefits of physical exercise, yoga's origins and underlying ideology are clearly Eastern and pantheistic. Yoga has become very popular, and even some churches offer yoga classes in their community. There are clear, spiritually safe alternatives to yoga, including fitness programs that combine the Christian disciplines of prayer and worship with exercise. More on that in Chapter 9.

Given that many of the alternative healing arts cross into the extra-dimensional spiritual realm for both diagnostic and therapeutic modalities, let's look at the biblical solution for our physical and emotional ills.

6 | What Does God Offer?

> *As Christ's death redeems men, including their bodies, from the consequences of the Fall... we should be looking now, on the basis of the work of Christ, for substantial healing in every area affected by the Fall.*

> Francis Schaeffer

The CBC National recently featured a documentary called "Livin' On" which spotlighted a retired science teacher who has made it his life's ambition to slow aging—he thinks he can live to be 120, and hopes medical science will by then have solved the mortality problem. He mixes a concoction of nuts and vegetables for breakfast, along with a fistful of vitamins and minerals, gets the right exercise (mostly disco dancing), and checks his blood sugar and blood pressure daily, even though he is not a diabetic or hypertensive. His days are almost all filled with attempts to stop the aging process and ensure his immortality.

Will science solve humankind's quest for immortality? Even if we do all live to be 120, overpopulation is likely to increasingly challenge the environment. Antibiotic-resistant bacteria will continue to threaten our health, and some new epidemic may yet sweep around the world before science can control it, as in the case of the AIDS virus. If we do survive the aging process, there is still the threat of natural disaster or trauma from accidents. Where alternative healers look to the spiritual realm for answers and the hope for reincarnation, given our Christian worldview, let's now look to the Bible for the answers God gives for our brokenness and mortality.

THE HEALING MINISTRY OF JESUS

In order to understand God's solution for sickness, aging, and death, we need to begin by looking at the ministry of Jesus Christ, His Son. The Gospels of Matthew, Mark, Luke, and John, first-hand accounts of the life of Jesus, are replete with stories of miraculous healings—forty-one in all, seventy-two including duplicates. Nearly one-fifth of these writings is apportioned to Jesus' healings and discussions occasioned by them. Why is this so?

In Chapter 1 we traced the spiritual roots of sickness, aging, and death. We saw that in the Fall we lost four blessings that God intended humanity to experience:

- Eternal fellowship with God;
- Lordship over the created order;
- Healthy interpersonal relationships;
- Health and immortality.

We saw that sin, or rebellion, was the root of this fall from God's favour. We then went on to explain that God was just and obligated to punish sin, but that He left a way out by promising the Messiah, a Saviour.

The gospel writers wanted to establish that Jesus was this Messiah, the Saviour of the world, the One promised by the prophets. Therefore, they spared no time in demonstrating that He reversed all four of these losses:

- He granted eternal life by forgiving sin;
- He exerted lordship over the created order;
- He healed relationships;
- He healed the sick and raised the dead.

Jesus granted eternal life

Jesus was executed by Roman crucifixion along with two other convicted criminals. While one of them joined the crowd and mocked Jesus, taunting Him to save Himself, the second criminal became penitent and said to the first:

> *Don't you fear God, since you are under the same sentence? We are punished justly, for we are getting what our deeds deserve. But this man has done nothing wrong.*

Recognizing Jesus' ability to forgive, he then turned to Jesus and said, *Jesus, remember me when you come into your kingdom.* Jesus replied in the affirmative, demonstrating that by forgiving sins He could grant eternal life: *I tell you the truth, today you will be with me in paradise* (Luke 23:39-43).

Jesus exerted lordship over the created order

The Sea of Galilee, known by its Hebrew name *Yam Kinneret* in modern Israel, is a lake thirteen miles long and up to seven miles wide which lies 695 feet below sea level. The Jordan River flows through it from north to south. The position of the lake in the depths of the Jordan rift and the surrounding hills renders it very liable to atmospheric downdrafts and sudden storms. Despite being an inland lake, its width makes for rough seas in a storm. Jesus and his disciples were caught in one of these storms and their boat was in danger of taking on water. Three of the gospel writers record the story and here is Luke's version:

> One day Jesus said to his disciples, "Let's go over to the other side of the lake." So they got into a boat and set out. As they sailed, he fell asleep. A squall came down on the lake, so that the boat was being swamped, and they were in great danger. The disciples went and woke him, saying, "Master, Master, we're going to drown!" He got up and rebuked the wind and the raging waters; the storm subsided, and all was calm. "Where is your faith?" he asked his disciples. In fear and amazement they asked one another, "Who is this? He commands even the winds and the water, and they obey him" (Luke 8:22-25).

Jesus also defied the laws of nature by walking on water and multiplying food to feed a multitude of people.

Jesus healed relationships

Jesus demonstrated that all the taboos associated with broken relationships and long-standing enmity were nonsense. One such feud in Jesus' day was between the Samaritans and Israelites. The Samaritans were a mixed race of primarily Jewish descent. The Jews felt the Samaritans were adulterated by non-Jewish blood and looked down on them. In fact, they were not on speaking terms. So Jesus broke the cultural prohibition and spoke to the Samaritan woman at the well. John records the story:

> When a Samaritan woman came to draw water, Jesus said to her, "Will you give me a drink?" (His disciples had gone into the town to buy food.) The Samaritan woman said to him, "You are a Jew and I am a Samaritan woman. How can you ask me for a drink?" (For Jews do not associate with Samaritans) (John 4:7-9).

Not only did John demonstrate Jesus' penchant for healing racial discrimination by relating this story, his record of Jesus' conversation with the woman at the well went on to reveal that she had her own relational problems, particularly with the men in her life. As the result of this encounter with Jesus, she and many of her people came to faith in Jesus as God's Son, the long-awaited Messiah. And by so doing, they experienced relational healing.

Jesus healed the sick and raised the dead

One of the gospel writers, Luke, was a Greek physician, probably trained in the tradition of Hippocrates. Fascinated by Jesus' healing ministry for obvious reasons, he recorded many healing stories with exacting detail. One was of the paralytic that was brought to Jesus by his friends. There was such a crowd around Jesus they couldn't get close to Him, so they took their sick friend up on the roof, removed one of the roof tiles and lowered him down in front of Jesus through the hole. Jesus was impressed by their insistence, and their faith, and proclaimed to the sick man, *Friend, your sins are forgiven.* This statement created quite a stir among the religious leaders present for the meeting. They grumbled something about the fact that only God could forgive sins. Jesus perceived their objections and addressed them:

> *Why are you thinking these things in your hearts? Which is easier: to say, "Your sins are forgiven,"or to say, "Get up and walk"? But that you may know that the Son of Man has authority on earth to forgive sins...."*

Then He turned to the sick man: *I tell you, get up, take your mat and go home.* He was instantly healed, walked out with his mat and began praising God. The people were impressed (Luke 5:18-25).

The correlation between sin and sickness, and pardon and healing, are clear in this narrative. Luke showed that Jesus not only had the authority to forgive sins, but by so doing, He could also offset the affects of sin—sickness. And not only sickness, but its ultimate end—death.

John records that account in intimate detail—the story of Jesus' good friend Lazarus, dead for two days in a hot country without embalming and then raised from the dead by Jesus' word. Jesus had said to Martha, the dead man's sister:

> *"I am the resurrection and the life. He who believes in me will live, even though he dies; and whoever lives and believes in me will never die. Do you believe this?" She replied, "Yes, Lord, I believe that you are the Christ, the Son of God, who was to come into the world"* (John 11:25-27).

Meaning what He said, He then clearly demonstrated His resurrection power by calling forth life into Lazarus' dead remains. John, the writer of this account, was one of Jesus' disciples. He was, in fact, one of Jesus' inner-circle favourites and therefore a firsthand witness to these events. He makes no bones about why he took the trouble to chronicle Jesus' life:

> *But these are written that you may believe that Jesus is the Christ, the Son of God, and that by believing you may have life in his name* (John 20:31).

The restoration of all four human losses is what the Bible calls *salvation*. Translated from the Greek *soteria*, it is the noun of the verb *sozo*, or "to save" in English. It means to be delivered or preserved from danger or disease, implying safety, health, and prosperity. It includes concepts of cure, recovery, redemption, remedy, and rescue. It includes spiritual and relational, as well as physical, deliverance—partly now, completely in the future. In essence, *sozo* means to be made whole.

Jesus uses the word in Luke 19:9 when He addresses Zacchaeus:

> *Today salvation has come to this house, because this man, too,*
> *is a son of Abraham. For the Son of Man came to seek and to*
> *save what was lost.*

Because Zacchaeus expressed regret for his sin and turned to
Jesus, Jesus was able to assure him of his rescue from the consequences of that sin. We clearly see Jesus as the *Soter*, or
Saviour. Luke confirms this in his other work, the book of
Acts: *Salvation is found in no one else, for there is no other name*
under heaven given to men by which we must be saved (Acts
4:18). And the writer to the Hebrews adds his weight to the
argument: *Therefore he (Jesus) is able to save completely those*
who come to God through him (Heb. 7:25).

What was it about Jesus that gave Him authority to forgive
sin and thereby offset its consequences and grant complete salvation? To understand that we need to examine another key
concept found throughout the New Testament Scriptures—
the "Kingdom of God." This phrase, or its equivalent the
"Kingdom of Heaven," is used over eighty times in the four
Gospels and is frequently found in Jesus' recorded teaching
and parables. Jesus begins His ministry by saying, *I must*
preach the good news of the Kingdom of God (Luke 4:43) and
He taught His followers to pray, *Thy kingdom come* (Matt.
6:10 KJV). Luke uses the phrase again in his second work, the
Book of Acts, when he describes the Apostle Paul's ministry:
Boldly and without hindrance (Paul) preached the kingdom of
God and taught about the Lord Jesus Christ (Acts 28:31).

THE KINGDOM OF GOD

When we think of kingdoms, we think of kings, or rulers,
or authority. In an earthly kingdom, if it is a monarchy, the king
has the ultimate authority. He has the rank and attributes that
give him the privilege, the right, and the authority to rule and

to be sovereign over the people and the wealth of his realm. Now the king may delegate authority to his Prime Minister for the daily affairs of the state, but he still has the ultimate authority.

In the realm of the Kingdom of God, it is God who has this ultimate authority—the rank and attributes to reign, to be sovereign. God's authority extends over the spiritual realm, as well the natural realm. Since God created the cosmos, He is the ultimate authority over it. He is the rightful holder of the scepter of rulership.

Satan's error, sometime before Genesis 1, was that he wanted the scepter. He longed to rise up the rank and acquire the attribute that would allow him to reign. His attitude is represented by the words the king of Babylon in Isaiah 14: *I will raise my throne above the stars of God; I will make myself like the Most High* (Isa. 14:13,14). God of course recognized his mutiny and expelled Satan from his heavenly Presence. *How you have fallen from heaven, O morning star, son of the dawn! You have been cast down to the earth* (Isa. 14:12).

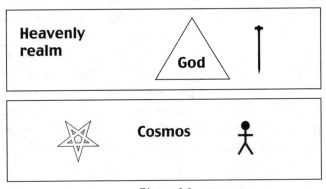

Figure 6.1
The Kingdom of God at creation

Figure 6.1 illustrates the authority structure at the time of creation. The scepter of rulership is with the triune God, the Creator who reigns over the heavenly realm, over the cosmos, over humankind, and over the fallen spiritual realm. God had a different plan, however, since the human race He created to bear His image, qualified them for delegated rulership:

> *Then God said, "Let us make man in our image, in our likeness, and let them rule over the fish of the sea and the birds of the air, over the livestock, over all the earth, and over all the creatures that move along the ground." So God created man in his own image, in the image of God he created him; male and female he created them. God blessed them and said to them, "Be fruitful and increase in number; fill the earth and subdue it. Rule over the fish of the sea and the birds of the air and over every living creature that moves on the ground"* (Gen. 1:26-28).

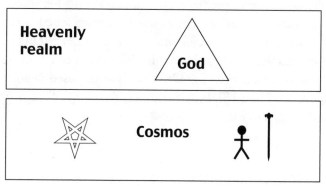

Figure 6.2
Kingdom of God—humanity has delegated authority

Figure 6.2 shows the scepter with the human race. Much like a Prime Minister in an earthly kingdom, mankind was given the delegated authority to rule over the created order, including the fallen spiritual realm. This was God's ultimate purpose for humanity.

Unfortunately, the events of Genesis 3 had severe effects on humanity's delegated authority. Satan, recognizing his own failure to ascend the throne, now focuses on God's delegated authority, Adam and Eve, and sees an easy target. He uses the same argument that caused his own fall:

> *You will not surely die, for God knows that when you eat of it (the forbidden fruit) your eyes will be opened, and you will be like God, knowing good and evil* (Gen. 3:4).

And so Satan tempts them to raise the rank just as he had tried before.

Adam and Eve fall for it. By eating the forbidden fruit at Satan's bidding, they subordinated themselves to Satan, thereby shifting their authority to him. They can no longer rule, having forfeited their right to the scepter, giving it to Satan who becomes *"the god of this age"* (2 Cor. 4:4). Figure 6.3 below shows the scepter in Satan's domain. This has placed the human race in a judgement position, having rebelled against God's authority. Separated from God and under Satan's rule is a worst-case scenario for humanity. The Bible calls this period *this age*, or *eon* (Matt. 12:32). This is juxtaposed against the *age to come* (Luke 18:30) which refers to the fulfillment of the Kingdom of God in the future.

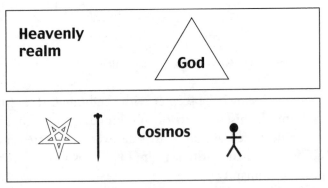

Figure 6.3
Satan is the ruler of this age

Thankfully God was not content to leave this sorry state of affairs. Within moments, He promises a solution, a way out. He says to Satan, referring to the promised Saviour:

And I will put enmity between you and the woman, and between your offspring and hers; he will crush your head, and you will strike his heel (Gen. 3:15).

Jesus came to earth about 2000 years ago as God incarnate, fully human and fully God. Because of His divinity, He automatically carried His Father's authority. Thus, early in His ministry He quotes Isaiah the prophet and declares that He is the fulfillment of that prophecy:

The Spirit of the Lord is on me, because he has anointed me to preach good news to the poor. He has sent me to proclaim freedom for the prisoners and recovery of sight for the blind, to release the oppressed, to proclaim the year of the Lord's favor... Today this Scripture is fulfilled in your hearing (Luke 4:18-19).

During His three-year ministry, Jesus demonstrated that authority by restoring the four losses mentioned above. Jesus' close friend and follower John put it this way: *The reason the Son of God appeared was to destroy the devil's work* (1 John 3:8). Jesus lived a perfect life, triumphing over Satan's temptation to rise in rank above His Father. He died to atone for the sins of the human race, thereby dealing with the legal requirement of God's judgement. And when He conquered death, Satan's claim to the scepter was broken, wrested away from him by Jesus who, for forty days following His resurrection, carried it as a clear demonstration of His rulership over the created order. Herein lay Jesus' authority to offer complete salvation—eternal life, rulership over the created order, healed relationships, and immortal bodies. Thus Jesus declared, *The kingdom of God has come upon you* (Matt. 12:28). Figure 6.4 shows the scepter taken from Satan by Jesus. Note that Satan has not been removed and still exerts some power and authority. His defeat by Jesus' resurrection was much like D-Day during World War II. When the Allies landed on the beaches of Normandy in June of 1944, Hitler was defeated, but he wasn't removed until V-Day in May of 1945.

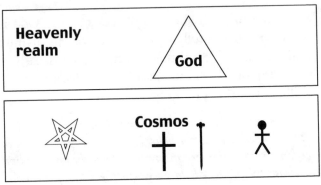

Figure 6.4
Jesus declares the Kingdom of God has come

At the end of His time on earth, Jesus clearly demonstrates His hold on the scepter when He says to the disciples, *All authority (delegated power) in heaven and on earth has been given to me* (Matt 28:18). But then He does an interesting thing as He prepares to leave earth to return to His Father's heavenly realm—He issues instructions to His followers and passes authority to them:

> *Therefore go and make disciples of all nations, baptizing them in the name of the Father and of the Son and of the Holy Spirit, and teaching them to obey everything I have commanded you. And surely I am with you always, to the very end of the age* (Matt 28:19,20).

Here are instructions to expand the Kingdom and again to subdue the earth, similar to God's original instructions to

Adam. And how is humankind equipped to fulfill this task? The answer lies in the Holy Spirit and the birth of the Church on the day of Pentecost.

Jesus had previously intimated His imminent departure from the earthly realm and had promised His disciples He would not *leave them as orphans,* but would *ask the Father* to send the Holy Spirit (John 14:16-18). On the day of His departure He again reiterates the promise of the Holy Spirit:

> *But you will receive power when the Holy Spirit comes on you; and you will be my witnesses in Jerusalem, and in all Judea and Samaria, and to the ends of the earth* (Acts 1:8).

Fulfilled on the day of Pentecost when the Holy Spirit was poured out on the believers, Jesus' delegated power in Matthew 28:18 is passed on to the Church which now holds the scepter on God's behalf. Figure 6.5 depicts the Church Age—the era we now live in—with the Church empowered by the Holy Spirit under the headship of Jesus, with instructions to liberate Satan's conquered territory. Just as the Allied troops needed to liberate Europe after D-Day country by country, so the Church must regain ground from Satan and bring it under its rightful ruler, God.

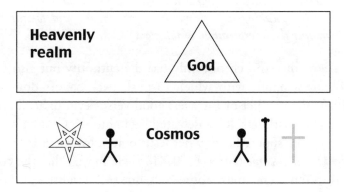

Figure 6.5
The Church Age—the conflict of the ages

And so, with the scepter in hand, the early Church continued Christ's redemptive work—preaching the gospel, healing the sick, restoring relationships, performing miracles. The Apostle Paul rephrases the concept of delegated authority with the ambassador paradigm: *We are therefore Christ's ambassadors, as though God were making his appeal through us* (2 Cor. 5:20). Ambassadors represent the authority and are accountable to the home government which sent them. Likewise, the Church represents the authority of, and is accountable to, Jesus who is called the *head of the Church* (Col. 1:18).

How is the Church equipped for this task? Not only had Jesus personally trained His disciples for three years, when the Holy Spirit was poured out on them, they received gifts of the Holy Spirit. The Apostle Paul talks about the importance of these gifts, also known as the gifts of grace.

> *Now about spiritual gifts, brothers, I do not want you to be ignorant. There are different kinds of gifts, but the same Spirit. To one there is given through the Spirit the message of wisdom, to another the message of knowledge by means of the same Spirit, to another faith by the same Spirit, to another gifts of healing by that one Spirit, to another miraculous powers, to another prophecy, to another distinguishing between spirits, to another speaking in different kinds of tongues, and to still another the interpretation of tongues* (1 Cor. 12:1,4,8-10).

Now the Church not only has the authority but also the tools or weapons with which to push back Satan's domain. This is the conflict of the ages: good versus evil, light illuminating the darkness. Jesus defeated Satan but the Church must mop up the spoils. That's what Jesus prayed for when He said, *Thy kingdom come* (Matt. 6:10 KJV). He prayed that the cosmos would increasingly come back under the rightful authority of His Heavenly Father. And that's what Paul means in Ephesians when he says:

Finally, be strong in the Lord and in his mighty power. Put on the full armor of God so that you can take your stand against the devil's schemes. For our struggle is not against flesh and blood (people), but against the rulers, against the authorities, against the powers of this dark world and against the spiritual forces of evil in the heavenly realms (Eph. 6:10-12).

How long will this battle last?

Then the end will come, when he hands over the kingdom to God the Father after he has destroyed all dominion, authority and power. For he must reign until he has put all his enemies under his feet. The last enemy to be destroyed is death (1 Cor.15:24-26).

The full realization of the Kingdom of God will come at the close of time when Christ returns, the dead are raised, the present cosmos is destroyed, Satan and his followers are forever removed, and God establishes a New Heaven and a New Earth. Although there are several steps in this fulfillment of the Kingdom, figure 6.6 depicts it visually.

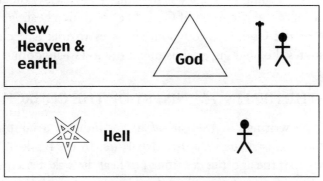

Figure 6.6
The Kingdom of God—the New Creation

Revelation 21 spells out the conditions of the New Creation:

Then I saw a new heaven and a new earth, for the first heaven and the first earth had passed away, and there was no longer any sea. I saw the Holy City, the new Jerusalem, coming down out of heaven from God, prepared as a bride beautifully dressed for her husband. And I heard a loud voice from the throne saying, "Now the dwelling of God is with men, and he will live with them. They will be his people, and God himself will be with them and be their God. He will wipe every tear from their eyes. There will be no more death or mourning or crying or pain, for the old order of things has passed away" (Rev. 21:1-4).

Here lies the ultimate answer to our mortality and sickness. Apart from becoming citizens of God's Kingdom, we cannot achieve a state of health where death and mourning and crying and pain have no part. And becoming a citizen of God's Kingdom is easy. Jesus bought our citizenship papers through His death and resurrection and He will hand them to you if you but ask Him. We just need to admit our need, repent of our sin and ask Jesus to fill us with His Holy Spirit (see Appendix A, "Finding Peace with God").

Jesus' healing ministry was to demonstrate clearly the inauguration of the Kingdom of God. The continued healing ministry of the Church throughout the ages to this day, clearly illustrates the ongoing establishment of God's Kingdom.

THE HEALING MINISTRY OF THE CHURCH

The writings of the early Church indicate a continued healing ministry after Christ's departure. In the book of Acts we see that the apostles continued to heal the sick. Perhaps the best known was the paralytic beggar at the temple gate who asked Peter and John for a contribution. Peter replied, *Silver or gold I do not have, but what I have I give you. In the name of Jesus Christ of Nazareth, walk.* With that Peter and John helped the man to his feet and Dr. Luke records that he joined them into the temple walking and jumping, and praising God (Acts 3:6-8). Later, Dr. Luke tells of the Apostle Paul's healing ministry:

> *God did extraordinary miracles through Paul, so that even handkerchiefs and aprons that had touched him were taken to the sick, and their illnesses were cured and the evil spirits left them* (Acts 19:11,12).

About 60 AD, James, Jesus' half brother, writing to Jewish Christians scattered throughout the Middle East, left these instructions about sickness and healing:

> *Is any one of you sick? He should call the elders of the church to pray over him and anoint him with oil in the name of the Lord. And the prayer offered in faith will make the sick person well; the Lord will raise him up. If he has sinned, he will be forgiven. Therefore confess your sins to each other and pray for each other so that you may be healed. The prayer of a righteous man is powerful and effective* (Jas. 5:14-16).

Here we see that the New Testament Church continued Christ's healing ministry. Subsequently, writings throughout the ages—from early church history through the Middle Ages, during the Reformation, during revivalism of the 18th and 19th centuries, right up to modern Pentecostalism—would indicate that the Church's healing ministry has continued.

The Church as a healing community today

Although God's plan of redemptive work has been delegated to the Church, it is my conviction that the Church has forfeited its responsibility in several areas, health and healing being one. This, in part, has been fueled by the historic tension between those who see the primary purpose of the Church as being evangelizing the lost and those who long to see the Church active in social issues, such as the alleviation of poverty and suffering. This debate intensified during the first half of the 20th century with theological conservatives on the one hand pitted against liberals on the other. This kind of dichotomist "either/or" thinking caused much of the evangelical church to forfeit responsibility in such areas as care of the poor, care of the elderly, health, education, and politics.

But some recent authors, particularly Francis Schaeffer, Howard Snyder, and Charles Colson, have argued that we need to end the dichotomist thinking of the past. They argue a position that attempts to view God's total plan for His creation as outlined in Ephesians 1:9-10:

> *He made known to us the mystery of his will according to his good pleasure, which he purposed in Christ, to be put into effect when the times will have reached their fulfilment—to bring all things in heaven and on earth together under one head, even Christ.*

Here one sees not two poles—evangelism and social action—but one cosmic design. This is Kingdom thinking—the view that God's rule needs to be established in all areas of life. Colson puts it this way in his recent book, *How Now Shall We Live?*

> The church's singular failure in recent decades has been the failure to see Christianity as a life system, or worldview, that governs every area of existence.... Is there yet time in this epic moment, at the dawn of the third millennium, to revive the church's sense of hope and to bear witness to the immutable truth of biblical revelation? Can a culture be rebuilt so that all the world can see in its splendor and glory the contours of God's kingdom? Emphatically yes.[49]

Such a unified view of the church in relation to its mission and God's purpose for the cosmos sees the church as a people, citizens of God's Kingdom, who in turn are the agents God uses to advance the Kingdom. Rather than the old institutional view of the church, this vision finds the proper biblical place for every legitimate Christian emphasis, whether evangelism, social action, church renewal, discipleship or healing.

We want to apply this Kingdom view of the church to the area of health and healing, looking more closely at the church's practical role as a therapeutic, healing community—first as a loving, caring community, and secondly as the agent through which the Kingdom of God is visibly advanced.

Some recovery is needed here, particularly in the developed West, as Christians from an earlier era and in other cultures, have demonstrated a healthier Kingdom consciousness. Historically, and in many mission fields, we find clinics, hospitals and primary health care systems founded by Christians with such view. In the West, after the turn of the 20th century, this Kingdom vision was secularized by social gospelers, while the conservatives spiritualized it. Consequently hospitals and health care have been largely relegated to secularists in government and science, with the church forfeiting its historic role. And not only is recovery needed because of this historical perspective, but now with the emergence of New Age Medicine, we need to take a serious look at the spiritual bankruptcy of biomedicine and the spiritual fallacy and danger of much of alternative medicine.

The Community of the King

We have already seen that the Kingdom of God is God's rule or dominion over the people and wealth of His realm. Here on earth, these people are all part of the Church of Jesus Christ, since they are born into the Kingdom through faith in Jesus. Thus we can think of the Church as the "Community of the King," a community of God's people.

And so, with this view clearly in focus, we want to look at the implications for the Church in the area of health and healing. I believe there are three. First, the King cares about the welfare of His subjects—He desires abundance rather than deprivation. Secondly, the people in the community care for each another, providing a milieu for healing. Thirdly, the community promotes the ethics of the King among its members.

The King cares for his subjects

One computer game my sons have enjoyed is SimCity. Here they get to be in charge of a virtual city, or kingdom, which they build. They learn that, in return for fair taxation, the leader must provide a kingdom in which people want to live, with healthy air, good services, and plenty of jobs. The industrial part of town must be far enough from the residential area to prevent air pollution. Roads, schools, police, and hospitals are all needed to service the population or else people will move to a better town. If taxation is too low, the city coffers run dry and services suffer—power plants fail due to lack of maintenance and roads riddle with potholes. If taxation is too high, people move away in disgust. Kids playing this game learn that a good leader, or king, must care about the welfare of the people in his kingdom.

So too in a real earthly kingdom, a just king is concerned about the welfare of his subjects. He ensures safety and security by maintaining the military and police. He encourages the economy of his kingdom through trade and sound fiscal policy, balancing taxation with services. He protects his kingdom from environmental mismanagement and disaster. A healthy food supply is guaranteed through sustainable farming methods. Health care is evenly distributed throughout his kingdom and the poor are looked after.

An unjust king on the other hand, exploits his subjects to his own benefit. History is replete with such unjust, selfish leaders lining Swiss bank accounts with the riches of their kingdom while their people suffer in poverty and misery.

Not so in the Community of the King, the Church, where

Jesus is the just ruler, the *Lord of lords and King of kings* (Rev. 17:14). He desires abundance for His subjects, not deprivation or exploitation. One of the biblical metaphors used to illustrate this abundance is *water*. In His conversation with the woman at the well in John 4:13 and 14, Jesus said:

> *Everyone who drinks this water will be thirsty again, but whoever drinks the water I give him will never thirst. Indeed, the water I give him will become in him a spring of water welling up to eternal life.*

The Old Testament prophet Jeremiah spoke similarly during a time when God's people were slipping far away from Him:

> *My people have committed two sins: They have forsaken me, the spring of living water, and have dug their own cisterns, broken cisterns that cannot hold water* (Jer. 2:13).

There are three principles in these "water" passages. First is the implication that people are thirsty—we have deep unmet longings. We were designed to enjoy the abundance Adam and Eve had in the Garden, and we rightfully long for what was lost in the Fall. God doesn't condemn us for thirst—it's okay to be thirsty. What matters is what we do with our thirst, as illustrated in the second principle—people move in wrong directions in response to their thirst. Rather than turning to God through Jesus Christ, people *dig their own cisterns*. They refuse to trust God to look after their thirst and develop wrong strategies to find the life they desire. Here we see the human tendency to self-sufficiency—picking up our shovels and finding likely places to dig our own muddy wells. Better to observe the third truth which is that only God will fully satisfy the deepest thirst and longings in our hearts, and that is through faith in Jesus Christ.

In the area of health, we are thirsty because we are mortal and we suffer because of sickness. Strained relationships add to our burden of ills, and deep emotional wants may leave us depressed and discouraged. We have already seen some of the wells we dig in order to quench our thirst for health—scientism or New Age. How do we turn to God and attempt to satisfy our thirst by drinking Jesus' water? We do it by daily exercising what we might call the *Spiritual Life Cycle*—a way of living which will change us from the inside out, fulfilling our most intense thirst and longings for eternity while promoting health to body and soul in the present.

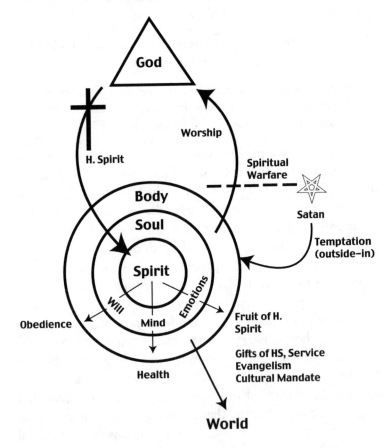

Figure 6.7
Spiritual Life Cycle

Spiritual Life Cycle

Figure 6.7 illustrates the Spiritual Life Cycle. The triune God is represented at the top by the triangle; tripartite humanity at the bottom by three concentric circles representing the spirit, soul, and body. The cycle is initiated when God's Holy Spirit convicts our spirit-man (the site of our conscience and God-consciousness) of the need for repentance—the realization that our sin has separated us from God and we need a Saviour. Our spirit is thus activated and influences our soul (mind, will, and emotions) to cry out to God in repentance (worship) expressed through our body, thus closing the first loop of the cycle. As the cycle closes in our repentance and worship, God fills us with His Spirit, quickening (making alive) our spirit-man which was dead in our unregenerate condition.

The first iteration of the cycle is regeneration or rebirth. It is the beginning of a daily "trip to God's well" in worship—loving God, prayer, meditation, surrender, obedience. Each iteration brings more of God's Spirit into our spirit-man, and the more we are filled with His Spirit, the more our soul comes in line with God's purposes, activating our bodies into obedience and service, producing the fruit of the Spirit as well as enabling us with spiritual gifts. This is called sanctification, and as we grow we should reach a crisis point when we give the reins of our life to Christ, making Him Lord as well as our Saviour. This so-called "second blessing" is referred to in some Christian circles as the baptism of the Holy Spirit, by others as entire sanctification.

We do, of course, have an arch-enemy whose aim is to interrupt each iteration of our Spiritual Life Cycle. Represented by the pentagram in our diagram, he will try to hinder our worship because he knows worship will promote the flow of God's Spirit into our lives. This is known as spiritual warfare. His tactics are well known by those who strive to faithfully exercise this cycle: sleeping in, mind wandering,

Sunday-morning fatigue, the golf course. He also attempts to arrest the inside-out flow of God's Spirit in our soul by implanting lies in our minds.

There are many Scriptures which support this Spiritual Life Cycle concept:

> *Come near to God and he will come near to you.... Humble yourselves before the Lord, and he will lift you up* (Jas. 4:8,10).

> *(God) rewards those who earnestly seek him* (Heb. 11:6).

> *You will seek me and find me when you seek me with all your heart* (Jer. 29:13).

> *If you seek (the LORD), he will be found by you, but if you forsake him, he will forsake you* (2 Chron. 15:2).

> *For the eyes of the LORD range throughout the earth to strengthen those whose hearts are fully committed to him* (2 Chron. 16:9).

Each Scripture teaches that the upward arm of the cycle is rewarded with the downward arm of God's blessing. Oh that we would develop such a deep passion in our devotion to God so He can truly pour out His life and power into our lives.

How does this relate to health and healing? This is illustrated in our diagram by the arrow from our spirit-man, through our mind, to our body. Validated by science, this is the *psychoneuroimmunology* (PNI) pathway, the so-called mind-body connection. The November 7, 1988 issue of *Newsweek* headlined: "New discoveries linking the brain to the immune system suggest that state of mind can affect us right down to our cells." In his book, *Psychoneuroimmunology: The new mind/body healing program*, Dr. Elliott Dacher describes how the brain releases neuropeptides, small hormone transmitters which directly affect immune cells and other hormone-producing cells. Their release is affected by what preoccupies our mind—anxiety and stress have negative affects, while peace and harmony enhance their positive affects.[50] The immune system obviously helps protect our body from infection and cancer. The various hormones released help us maintain balance in such areas of metabolism, emotions and sexuality.

Numerous books have now been written about this mind-body connection and many studies have positively linked active spirituality with positive health—abundance rather than deprivation. I propose a new word, *pneumapsychoneuroimmunology* (PPNI), representing a spirit-mind-body connection within the Spiritual Life Cycle paradigm. It is activated by faith (upward arm of cycle) and mediated through Christ by the Holy Spirit connecting with our spirits. Faith here is not possibility-thinking, or faith in faith. It is faith in Almighty God to heal us from the inside out.

Obviously God is not limited to the PPNI pathway. He has the power to heal the mind or body directly and suddenly as well as to raise the dead.

As constituents of the Community of the King, let us daily reap that abundance by vigorously exercising our Spiritual Life Cycle. Then, as people being transformed from the inside out, we will be ready to live in loving community, another health enhancer.

A caring community

Just as research has validated the mind-body connection, vast amounts of research and experience show that healthy relationships promote mental and physical health. Take the Alcoholics Anonymous (AA) experience for example—by entering into meaningful, caring relationships, and holding each other accountable, many have been helped in their addiction to alcohol. Similarly, studies have shown the positive effects of regular church attendance on health. Thus, we want to explore how the Community of the King may be a therapeutic community through caring relationships. I believe we have barely begun to understand the healing potential of the Church in this area, a view shared by Larry Crabb in his book *Connecting*:

> *The idea is this: When two people connect... something is poured out of one and into the other that has the power to heal the soul of its deepest wounds and restore it to health... In recent days, I have made a shift. I am now working toward the day when communities of God's people, ordinary Christians whose lives regularly intersect, will accomplish most of the good that we now depend on mental health professionals to provide.*[51]

Although Dr. Crabb's area of expertise is mental health, I believe his conclusions are just as valid for physical health. Since the mind and body are inextricably linked, it's a fair conclusion that the benefits of community on mental and spiritual health will spill over into physical health. This is the view of many contemporary thinkers and writers. In *The Four Pillars of Healing*, Dr. Leo Galland cites *relationship* as the first pillar, observing that "inadequate social support is analogous to nutritional deficiency."[52] He goes on to explain how this might work: "Satisfying relationships may buffer the impact of stress, actually lowering the levels of chemical mediators, decreasing the strain on mind and body."[53]

In addition to his arguments for the benefits of community, I would strongly contend that the Church is not just any social club. No, our Kingdom view insists that the Community of the King has a supernatural element, namely the Holy Spirit of God. Our leader, King Jesus, provides what no earthly leader can give his community or organization— the very *Pneuma* or Wind of God—a spiritual "Life Force" that was poured out on the day of Pentecost in Acts 2. I believe there are primarily two ways in which the Church is unique and produces the healing no earthly organization can: the fruit and the gifts of the Holy Spirit

A community with fruit

First, when individuals exercise their Spiritual Life Cycle, they produce the fruit of the Holy Spirit—*love, joy, peace, patience, kindness, goodness, faithfulness, gentleness and self-control* (Gal. 5:22,23). Now a relationship in which at least one person vigorously exercises her Spiritual Life Cycle, that person doesn't need to look to the other person for needs. Because she goes to God regularly, she is free to give unselfishly to the other and start to minister God's healing power in the other person's life.

The key concept which makes this work is biblical *agape* love. Only regular trips to God's well produce this in your life, but with it you can unselfishly love other people within the context of community. Larry Crabb continues in his optimism that this can truly begin to happen:

> (God) has deposited within us an energy that can heal soul disease, a power that is released to do its miraculous work as we relate in certain ways with each other. Our difficulty is that we don't believe it and therefore haven't thought much about it. But that could change. I envision a community of people who intentionally mingle in settings where these nutrients are passed back and forth, where I pour into you the healing resources within me and you pour into me what God has put in you.[54]

Two crucial elements resulting from community life where the fruits of the Spirit are cultivated are *acceptance* and *forgiveness*. Acceptance builds esteem and self-worth, thus making a person more open to God's love and forgiveness. This is powerfully therapeutic for soul and body. Similarly, forgiveness has been shown by even secular researchers to boost the body's healing abilities. Biblical Christianity promotes a level of unreserved forgiveness found nowhere but in the Community of the King.

A community with gifts

It is my contention from Scripture that for *agape* love to be expressed within the context of community, individuals need to be exercising their *spiritual gifts*. I say this because some of the greatest "love" passages in Scripture are linked to, or found within, teaching on spiritual gifts. Take 1 Corinthians 13, the great love chapter often read at weddings, for example—it is between two chapters completely dedicated to teaching on spiritual gifts. Similarly, in Romans 12 several verses on the gifts of the Holy Spirit are directly followed by the statement: *Love must be sincere* (Rom. 12:9). In his first letter, Peter admonishes us to *love each other deeply* and immediately following that he exhorts us to *use whatever gift (we have) received to serve others* (1 Pet. 4:8,10). The same thing happens in Ephesians 4 where the verse, *Be completely humble and gentle; be patient, bearing with one another in love* (vs. 2), is followed by:

> It was he who gave some to be apostles, some to be prophets, some to be evangelists, and some to be pastors and teachers, to prepare God's people for works of service, so that the body of Christ may be built up until we all reach unity in the faith and in the knowledge of the Son of God and become mature, attaining to the whole measure of the fullness of Christ (vs. 11-13).

I believe this association of love with the gifts is highly significant for two reasons—you need to use your gifts to truly express *agape* love practically and the gifts are dangerous if exercised without it—they are open to selfish abuse.

The best way for you to pour your life into that of another is in the area where you are strongest, likely the area of your gifting. Take the gift of *mercy*; with it you can come alongside someone in a powerfully empathetic way. Similarly, the gift of *encouragement* will allow you to encourage a struggler. So these gifts allow you to express love in a deeper, more powerful way. In essence, they deepen the care of the community.

Let's take a closer look at how the gifts of the Holy Spirit may augment the milieu for healing. While alternative healers use medical intuition and Therapeutic Touch to heal, we need to offer the biblical spiritual gifts that are the proper replacements for these methods.

Medical intuition (a.k.a. psychic healing) is the ability to look beyond the natural realm into the extra-dimensional realm of the spirit world and find answers to physical or emotional problems. The proper biblical expression of that is *the word of knowledge* (1 Cor. 12:8 KJV). Here a person with this gift may be given insights into another's physical, emotional, or spiritual illness through the Holy Spirit. Exercised within a caring community, with opportunity for repentance and prayer, this can be powerfully therapeutic. To replace Therapeutic Touch we need to exercise the biblical concept of laying on of hands. Within the context of caring community, people who have healing gifts or spiritual leaders within the Church with authority to lay on hands, need to use this therapeutic modality in combination with anointing with oil as clearly instructed in Scripture.

We have long been warning Christians about the dangers of New Age Medicine, and some very informative books have been written. My criticism of some of these books is that while they are long in identifying the ills of New Age Medicine, they are short in promoting true biblical alternatives. So people are forced to turn to science and biomedicine, which we have already seen to be spiritually bankrupt. Hence the encouragement in this work for the Church to rediscover its historic role as a therapeutic community. But it can't be a weakened Church—it needs to be empowered from on high.

Promote Kingdom ethics

We will see in chapter 9 that Kingdom ethics—the set of moral values and principles espoused by the King—are health-promoting. What is so powerful about living in community is that these ethics are held as the standard of community life. Here now is the opportunity for accountability—I will hold you accountable to live out the King's ethics, while you hold me accountable. We give each other the right to call us to task.

We have a long way to go here. Promise Keepers, the Christian men's movement, has been promoting accountability relationships between men where each asks the other tough questions, all designed to promote healthy marriages and relationships and holy living. Appendix D lists some sample questions that might be used in such accountability relationships. However, in the greater Christian community this is sorely lacking.

Promoting Kingdom ethics also involves accountability against syncretism—the intermingling of various belief systems. Since its earliest days, concepts from other religions have crept into Christianity. In the first century it was Gnosticism; in the Middle Ages it was ritual. Today's New Age concepts and beliefs are becoming mainstay within Christianity—something we must guard and speak against passionately. False beliefs will surely weaken our impact as agents of the Kingdom, severely restricting our mandate to make disciples of all nations.

The Church as the agent of the Kingdom

When we say the Church is the agent of the Kingdom, we mean it is God's chosen means through which more and more of the world comes under God's rule—it is the medium through which He expresses Himself to the world and reconciles it to Himself. It is God's redeeming agency in the earth— His chosen vessel for evangelizing the world. It is also the means through which the Christian worldview is established as the most rational, logical explanation for all of reality. As such, in the area of health and healing, science and medicine, it is the agency through which God's rule needs to be established here as well. We want to explore some practical ways in which the Church can be the agent of the Kingdom in the area of health, both inside and outside the traditional boundaries of the Church? It most certainly begins with praying for the sick.

Provide healing through prayer

We have already seen the injunction in James to pray for the sick:

> *Is any one of you sick? He should call the elders of the church to pray over him and anoint him with oil in the name of the Lord. And the prayer offered in faith will make the sick person well; the Lord will raise him up. If he has sinned, he will be forgiven (Jas. 5:14,15).*

Christ and the early Church exemplified our role: *They... anointed many sick people with oil and healed them* (Mark 6:13). Science has validated the power of faith in healing. In his book *The Healing Power of Faith*, Dr. Harold Koenig summarizes the findings of his research into the relationship of faith and health:

> *Now I am amazed at what science has discovered about the wide-ranging effects that devout religious faith and practise may have on mental and physical health and on quality of life for individuals, families, and communities. Almost every area of life and health appears to be affected by deep religious faith that is lived within in a community of believers.*[55]

Also, the Church's recovery of spiritual gifts in the last century reaffirmed the gift of healing. History and personal testimonials have substantiated it throughout the centuries, with many being medically confirmed.

Biblical praying for the sick often involved the practice of touch—either laying on of hands, anointing with oil or otherwise touching the healee. Both laying on of hands and anointing with oil are sensory aids to illustrate physically what happens in the spiritual realm. A friend recently shared her experience with the power of touch while she was in hospital isolation because of an infectious illness. An empathetic nurse did her care, all gowned and gloved as per hospital policy, but at the end removed her gloves and touched my friend and said, "Now do you feel better?" Indeed she did.

Let's look at the practice of touch in healing from a biblical perspective.

Laying on of hands

In Hebrews 6:1-2, the laying on of hands is listed with the *elementary* doctrines:

> *Therefore let us leave the elementary teachings about Christ and go on to maturity, not laying again the foundation of repentance from acts that lead to death, and of faith in God, instruction about baptisms, the laying on of hands, the resurrection of the dead, and eternal judgment.*

Within early Christianity, the laying on of hands was a frequently-used, basic technique. Jesus used it to heal the sick in Mark 6:5; the apostles used it when commissioning the seven workers in Acts 6:6 and when praying for people to receive the Holy Spirit in Acts 8:18; Paul used it in his healing ministry in Acts 28:8; Timothy was the recipient of it when Paul prayed over him for a particular spiritual gift (1 Tim. 5:22); the church at Antioch laid hands on Paul and Barnabas when they were commissioned as missionaries (Acts 13:2).

The laying on of hands has its roots in the Old Testament. There we see it used to confer a blessing (Gen. 48:13-20), transfer guilt from a sinner to a sacrificial animal (Lev. 1:4), and commission a person to a new service (Num. 27:23). By using both the sense of touch and the sense of sight, it represents a transfer of a spiritual nature. Jesus noticed this transfer in Mark 5 when the woman who had been subject to bleeding for twelve years touched His clothing: *At once Jesus realized that power had gone out from him* (Mark 5:30). The word for power here is *dunamis*, the same word used in Acts 1:8 describing what would happen when the Holy Spirit would be poured out: *But you will receive power when the Holy Spirit comes on you.* So what we see in the laying on of hands is an outward sign of an inward transfer of the power of the Holy Spirit. Using our Spiritual Life Cycle paradigm, the person ministering the laying on of hands transfers God's power via his spirit-soul-body connection, through his hands, to the person receiving ministering. I believe this is not a magical, but a visible, representation of the flow of God's Spirit.

I do believe that we need to practise the laying on of hands frequently, but must have the spiritual authority to do so— first through church-leadership sanction and secondly, before God. We must be exercising our Spiritual Life Cycle. If we are not in right relationship with God ourselves, we are hypocritical in attempting to impart God's blessing on someone else.

Anointing with oil

Oil was used scripturally in both medicinal and symbolic ways. In the parable of the good Samaritan, he bandaged the injured man's wounds, *pouring on oil and wine* (Luke 10:34). We know from the ancient Greek physician Galen that olive oil in particular was used therapeutically, as well as being a carrying agent for medicinal herbs. In Isaiah 1:6 oil is also mentioned as being soothing for *wounds and welts and open sores.*

Symbolically, oil was used in anointing to set people or objects apart for service to God—to *consecrate* them, to make them holy. It was an act done on behalf of God and meant to be a bestowal of divine favour, or appointment to a special place of function in the purpose of God. It was associated with the outpouring of the Spirit of God. For example, Samuel used oil to anoint David as the future king:

> *So Samuel took the horn of oil and anointed him in the presence of his brothers, and from that day on the Spirit of the LORD came upon David in power* (1 Sam. 16:13).

I believe we see here then, scriptural grounds to use oil both medicinally and symbolically. Within the context of prayer for healing, because we no longer use it medicinally, it is the symbolic power of the Holy Spirit that we utilize, this time on behalf of God. Hence I believe James' insistence on elders with appropriate spiritual authority being given this responsibility.

Let's look then at implementing prayer and touch practically in the context of church life.

Where to pray

The place to begin prayer for healing is in worship. In our corporate worship, prayer needs to be an integral part of our encounter with God. Churches that have successful healing ministries probably use it in some of the following ways, and if you are sick you need to be there:

- *Regular Sunday worship services.* Many churches with success in this area have a ministry time following the service either at an altar at the front of the church or in an adjacent prayer room. The adjacent room is preferable.

- *Special services with a healing theme.* Services like this use worship music, Scripture readings and a sermon, all focussed on healing. Usually prayer for healing is ministered at the front of the church.

- *Communion.* The Lord's Supper can be used therapeutically in a powerful way. It adds the extra senses in the healing experience. The elements of bread and wine can be viewed as medicine.

- *Cell groups.* Cell groups are small groups which often meet in homes and are one of the best places to pray for the sick. Here the added power of caring relationships augments the impact of prayer.

- *Weekend retreats and conferences.* These are wonderful means to emphasize health and healing. Teaching on health is supplemented with counselling and prayer.

- *Camps.* Christian camps for all ages provide a wonderful milieu for healing, particularly in a natural, serene setting.

Other places to pray for the sick are obviously the bedside in the hospital and nursing home, or the homes of shut-ins. Christian support groups for addictions of all types all need prayer for healing. We need to teach our children at an early age to experience the power of healing prayer. We need to teach them that we have an enemy who wants us to kill ourselves by destroying our bodies.

Spiritual warfare

Jesus taught us well when He taught us to pray *deliver us from the evil one* (Matt. 6:13). He knows the evil one intimately—He had a couple of rounds with him in the desert, on the temple roof, on the mountain, and in Gethsemane... and won! The biggest battle of all was the three days He was separated from His Father, but He triumphed victoriously there too, revealing that Satan no longer has power over death. Jesus declared to John in his vision: *I am the Living One; I was dead, and behold I am alive for ever and ever! And I hold the keys of death and Hades* (Rev. 1:18). He holds the sceptre and now calls His followers to complete what was won by His death and resurrection—the mop-up operation we talked about earlier. We now hold the sceptre on behalf of the King, and we fight for Jesus, draftees regardless of age, race, or social status. The old hymn put it this way:

> *Onward Christian soldiers, marching as to war,*
> *With the cross of Jesus going on before...*

The Apostle Paul puts it this way:

> *Finally, be strong in the Lord and in his mighty power. Put on the full armor of God so that you can take your stand against the devil's schemes. For our struggle is not against flesh and blood, but against the rulers, against the authorities, against the powers of this dark world and against the spiritual forces of evil in the heavenly realms. Therefore put on the full armor of God, so that when the day of evil comes, you may be able to stand your ground, and after you have done everything, to stand... And pray in the Spirit on all occasions with all kinds of prayers and requests* (Eph. 6:10-13,18).

Learning to pray for healing involves recognizing who the enemy really is and taking a stand against him. Not every emotional or physical sickness is a direct result of demonic attack, but some are. Other illnesses may certainly be used by the enemy to distract us from our call, leaving us rag-tag soldiers at the back of the army, uniforms shoddy, limping along, barely able to hear our Commander-in-chief's orders. Take illnesses such as fibromyalgia, chronic fatigue, depression, or multiple chemical sensitivities—they leave many a warrior feeling defeated and wounded.

So how do we wage war against our enemy in the area of illness? It begins, according to Ephesians 3:10-11, by daily reminding and showing the demonic realm who is victor.

> *His intent was that now, through the church, the manifold wisdom of God should be made known to the rulers and authorities in the heavenly realms.*

It's as if we're to hold Satan's ultimate defeat over his head, reminding him of that word spoken in Genesis 3:15: *(Jesus) will crush your head.* It's staring down the enemy just as boxers do in the ring before round one. Then we don our armour. To do this we need to take off our unrighteousness. *So let us put aside the deeds of darkness and put on the armor of light* (Rom. 13:12). It's part of the Spiritual Life Cycle—as we draw near to

God in repentance, in surrender, in obedience, He, in turn, draws near to us in forgiveness, in cleansing, in filling us with His Spirit. Then each piece of armour readies us to do battle—truth, righteousness, peace, faith, salvation, Word of God—each piece designed to thwart the enemy.

Having donned the armour, we need to recognize that we are not alone in the battle. Besides our fellow earthbound soldiers, there are angels who war on our behalf. *Are not all angels ministering spirits sent to serve those who will inherit salvation?* (Heb. 1:14). *The angel of the LORD encamps around those who fear him, and he delivers them* (Ps. 34:7). Although there is no scriptural basis for praying to angels, we can ask God to send them to minister to us or the person we are praying for. Angels have recently been depicted in various popular media, probably as result of postmodernism, but most of this material is not from a Christian source and may be deceptive or frankly New Age.

In the area of spiritual warfare, there is an important principle which we can learn from David in the Old Testament. David used Goliath's sword, which would have used against him, to remove Goliath's head. The weapon the enemy tries to use against you will become your offensive weapon in advancing the Kingdom against him. Take childhood abuse for example. After being delivered and healed of the pain of that through genuine forgiveness, in Christ you may be used to help many others through deliverance. A preacher I heard recently shared about his extreme introversion as a young person; now he preaches to thousands.

Victim or target—which would you rather be? You are either a victim because of cowardly retreat or a target because, like David, you take your stand against the enemy, advancing the Kingdom. It is much better that the target engages the enemy head-on and drives him back to his destined position—defeat!

Persistence in prayer

It is a fact of life that not everyone we pray for will experience sudden divine intervention, nor will we be instantly healed of every disease we request prayer for. That should not hinder us from being obedient to Scripture in continuing to pray and believe. The answer to why some are healed and some are not may be found in asking the questions we looked at in Chapter 4. Yet sometimes the answer to all the questions is "no" and still healing doesn't come. Obviously the faith of people praying and the healee are factors. Scripture is clear on the relationship between faith and answered prayer: *the prayer offered in faith will make the sick person well* (Jas. 5:15). Jesus Himself said, *If you believe, you will receive whatever you ask for in prayer* (Matt. 21:22). But despite faith, even faith as strong as the Apostle Paul's, there may be times when God says, *My grace is sufficient for you, for my power is made perfect in weakness.* This was God's answer to Paul after he prayed three times to God for healing for his *thorn in the flesh* (2 Cor. 12:7-9). Until we get as clear a sense to cease praying as Paul did, I would advocate taking the Canaanite woman in Matthew as our example:

> *A Canaanite woman from that vicinity came to him, crying out, "Lord, Son of David, have mercy on me! My daughter is suffering terribly from demon-possession." Jesus did not answer a word. So his disciples came to him and urged him, "Send her away, for she keeps crying out after us." He answered, "I was sent only to the lost sheep of Israel." The woman came and knelt before him. "Lord, help me!" she said. He replied, "It is not right to take the children's bread and toss it to their dogs." "Yes, Lord," she said, "but even the dogs eat the crumbs that fall from their masters' table." Then Jesus answered, "Woman, you have great faith! Your request is granted." And her daughter was healed from that very hour* (Matt. 15:22-28).

Here we can see four points to learn from:

- *She recognized the source of her daughter's misery.* The daughter's condition seemed hopeless, but the mother recognized it was the result of the enemy's work.

- *She recognized Christ as her source of hope.* The only antidote for Satanic oppression is the power of Jesus Christ.

- *Her faith persevered despite an initial "no" from Jesus.* Perseverance was her key to deliverance. We too may get an initial "no," but persevere in faith.

- *She reaped a wondrous blessing as a result of her persevering faith.* We too will reap a blessing, if not in the here and now, certainly in the New Creation.

When healing is delayed, or denied, the Church should guard against neglecting people who are not healed. We need to provide the best care good science and empathy can bring. And we shouldn't just turn them over to secular healers. This is where some recovery is needed by evangelical churches today.[56]

Healing for the nations

There is a beautiful picture in Revelation of the water metaphor we've already developed (living water bearing the empowerment of God as healing to the nations):

> *Then the angel showed me the river of the water of life, as clear as crystal, flowing from the throne of God and of the Lamb down the middle of the great street of the city. On each side of the river stood the tree of life, bearing twelve crops of fruit, yielding its fruit every month. And the leaves of the tree are for the healing of the nations* (Rev. 22:1).

The word "healing" in this verse is *therapeia* in Greek, from which we obviously derive our words "therapy" and "therapeutic." The Church is to be the agent, the deliverer, of that *therapeia*. How does this happen powerfully? Jesus' high priestly prayer gives us some clues:

> *My prayer is not for them alone. I pray also for those who will believe in me through their message, that all of them may be one, Father, just as you are in me and I am in you. May they also be in us so that the world may believe that you have sent me. I have given them the glory that you gave me, that they may be one as we are one: I in them and you in me. May they be brought to complete unity to let the world know that you sent me and have loved them even as you have loved me* (John 17:20-23).

Jesus here prays for *those who will believe*—all Christians of all time that came after Christ, including us! Then He prays for *unity to let the world know*. There is power, healing power, in true Christian unity where brothers and sisters, born from above, stand together against the common enemy of our souls.

This is happening in many communities around the world which are featured in a video entitled *Transformations* by George Otis Jr.[57] In communities such as Cali, Columbia and Almolonga, Guatemala, Christians are standing together in unity and corporate prayer, breaking the generational curse over their communities by confessing the sins of the past, resulting in radical social change in these communities. In Almolonga, prisons were closed due to reduced crime and the agricultural production increased by 1000 percent!

In summary then, God's solution to the problem of sickness, aging, and death is salvation in Christ. Ultimately, this means immortality and freedom from sickness. In the here and now, the Church has a continued responsibility to be involved in healing ministry. Part of that responsibility is to help people carefully choose who they go to for healing.

Choose
7 | Your Healers
Wisely

Just as the search for self becomes a search for health, so the pursuit of health can lead to greater self-awareness.

Marilyn Ferguson

You have just hurt your back while shoveling heavy, wet snow. The pain hit you suddenly like a knife, and every time you move, you feel your back muscles tightening, causing even more pain. You go in the house and try to get comfortable on the couch. First you try cold, then heat, all to no avail. You raid the medicine cupboard for some Advil®. Before long, the pain is radiating down one leg and you can hardly move. You spend a terrible night trying to get relief. All your Advil® are gone, and by 6:00 a.m., you have had it. You grab the phone book and start leafing through the yellow pages. Which section should you turn to—physicians, chiropractors, physiotherapists, acupuncturists, naturopaths, or massage therapists? Or should you call the elders of your church to anoint you with oil?

This chapter will help answer that question. With so many treatment options available and with scientific healthcare as stretched as it is in Canada, how do you choose your treatment options safely? Not only do you care about being restored physically in short order, but if you are a sincere believer in Christ, you must also consider your spiritual health—probably more importantly. Life on earth is short compared to eternity.

The choices we make may impact not only our own physical and spiritual health but also the well-being of our children and grandchildren. Many Christians don't recognize the occultic methods used by many CAM practitioners. When considering your options, here are the questions to ask:

- Should I trust God for healing?
- What is the practitioner's worldview?
- Are there methods denounced by Scripture?
- Does science validate the healing discipline?
- Is the practitioner a "mixer"?
- What is the role of financial gain?
- Is there any doctor bashing?
- Is there unethical promotion or advertising?
- What about healing crusades?

Should I trust God for healing?

The first question we need to address is whether God allows natural means to advance His Kingdom. Are we discouraged scripturally from the use of technology? Is supernatural healing better than healing through medicine?

Nowhere does the Bible prohibit technology, and this has been the historic Christian stand. The printing press revolutionized the distribution of the Bible—no one argued that handwritten scrolls were superior or more "inspired." Likewise, electronic media such as radio and television have been used extensively for evangelism. We recognize technology in these instances as a gift from God. We're thankful for inventive minds to advance the Kingdom and alleviate suffering. *Every good and perfect gift is from above, coming down from the Father of the heavenly lights* (Jas. 1:17).

Similarly, in the area of health, no censure is made of physicians or medicine. Dr. Luke accompanied Paul on his later missionary journeys, possibly as his personal physician to attend his "thorn in the flesh." Paul also gave Timothy advice to use a natural means for his gastric problems and frequent sickness: *Stop drinking only water, and use a little wine because of your stomach and your frequent illnesses* (1 Tim. 5:23). This advice may have been a mixed blessing—wine probably didn't do much for his stomach, but it may have helped prevent waterborne diseases such as cholera or gastroenteritis. Jesus never condemned doctors. Although, He did rescue people whose physicians had failed them, as in the case of the woman with vaginal bleeding.

What we do see though, in the story of King Asa in the Old Testament, is an indictment for seeking natural healing *only*. Asa began his rule as a sincere follower of God, tearing down idols and calling people back to the true worship of God. God blessed him and his people by defeating their enemies. Later in life, however, his zeal for God wavered, and when confronted with a threat from a neighbouring enemy, he bought them off with savings from the temple treasury. When God's prophet confronted Asa for his lack of faith, Asa became angry and imprisoned the prophet. Rather than repent, Asa reaped the consequences of his rebellion. God then tried to get his attention through sickness.

In the thirty-ninth year of his reign Asa was afflicted with a disease in his feet. Though his disease was severe, even in his illness he did not seek help from the LORD, but only from the physicians (2 Chron. 16:12).

Here is the point: don't place your trust in technology or natural means alone. Whether naturally or supernaturally, it is still God who must heal. It is God who created natural laws, as well as spiritual laws. So, pray for healing first. Seek God, and ask Him the *why* questions. Ask for people to pray for you. Call the elders as James suggests. Then God, through His Holy Spirit, may give you direction regarding who to seek for healing in the natural realm.

As I personally sought the Lord about supernatural versus natural healing, He led me to the passage on Jesus' temptation by Satan. The second temptation was for Jesus to defy God's natural law of gravity by jumping off the highest point of the temple and to rely on God's supernatural laws for protection. Jesus' answer was a quote from Deuteronomy 6:16: *"Do not put the Lord your God to the test"* (Matt. 4:7). From this, I understood that insisting on supernatural healing alone, when natural means are easily available, is *putting God to the test*.

What is the practitioner's worldview?

As you pray for leading regarding which healing practitioners to turn to, consider first his or her worldview. Healers with worldviews other than the Christian one may influence you at an intellectual level and possibly at a spiritual level to waver from your commitment and zeal in Christ. One of the purposes of this book is to warn Christians about the dangers of alternate worldviews and their prophets, masquerading as alternative or medical healers. I believe New Age healers are a major threat to Christianity and are a subtle means whereby Satan is influencing the Church. This chapter's opening quote by Marilyn Ferguson illustrates that. Similarly, scientism is influencing Christians; no longer is Christ their hope for salvation.

In order to assess the practitioner's worldview, ask the following questions:

- ***Do disease etiology theories and proposed solutions coincide with a Christian worldview?*** Before you consent to any evaluation or treatment, ask the practitioner what he or she views to be the cause of illness, or research it yourself. Review Chapter 1 to evaluate non-Christian disease theories, and check the chart in Appendix B. Healing traditions with an "energy" model of disease—*yin* and *yang* of Taoism, *prana* of Hinduism—should be avoided. Scientifically questionable disease theories are also safest to avoid. Where naturalism excuses sin, such as alternate lifestyles, promiscuity, and disbelief in God as Creator, avoid practitioners with that view.

- ***Does the practitioner's personal life reflect a biblical lifestyle, or are there connections to humanism, New Age, or occultism?*** You can know someone by the books he or she reads. You may be able to scan the practitioner's library while waiting. Waiting room materials may give clues, and any articles or books he has written should be reviewed. Look for New Age buzzwords such as *transpersonal psychology, non-local mind, holistic, readings, medical intuition,* and examine the authors he quotes. Which religion does she practise, or is she an atheist with a naturalistic worldview? Are there New Age symbols in the office? Which associations is he a member of? Where was she trained? In what type of media does he advertise? Does she participate in Psychic Fairs?

- ***What were/are the founder's beliefs and practices?*** Most healing arts can be traced back to a founder, some of whom were prolific writers and outspoken advocates of their healing theories. Here you may find evidence of worldviews and disease etiology theories which run contrary to biblical Christianity.

- *Does the healing art encourage the establishment of the Kingdom of God, or does it root for the kingdom of this age?* Where does hope for a better future lie? Is it in science? Is it in a New Age hope of peace and harmony on earth? Or is it in the Christian hope of the establishment of the Kingdom of God on earth, to be completed in the age to come.

Even with these questions before you, it may not be easy to reach an accurate conclusion. A practitioner may profess Christ and yet use New Age methods. Discernment is critical. Ask for advice from mature believers, and pray for wisdom. Above all, listen to your conscience, and follow any checks the Holy Spirit may impress upon you.

Are there methods denounced by Scripture?

In the first instance, examine the healing art for occultic practices which the Bible clearly denounces:

> *Let no one be found among you who... practices divination or sorcery, interprets omens, engages in witchcraft, or casts spells, or who is a medium or spiritist or who consults the dead. Anyone who does these things is detestable to the LORD* (Deut. 18:10-12).

The two practices which are often found in alternative medicine are *divination* and *sorcery*.

- *Divination* is the attempt—either while in a trance or through the interpretation of external signs or omens—to discern knowledge or events that are distant in time or space. Other terms for divination are *clairvoyance* or *ESP*. Palm reading, astrology, and more than 900 psychic lines are examples. As well, a *reading* done by a *medical intuitive* is divination, as is the *centering* of Therapeutic Touch. Several other contemporary alternative healing arts use this method to reach diagnoses, similar to the ancient liver diviners of Babylon referred to in Ezekiel 21:21.

For the king of Babylon will stop at the fork in the road, at the junction of the two roads, to seek an omen: He will cast lots with arrows, he will consult his idols, he will examine the liver.

Clay model livers, inscribed in fifty-five sections, have been unearthed. They were used as a guide in examining cadaver or animal livers for omens. Iridology, reflexology, and pulse diagnosis in TCM have similar ancient roots—all scientifically unverifiable.

- *Sorcery* is attempting to influence people and events by supernatural or occult means. An example of this is Shamanism, in which the shaman uses magic to cure the sick or control events. Many traditional healing arts of aboriginal people groups use Shamanism—we frequently saw it used by African traditional healers. In alternative medicine, those healing arts which manipulate the *vital force* or *human energy fields* by various means draw on this practice. The most obvious example is Therapeutic Touch, where the practitioner attempts to control a person's energy field by using one's hands to direct energy flow.

Carefully scrutinize any healer that you are considering to patronize for any of these practices, even if they claim to be Christian. Scripture is clear about the dangers of mixing occultism with Christianity.

You cannot drink the cup of the Lord and the cup of demons too; you cannot have a part in both the Lord's table and the table of demons. Are we trying to arouse the Lord's jealousy? (1 Cor. 10:21,22).

The danger, of course, is giving the demonic realm legal access to you and your descendants. Such legal access can cause what Scripture calls a *"stronghold"* (2 Cor. 10:4) and may wreck havoc in your life by causing spiritual blindness.

Secondly, look for man-made rules that are contrary to Scripture. We are warned about this by the Apostle Paul in his letter to Timothy:

> *The Spirit clearly says that in later times some will abandon the faith and follow deceiving spirits and things taught by demons. Such teachings come through hypocritical liars, whose consciences have been seared as with a hot iron. They forbid people to marry and order them to abstain from certain foods, which God created to be received with thanksgiving by those who believe and who know the truth. For everything God created is good, and nothing is to be rejected if it is received with thanksgiving, because it is consecrated by the word of God and prayer* (1 Tim. 4:1-5).

Esoteric food rules, extreme self-denial, and unscriptural religious practices should all be suspect. Some food rules you may encounter have roots in the healing arts of Hinduism or Taoism. Similarly, supplements that promise all but immortality may feed a humanistic zeal for salvation. Watch for a balance that is true to Scripture and the best science.

Thirdly, watch for the use of mind-altering drugs or herbs. A favourite method of traditional African healers is to administer mind-altering herbs to the patient, as well as to themselves, thereby encouraging altered states of consciousness to invoke their healing sorcery. Interestingly, in Galatians 5:20, the original Greek word for *witchcraft* is *pharmakeia,* which is where the root of our English *pharmacy* and *pharmaceutical* originates. The ancient practice obviously mixed herbal potions with magical spells, which later became legitimized as pharmaceuticals. The resurgence of herbalism in CAM needs to be scrutinized carefully. While many herbal remedies are legitimate and helpful, others are potent, not only in their addictive potential, but also in their toxicity. Similarly, MDs have a large armamentarium of mood-altering drugs at their disposal, which can be just as addictive and spiritually damaging.

The biblical alternative is to be filled with the Holy Spirit—to exercise the Spiritual Life Cycle. *Do not get drunk on wine.... Instead, be filled with the Spirit* (Eph. 5:18).

Does science validate the healing discipline?

Although science is in danger of trying to become the sole means of evaluating reality because of its denial of an extra-dimensional realm, it is nevertheless a helpful tool to separate natural healing from supernatural or spiritual healing. Likewise, it is helpful to validate or invalidate diagnostic and therapeutic measures. In other words, science is a useful tool in separating quackery from legitimate healing and natural from spiritual healing.

Christianity is not anti-science, and we should not shun scientific analysis. It is the means to discover the Creator in the created. Currently, we are seeing more scientific analysis of the effect of Christian spiritual healing, such as prayer and worship, on health and well-being. Alternative healers should therefore not be afraid of having their work examined under the microscope of science.

Here are the questions to consider:

- *Is there a plausible scientific explanation for the diagnostic method or the therapy?* Do the methods concur with common sense and known physiology? Is it plausible that examination of an iris will yield diagnoses of organs far removed, even though the disease causes no systemic effects and the affected organ has no direct connection to the eye? Some argue that a yet undiscovered natural explanation exists, often in the realm of quantum mechanics or in energy imprinting. Others argue pragmatism—if it works, it is okay. The thesis of this book is that just because it works, doesn't mean it's spiritually safe.

- *Have double-blind placebo controlled trials been done?* This is the gold standard for scientific evaluation. Even so, a positive result does not rule out a potentially harmful treatment. There are some cases where studies have been done and failed to show statistical results, but the methods have still been used, sometimes even by Christian healers or doctors. For example, some Christian clinics in Mexico use the drug Laetrile for cancer treatment.

Is the practitioner a "mixer?"

Many CAM practitioners mix therapies from several disciplines. For example, a chiropractor may combine traditional chiropractic manipulation with herbs, dietary supplements, and Therapeutic Touch. Similarly, an MD may recommend yoga or Transcendental Meditation for relaxation. We are seeing some of this in Palliative Care units. The discerning Christian should beware of the potential mix of valid natural healing with either quackery or outright sorcery. Question your practitioner on the first visit regarding which methods he supports or uses. Avoid any healer who uses energy-based methods or methods that you question or feel uncomfortable with. This is even a question to ask your dentist. A Christian acquaintance recently encountered TT during a dental appointment. With her mouth full of dental equipment she was unable to object but wisely chose to pray for spiritual protection.

What is the role of financial gain?

It is no secret that baby boomers make up a huge market for purveyors of wellness and healing. Startup-supplement companies have already amassed fortunes. Multinational pharmaceutical giants charge exorbitant amounts for new drugs under the guise of recovering their research costs. However, many are "me-too" drugs—classes of drugs already in the marketplace which are then promoted with expensive advertising campaigns. Many a surgeon has lined his pocket doing unnecessary surgical procedures. Some spiritual healers have not been above reproach either in their financial dealings and fund-raising techniques.

Here are questions to ask and steps to take to protect your family from financial pilfering.

- *Do financial incentives influence the practitioner's ability to diagnose objectively?* This may come to light in the frequency of certain diagnoses. For example, some CAM practitioners virtually always diagnosis yeast overgrowth, possibly because they market anti-yeast products. Some orthopedic surgeons may virtually always diagnose a meniscal injury (knee cartilage) because arthroscopic examination and repair of the cartilage generates lucrative income.

- *Does the practitioner routinely sell supplements or treatments as part of their practice?* Practitioners who sell these products may recommend them inappropriately. In addition, such products may be substantially more expensive than similar ones in drugstores.

- *Get an opinion from a "non-cutting" doctor about the need and benefits of proposed surgery.* Talk to your family doctor or an internist if you have seen a surgeon who is recommending surgery. Similarly, good medical information is available on the Internet which may help you decide about the need for surgery.

- *Avoid network marketing schemes.* Many alternative products are marketed this way. Typically, you will be handed a cassette or literature expounding the virtues of the products being sold. Not only may you buy them for your family, there is an incentive to become a seller and to recruit your friends into selling as well. With this scheme, the incentive to sell will far outweigh objective assessment of need in the vast majority—it is simply human nature.

Obviously, health practitioners deserve a wage for their expertise and knowledge as well as their investment in training. Maybe the best are those who do it as a calling rather than those with a get-rich-fast mentality. As practitioners, we need to repeatedly check our motives and goals. I would encourage any Christian practitioner in any discipline—whether a doctor, nurse, dentist, or physiotherapist—to make time for a Third World or mission experience.

Is there doctor bashing?

The scientific healthcare community is certainly not above the need for criticism and accountability. A recent study documenting iatrogenic (medically caused) misdeeds showed astounding problems in health care. An article in the December 13, 1999 issue of *Time* reported that medical errors kill up to 98,000 Americans yearly.[58] Obviously this is fodder for alternative healers trying to forge a niche for themselves in the marketplace. There are some who go beyond valid criticism and make "doctor bashing" their main objective. Books like *Dead Doctors Don't Lie*,[59] and *What Doctors Don't Tell You*,[60] are unusually critical of scientific medicine. Obviously as an MD, I will be perceived by some readers as biased. However, consider the following suggestions to protect yourself and your family:

- *Watch for criticism of epidemiologically proven preventions.* There is a trend, for example among many CAM practitioners, to advise families not to immunize their children. However, no one can argue about the positive effects of smallpox, tetanus, and polio vaccination—these diseases are virtually eradicated (smallpox, altogether). What is at stake here is "herd immunity." Should there be a critical drop in the number of people immune to polio for example, we will likely see its recurrence. Many people have never seen tetanus or polio. I have and I would not hesitate to immunize my children against them. Similarly, there is opposition to pasteurization of milk.

- *Watch for criticism of scientifically proven treatments.* Sometimes surgery, chemotherapy, and radiation are portrayed as barbaric treatments, on par with the bloodletting of yesteryear. True, they are toxic, wrought with side effects, and may even be disfiguring. However, some cancers are highly curable with them and I don't recommend you ignore these treatments. Ask for the cure statistics (usually in five-year survival rates) and prayerfully consider your options given your age.

- *Beware of the argument that natural is always better than artificial.* This is an invalid argument. Some natural substances are highly toxic—nicotinic acid is highly poisonous and very effective as an insecticide. Opiates from the poppy plant are highly addictive. Even pure salt (NaCl) or water (H_2O) can be toxic to the body merely by their excess. On the other hand, artificial insulin produced through genetically modified bacteria is pure, identical to human insulin and far superior to the animal insulins extracted from the pancreases of cows and pigs. Many CAM practitioners use this argument to promote their products. Similarly, don't take any pharmaceutical from an MD without knowing its intended purpose, its potential risks, and the proposed benefits. Every treatment is a balance of potential benefit against potential risk.

- *Beware of spiritual healers who advise you to avoid proven treatments.* Most reputable healers and Christian ministries seek to co-operate with whatever natural means are beneficial and spiritually safe. Cults and sects, on the other hand, may demand separation from family or established codes of medical practice. Avoid them.

- *Don't buy into the conspiracy theory that CAM practitioners are persecuted by orthodox medicine.* Most MDs today are open to alternative therapies that are scientifically verifiable. Nevertheless, we all need to be on the lookout for quackery as it has been around for millennia and is likely to continue into this one.

Is there unethical promotion or advertising?

We are all aware of the power of advertising. Companies know that well-spent advertising dollars yield high dividends in sales. We are seeing more and more advertising of health-care products and services. Here are some guidelines for assessing these claims:

- *Watch for false claims about the safety of our food.* Our food supply is probably safer than ever and some of the claims made by CAM practitioners are simply not verifiable scientifically.

- *Watch for false claims about the superiority of products.* Most supplement lines make their own claims of superiority, most of which can't be substantiated scientifically. Overall, the supplement and herbal industry is under-regulated without nearly the quality control of the pharmaceutical industry.

- *Be careful with the use of health questionnaires.* Some practitioners have designed questionnaires to inform patients about possible nutritional deficiencies. However, the symptoms being scored are likely to be secondary to conditions unrelated to nutrition such as depression. One would require a physical examination and prudent laboratory investigations to verify the diagnosis. Some questionnaires about nutrition are scored so that everyone who takes the test is judged deficient.

- *Look out for promises of quick, dramatic, or miraculous results.* Most claims are based on testimonials—people who have used the product or treatment and testify of its benefit in their lives. Virtually every healing art has its adherents. Every healer has his success stories. But because some people were helped, doesn't necessarily mean that you will be, or that it is spiritually safe for you.

- *Scrutinize Christian ministries that make grandiose or unproven claims.* Although encouraging an attitude of faith and hope for the future are highly beneficial, holding out unrealistic expectations for families is cruel. No healer can guarantee a healing—not everyone is healed at a healing crusade. Ministering to the unhealed is just as important as highlighting those with miraculous results.

What about healing crusades?

I know many Christians who, in the desperation of an unyielding illness, have traveled across the continent to a healing crusade. Parachurch healing ministries, such as Benny Hinn today and Kathryn Kuhlman before him, have arisen primarily out of a lack of successful healing ministries at the local church level. It is my conviction that the local church is the ideal therapeutic community. Nevertheless, you may be advised by well-meaning friends to attend a healing crusade and go forward for healing prayer. Should you? Here are some questions to consider.

- *Does the healing evangelist preach Jesus Christ as the only means to the Father, and is he healing in Jesus' name?* Here we may identify with Paul as he considered some of the other preachers of his day:

> *It is true that some preach Christ out of envy and rivalry, but others out of goodwill. The latter do so in love, knowing that I am put here for the defense of the gospel. The former preach Christ out of selfish ambition, not sincerely, supposing that they can stir up trouble for me while I am in chains. But what does it matter? The important thing is that in every way, whether from false motives or true, Christ is preached. And because of this I rejoice* (Phil. 1:15-18).

But do watch for biblical soundness. Some have wandered to the fringes of historic Christianity. There are strong warnings in Scripture about false prophets in the later days, some which could deceive even committed Christians. Avoid any healing ministry connected to a sect or cult, no matter how successful it is.

- *Is there any evidence of sorcery?* We have already seen that sorcery involves the use of faith-producing techniques for gaining spiritual power—attempts to manipulate reality through occultic means. Some authors argue that Christianity is being infiltrated by such techniques, particularly in the areas of possibility thinking, prosperity, and healing. Especially watch for faith in faith rather than faith in God.

- *Is the healing evangelist and his organization financially accountable?* Reputable ministries are open about their financial accountability. Does the evangelist make his own offering appeal? How much time is spent on offering appeals? How often are there mail appeals for money? Is he building his own empire or the Kingdom of God?

- **Will there be ministry for the disappointed?** Inevitably, after every healing crusade, some go home in their wheelchairs or with their pain. Not everyone is called to the platform to tell their story under the TV lights. Many, in the darkened parts of the arena, will turn in disappointment and are in need of intense ministry. Counselors should be available for them. Here is one of the strongest reasons for insisting that healing ministries be within the context of loving church community.

- **Is there a spirit of humility about the evangelist who gives complete credit to God?** Giftedness can be heady, leading to pride and arrogance. The evangelist's personal life should emulate that of Christ...

  who, being in very nature God, did not consider equality with God something to be grasped, but made himself nothing, taking the very nature of a servant, being made in human likeness. And being found in appearance as a man, he humbled himself and became obedient to death—even death on a cross (Phil. 2:6-8)!

- **Is there medical accountability to verify miraculous healings?** One of my patients attended a crusade and was called forward to share her story. Later, as her family doctor, I received a form requesting medical confirmation of her healing. I certainly appreciated this accountability.

Having scrutinized healing a art, you should be in a position to determine if it promotes holiness. As stated before, there is a great risk of the Church losing its focus and calling by becoming defiled by unholy practices. In closing this chapter, let's look at some of the arguments used by Christians who promote these practices.

"BE HOLY"

Christians who promote spiritually questionable healing methods rationalize their use with the following arguments.

- *It works, and since God is the Healer, it must be God who uses and endorses the method.* This is the argument of pragmatism (if it works, it must be good) that Nesamoni Lysander in his book *First Choice for the Next Millennium* uses in his discussion of Ayurveda:

Both (Ayurveda and Siddha) were developed by Indian sages whose religion was Hinduism. There is no doubt that these health care disciplines stressed the need to have faith and reliance in God. As a result, many people identify them with Hinduism and refuse to take these medicines. This is unfortunate. There are numerous practitioners of Ayurveda and Siddha who belong to other religions. God does not and will not withhold any good thing from His creation because of religious preferences or cultural differences. ...These treatments are found to be effective and useful.[61]

- *We use the method but don't believe the spiritual ideology behind the method and are, therefore, protected from spiritual danger.* This argument was recently brought to my attention through a professing Christian who practices CAM by combining therapeutic massage, colon therapy and Reiki, a form of Japanese spiritual healing. This person believed that the energy manipulated is an unidentified component of God's creation, not connected to spiritism or the occult.

To these arguments I would make the following observations.

- *New Age leaders see the holistic health movement as a means of legitimately proselytizing converts.* In *The*

Aquarian Conspiracy, Marilyn Ferguson observes how those treated with New Age Medicine easily become New Age converts:

Illness... is potentially transformative because it can cause a sudden shift in values, an awakening... For many Aquarian Conspirators, an involvement in health care was a major stimulus to transformation. Just as the search for self become a search for health, so the pursuit of health can lead to greater self-awareness. All wholeness is the same. The proliferating holistic health centers and networks have drawn many into the consciousness movement.[62]

Many alternative healing leaders and spokespersons are false prophets preaching a false doctrine. As in the case of cultists, truth gets mingled with small amounts of deception, to be followed by ever-increasing amounts of untruth. We are sharply warned against false prophets in Scripture, particularly in the last days.

- *You cannot have undivided loyalty when supporting opposing worldviews.* Jesus prayed, *Your kingdom come*, and, *Deliver us from the evil one*, in the same prayer. The Kingdom of God which Jesus prayed for and the kingdom New Agers envision as well as the new world order of the non-theistic humanist, are all mutually exclusive by their very premises. (There either is a god, or there isn't, and if there is, he is either a personal god or an impersonal one.) You cannot be a warrior for Jesus Christ while promoting New Age pantheism without being a defector.

- *Nowhere does Scripture condone syncretism* (the combining of differing belief systems). To the contrary, we are strictly warned against it:

What agreement is there between the temple of God and idols? For we are the temple of the living God... "Therefore come out from them and be separate," says the Lord. "Touch no unclean thing, and I will receive you" (2 Cor. 6:16,17).

- *God is holy and He desires a holy people.* To be holy means we are set apart for God. It means being free from the contamination of sin. The Church is called to purity and Jesus is looking for a "spotless bride." Within the Church, individual sin is likely to beget corporate sin, thus opening the door to the demonic realm.

But just as he who called you is holy, so be holy in all you do; for it is written: "Be holy, because I am holy" (1 Pet. 1:15,16).

- *Pragmatism is a forerunner of liberalism.* The argument, "If it works, it must be okay," has been used in other areas of the Church, particularly in evangelism and church growth. Some justifiable criticism has been directed toward purveyors of a candy-coated gospel used to lure people into large churches which lack spiritual depth. Whenever pragmatism influences the Church, discernment evaporates and questionable practices become acceptable methods leading to liberal theology.

- *New Age Medicine is, at its heart, idolatry.* This is the very danger of New Age, the subtle lie which Satan uses to deceive. That Christianity and Eastern thought can coexist without conflict is an oxymoron. God is a jealous God. He has given us the means for healing Why do we need to turn to the enemy camp for more?

So to who do you turn to help your sore back? Pray first. Rest in the presence of the Lord and relax your muscles. Some prudently administered analgesics (pain killers) from your family doctor will give you quick relief from the pain. A "pure" chiropractor or a physiotherapist can help with some physical modalities. I would avoid acupuncture from a practitioner who practises Traditional Chinese Medicine (TCM) for spiritual reasons. Similarly, avoid healers who wish to manipulate your energy fields through TT or who recommend martial arts-type exercises such a Tai Chi or yoga. Where spiritual healing is invoked, submit to biblical, Christ-centred healing only.

PART III:

Your Personal Journey Toward Wholeness

Wholeness—physical health, emotional happiness, deep loving relationships, peace and meaning in life—begins in harmonious living that properly balances the four basic human needs: physical, social, mental, and spiritual. Each of these needs is vitally important. Any one of these needs unmet, reduces quality of life. Like four quadrants on a wheel, each must be equally represented and weighted to run smoothly. If a quadrant is missing (an unmet need), or another is too heavy (a dysfunctional, overemphasized need), the wheel will bump mercilessly along life's road.

We will begin our journey to wholeness by examining the spiritual quadrant, often the most neglected though most important. For the reasons shared in Chapter 3 on worldviews, we accept the Christian worldview as ultimate reality with the best answers to life that accord with common sense and the most advanced science. And our worldview paradigm is one that properly balances the findings of science and written revelation—science that reveals the Creator and helps alleviate suffering, but which is subject to biblical ethics. This worldview acknowledges that there are spiritual, or moral laws, as well as natural laws, both of which lead to brokenness if disregarded—brokenness spiritually, emotionally, and physically. We will see how recovering and adhering to these laws leads to holism.

The Christian worldview stands diametrically opposed to the secular worldview of naturalism which holds that natural causes alone are sufficient to explain everything that exists, as well as the New Age worldview of pantheism which sees the divine in all of nature. They are mutually exclusive. Any truly holistic approach to health and healing must avoid the pitfalls of both of these errant worldviews, leading to false hopes for immortality and outright damage spiritually.

As you read the following pages, may you stay well, live victoriously above your circumstances, and, at the end of your life, face death with confidence and assurance.

8 | Finding Your Place in the Cosmos

A Bible falling apart probably belongs to someone who isn't.

Charles Haddon Spurgeon

There are two kinds of people—people who read manuals and people who don't. I am one that does. When a new car is brought home, it doesn't leave the driveway until the owner's manual is studied, every feature appreciated, and the maintenance schedule firmly ingrained in my mind. I faithfully try to follow the advice I read. When the manual advises a break-in period of careful driving without excessive speeds or constant speeds for lengthy periods, I do as it suggests. When it advises oil changes every 5,000 kilometers, I do it. I avoid the redline on the tachometer as instructed. I figure that's why I can easily get over 300,000 kilometers on my vehicles before we trade.

Now, I know a few people who feel manuals are a waste of time. When they purchase a bike that needs some assembly they wonder why they have a part left over. "Oh well," they shrug, and throw it in the toolbox. They show me their camera and ask, "What is this button for?" They wonder why their car starts giving them trouble at only 80,000 kilometers. When a recipe calls for a different microwave power setting, they throw their arms up in despair. They never learn all the features on their VCR and the flashing 12:00 is the telltale sign.

Owner's manuals are documents written by the product's maker, for the buyer's good, to help us get the most out of our new purchase whether it be a car, camera or microwave oven. First of all, they help us to *know* our purchase—understand its features, strengths, and weaknesses. Secondly, manuals give us *directions*—do's and don't's that will protect our purchase from damage, lengthen its life expectancy and yield the highest returns for our investment.

Our Maker has given us an "owner's manual" for our good. The Bible is a written document which will help us know God and ourselves and which gives us directions that will protect us from damage, lengthen our lives, and give us the greatest yield of productivity and fulfilment. We want to see how following this manual will help us to live and stay well.

KNOW GOD

Until the early 1990s when the Toronto Blue Jays won the World Series, most Canadians were rather bored by that great American pastime known as baseball. But during those glorious days for Canada, I, like many others, followed the Blue Jays to supremacy. What struck me during the World Series broadcasts was how the World Series trophy was portrayed repeatedly as an object of worship, with camera angle and lighting manipulated to give it a look of divinity. It made me think back to my days in Africa when a friend took me to his home compound and showed me the idol that some of his animistic relatives still worshiped—a clay image set up in a hut dedicated as a shrine with just the angle and light to convey deity. Seems like an inclination to worship exists in Africans and Americans alike.

Humanity in general has an innate desire to worship. Within every human being is a deep, ongoing search for meaning and significance. We all question, "Who am I?" and, "What gives my life meaning?" It seems to be part of our nature, that part of us which the Genesis account of origins says is the image of God—a religious imprint that remains even if we flee God. Sociologists and anthropologists have long known that within the human heart there exists a profound propensity to worship; everyone worships some kind of god, believes in some kind of deity. Whether that deity is science, or sport, or a celebrity, or religion, people everywhere identify an object, a body of knowledge, or an activity that gives their life meaning, direction, and hope.

Our personal journey to wholeness starts with the correct identification of our object of worship and who we are in relation to it. Our manual clearly teaches that Jehovah God, the triune God, is to be the sole object of our worship: *You shall have no other gods before me* (Exod. 20:3). Many other gods clamor for our obeisance, including the god of scientism peddled by the scientific humanist and the pantheistic god of the New Age mystic.

Be a worshiper

Worship, by definition, is honour or reverence offered to a divine being or supernatural power. In English it is derived from "worthy" and we direct our worship to whoever/whatever is worthy of our respect and allegiance. Within the Christian worldview, it is only the transcendent, infinite God of the Bible who has this worth. Worship acknowledges that we humans are not ultimate beings in the universe, that we neither created ourselves nor are the result of purposeless natural forces, but that we were created by a Supreme Being, greater than we, who deserves our obeisance, our respect, and our submission.

Earlier we saw four blessings that God intended humanity to enjoy: eternal fellowship with God, lordship over the natural laws of the universe, fulfilling human relationships, and perfect health and immortality. These four blessings were sustained by worship—the creature was to worship the Creator, to show submission and obedience. In Genesis 3, however, right worship was defiled. Worship, obeisance, and submission were replaced by rebellion and disobedience. What right worship sustained, defiled worship overturned resulting in spiritual death, subjection to the natural laws of decay, broken relationships, and sickness and death.

But God, in his infinite love, set in motion a redemptive plan in the promise of a Saviour, His own Son, and presents a program of revived worship through Him. What defiled worship lost, God's program of reinstated worship in Jesus Christ restores.

What is God's program of reinstated worship in Christ? It is restored access to God through faith in Christ. Jesus said, *I am the way and the truth and the life. No one comes to the Father except through me* (John 14:6). He died on the cross and rose from the grave, paying the penalty for our sin and bridging the gap between God and humankind. Does everyone have automatic access to God? No, we must appropriate this through personal invitation and faith in Jesus. *Yet to all who received him, to those who believed in his name, he gave the right to become children of God* (John 1:12). This is what the Bible calls a rebirth, sometimes referred to as regeneration, and through it we are adopted as God's children. As children, we regain access to the Father and begin a personal relationship with Him. See Appendix A for details on how to receive Christ personally.

Worship personally

Genuine worship is the nurturing of a relationship—a love relationship between you and your loving God. Like any human relationship, it requires time and commitment. Personal worship

involves spending time in prayer, communicating with God, and
listening to Him. It involves spending time in His love letter to
you—the Bible, meditating on it, assimilating its truths, recognizing it as a guide for living, the basis for morality and ethics.
Some people journal their thoughts during this time, particularly as they hear God speaking to them. Others enjoy writing, listening to, or singing Christian music. Some review, or refine, a
personal mission statement—a written document sketching
one's highest purposes and goals.

Often called a quiet time, even secular time-management
authors agree that a time of solitude for reflection, gathering
inner strength, and planning is not only very healthy, it also
profoundly bolsters productivity all day long. It helps focus
your day, creates inspiration, and gives life deep meaning.
Time management expert Charles Hobbs, author of *Time
Power*, suggests that solitude helps you daily focus on your
"unifying principles," the highest priorities in your life.[63] He
suggests examining your behavior daily for congruence with
your unifying principles. Another time management guru,
Stephen Covey, calls this "principle-centered living"—living
purposefully around your core values which, for the committed Christian, must be God's timeless truths.[64]

During a regular quiet time you will grow in love and in
understanding of who God is. The Trinity will take on new
meaning—you will experience the loving provision of God the
Father, you will love Jesus the Son as personal Saviour and
friend, the Holy Spirit will be your daily guide, comforter, and
source of giftedness. God's attributes of omniscience (all
knowing), omnipresence (everywhere present), and omnipotence (all powerful) will fill you with awe, and His sovereign
rule over all creation will buoy your faith. You will sense His
endless love, but also fear His justice and wrath toward sin and
disobedience. You will want to spend time with Him just as
you would a lover.

Passion like this has inspired many of the writers of Scripture. The writer of Psalm 42 put his intense feelings for God in this poetic form:

> *As the deer pants for streams of water,*
> *so my soul pants for you, O God.*
> *My soul thirsts for God, for the living God.*
> *When can I go and meet with God?* (Ps. 42:1,2).

The Apostle Paul displayed this kind of fervor for God. He admonished the Roman Christians to *never be lacking in zeal, but keep your spiritual fervor, serving the Lord* (Rom. 12:11) and clearly demonstrated this loyalty and uncompromised devotion to God himself when he declared he was ready to forsake all to be a follower of Christ:

> *But whatever was to my profit I now consider loss for the sake of Christ. What is more, I consider everything a loss compared to the surpassing greatness of knowing Christ Jesus my Lord, for whose sake I have lost all things. I consider them rubbish, that I may gain Christ and be found in him* (Phil. 3:8,9).

Should we find ourselves this passionate after God we will experience deep, deep meaning in life and a genuine desire to be part of God's cosmic plan for the universe.

Worship corporately

When we are born into God's family through faith in Jesus Christ, we automatically become part of God's worldwide family, sometimes called the Body of Christ and otherwise known as the Church. One of the true joys of Christianity is to be able to go almost anywhere in the world and immediately sense a oneness with other Christians, regardless of language, colour, or race. Since we share the same spiritual Father, we are brothers and sisters. We have already looked at the

Church's mandate to make disciples of all nations and to advance the Kingdom of God.

Corporate worship is meeting together with other Christians for celebration and praise, prayer, instruction, and fellowship. Scripture clearly instructs us to do so:

> *And let us consider how we may spur one another on toward love and good deeds. Let us not give up meeting together, as some are in the habit of doing, but let us encourage one another* (Heb.10:24,25).

Praise is one of the key components of corporate worship. It is the exultation of God through words, music, and bodily actions such as kneeling, raising hands, or dancing. In Hebrews 13:15, we are persuaded to *continually offer to God a sacrifice of praise—the fruit of lips that confess his name.* The psalmist, addressing God in Psalm 22:3, says, *Yet you are enthroned as the Holy One; you are the praise of Israel.* When God's people praise Him, they invite His rule into their midst, thereby enthroning Him and willingly submitting in obeisance to that rule. That is how God's Kingdom is advanced. Another key component of corporate worship is instruction—the teaching and preaching of God's Word in the language of the people. This helps people live according to God's timeless principles as we will see later. It encourages and edifies (builds up) believers and challenges unbelievers to take the first step of faith in Christ. Fellowship is a sense of belonging, the family feeling Christians have together, realizing a joint destiny and the need to help and support each other. Herein lies some of the great therapeutic milieu offered by the community of believers to its adherents.

Health benefits of being a worshiper

There is growing research evidence that being a worshiper is healthy. According to Statistics Canada,[65] worshipers on the whole are happier in their family relationships and both physically and mentally healthier than the rest of Canadians. In fact, they were 1.7 times as likely to feel "very satisfied with their lives" and 1.5 times as likely to have a "very happy marital relationships." Studies show that worshipers are less likely to abuse alcohol and drugs, to commit crime, suffer less from depression, stress, and suicide, have better sex, and are physically healthier.[66] Science seems to be confirming the teaching of Proverbs: *The fear of the Lord adds length to life"* (Prov. 10:27).

Why is being a worshiper good for your health? Worship affirms God's sufficiency as the source of our needs. As we've seen, praising God and worshiping Him enthrones Him—it places God on the throne of our lives and by declaring His Kingdom rule. We affirm that we are children of the King and, as such, God the King is the supplier of all our needs. In such a way, worship becomes a two-way encounter—we serve God with our praise and God serves our needs with His sufficiency. Obviously then, church attendance and worship should be our highest priorities, not only when we are well but especially when we are sick.

Being a worshiper is also healthy because it gives you a reference point for discovering who you are. This is the highest purpose for humanity—to discover one's place in the cosmos. This adds meaning and purpose to life, gives hope, a positiveness toward living, and an eternal perspective that gives you passion for living and joy in the journey. When God is the object of this worship, your self-discovery is based on ultimate reality and truth—a great source of security.

An undivided heart

Exodus 20 records God's ten timeless words for His people—the Ten Commandments. The first two deal with the issue of false gods and idolatry:

You shall have no other gods before me. You shall not make for

yourself an idol in the form of anything in heaven above or on
the earth beneath or in the waters below (Exod. 20:3,4).

Obviously of utmost importance to God is that He is the sole
object of our worship and supplier of our needs. He wants
undivided hearts. God's people of Moses' era were notorious for
worshiping other peoples' gods or fabricating their own idols.
This despite God's obvious provision for them and deliverance
from slavery in Egypt. Years later Jesus reiterated these commandments when He said, *It is written: "Worship the Lord your*
God and serve him only" (Luke 4:8) and, *Love the Lord your God*
with all your heart and with all your soul and with all your mind
and with all your strength (Mark 12:30). A person whose heart
is divided is often devoted horizontally toward something of
this world, instead of vertically toward God. Jesus said:

> *No one can serve two masters. Either he will hate the one and*
> *love the other, or he will be devoted to the one and despise the*
> *other. You cannot serve both God and Money* (Matt. 6:24).

Do we have an undivided heart? What are our false gods,
our idols? It could be anything that takes preeminence over
our worship of God—money, work, possessions, sports, family. It may be an addiction around which our whole world
revolves, such as alcoholism or gambling or even the recovery
program that's become our lifeline. Maybe we live for food,
whether it's craving too much, or anorexia, or an obsession
with just the right kind to guarantee longevity. There may be
TV programs we just can't live without, whether news, talk
shows, soap operas, the latest episode of "Survivor," or the latest thriller movie. Maybe we, like the Israelites of old, have
taken the gods of other people such as the Hindu, Buddhist or
Taoist philosophies of the New Age Movement. There might
be some who consult their horoscopes for daily guidance or
their psychics for major decisions.

In and of themselves, some of these are not harmful. But addictions are, and the worship of any deity other than God is strictly prohibited in Scripture. The others become idolatry or strongholds, as they are sometimes called, when they become the centre of our lives around which all other parts revolve. Take money for example. When all we think and dream of is accumulating more wealth, when relationships are built around business deals, and when the week's work hours approach three digits, it has obviously become an idol. In the area of health and healing, when we place more hope for longevity and health in our exercise program, our diet, our supplements, medical science, or alternative medicine than in God, we are guilty of idolatry.

If there is one thing Scripture is very clear about from Genesis to Revelation, it is that there are serious consequences to the sin of idolatry. The Exodus 20 passage listing the Ten Commandments goes on to discuss these repercussions:

> *You shall not bow down to them (false gods or idols) or worship them; for I, the LORD your God, am a jealous God, punishing the children for the sin of the fathers to the third and fourth generation of those who hate me, but showing love to a thousand generations of those who love me and keep my commandments* (Exod. 20:5,6).

Idolatry may result in generational curses such that the choices we make today may affect our children, right down to our great-grandchildren. Conversely, being a worshiper of the true God yields blessings for generations to come. Presumably this includes physical as well as spiritual blessings.

Know your enemy

As we nurture our heart in undivided devotion to God, we soon realize that there is a force in the universe that opposes itself to God. Historically, this has sometimes been personified in human flesh, such as Hitler in Nazi Germany, or Pot of the Khmer Rouge in Cambodia, both of which committed the unprecedented atrocities of mass genocide. More recently, Canadians have seen it in the evil perversions of the murderer/rapist Paul Bernardo and Americans, in the senseless shooting at Columbine High School. Others may recognize this opposition to God as temptation, a lure to break God's moral standards or to exercise our selfish rights.

The Bible teaches that Satan and the demonic realm are the root of this antagonism to God. As we have already seen, this answer, provided by a biblical worldview to the problem of evil and suffering in the world, is (in my estimation) the best, accounting for the universal human experience better than any other belief system. The better we get to know God, the more real this enemy becomes and the more intense the struggle becomes. Paul puts it this way:

> *For our struggle is not against flesh and blood, but against the rulers, against the authorities, against the powers of this dark world and against the spiritual forces of evil in the heavenly realms* (Eph. 6:12).

What Paul is saying here is that the enemy is not other human beings, or even the failure or frailty of our human bodies, but that there is a spiritual realm opposing itself to God and His followers. We need to recognize this enemy because knowing him will equip us fight.

> *Finally, be strong in the Lord and in his mighty power. Put on the full armor of God so that you can take your stand against the devil's schemes* (Eph. 6:10,11).

Daily putting on this "spiritual armour" is one way of maintaining physical and emotional wellness—it protects from spiritual attack against our bodies and minds. We also need this armor to protect us from the healers we may choose when we are unwell. Some operate outside the framework of the Christian worldview and stand to do us spiritual harm, despite their impressive physical results.

This battle has been dubbed "spiritual warfare" by many Christian writers. Experientially, any believer who seriously seeks to follow the Lord will encounter the reality of this warfare. But we can be prepared, fully equipped to safely do battle. Appendix C has a prayer that you can use daily to prepare for battle and it begins each and every day by knowing who we are in Christ.

KNOW YOURSELF

From the outside, Sally seemed to have it all together in her last year of high school. She was a beautiful girl with a slim figure, lovely blonde hair, and not a hint of acne. The youngest in a family of high achievers, the pressure was on her to perform academically which she did, staying near the top of her class. She wasn't a bad athlete either with an impressive record on her school's senior girls basketball team. She played the flute and had a wonderful singing voice, often being asked to sing in church. However, she was not happy—in fact she was frankly depressed, suffered from anorexia and had thoughts of suicide. Why was a girl who had it all so unhappy?

Sally's home life had been completely performance driven—love had been conditional and her father in particular was a driven man, a workaholic with high expectations and little affection. Sally had been led to believe the lie that her outward appearance and performance in sports and academics were what really mattered in life. Although she went to church, she never learned who she was in God's eyes—she had no sense of worth before God. In fact, as her school year ended, she became more and more tormented by guilt.

I caught up with Sally as her school year closed. She had taken to smoking in an attempt to maintain her weight—friends had told her cigarettes would make it easy to stay slim. Her taste in clothing had turned to more revealing outfits and she became an easy catch for any guy who gave her attention. In fact, she became frankly promiscuous, got pregnant, and without her parents' knowledge had an abortion. Guilt and despair set in and a botched suicide attempt landed her in hospital.

Sally is one of many who are being deceived about who they are. One of the main areas of spiritual warfare we find ourselves in is the realm of self worth—how we esteem ourselves. On the one hand the naturalistic worldview deceives us into thinking we are merely animals—an accidental conglomeration of atoms, chromosomes, and cells. On the other, Eastern pantheism deceives us into thinking we are divine along with the rest of nature, only waiting to be discovered. Even Christians are assaulted with deception that keeps them from knowing who they really are in Christ and robs them of the maturity and freedom which is their inheritance as children of God.

Not an animal

In 1996, the Copenhagen Zoo announced a new exhibit. In a glass-walled cage in the primate house, a pair of Homo Sapiens would be on display. When asked why a display of humans was appropriate in a zoo, especially given the fact that they could easily be observed around the globe, zookeeper Peter Vestergaard said he would force people to "confront their origins," causing them to "accept" that "we are all primates." After all, he added, "humans and apes share 98.5 percent of the same chromosomes."[67] Which may just prove we were designed by the same Designer!

Look at some of the results of this kind of thinking:

• A greater public outcry against the killing of baby seals, than against the slaughter of human unborn;

- Animal rights activism that opposes animal research;
- Euthanasia of humans in the way veterinarians deal with their incurable cases;
- Environmentalism that regards human needs as secondary to "Mother Nature's";
- Journalism that lowers humanity and elevates animals.

Scripture teaches differently: *So God created man in his own image... male and female he created them* (Gen. 1:27). Humans were given the stamp of the divine although they were not deities themselves. (Only Jesus was fully God and fully human.) What sets mankind apart from animals is a spirit—that innermost part where conscience and the innate need to worship reside. Thus, rather than being on par with the animal kingdom, God placed humans over the animals, telling them to *rule over the fish of the sea and the birds of the air and over every living creature that moves on the ground* (Gen. 1:28). Being image bearers also means that we are all equal before God: *There is neither Jew nor Greek, slave nor free, male nor female, for you are all one in Christ Jesus* (Gal. 3:28). Thus there is no theological justification for the caste system based on karma from previous lives as taught in the reincarnation theory of Eastern worldviews. Christians, of course, hold vehemently to an infinite afterlife— the soul lives on in heaven or hell resulting in the perspective that we invest this life into the next.

The biblical view of humankind as an image bearer of God, all equal before Him, gives human life a greater degree of dignity than any other worldview. This has profound implications in the area of health and healing.

- Stewardship of the environment: earth is the habitat for humanity, so we have an obligation to sustain it for the health of its peoples.

- Longevity is not the highest ideal. *For to me, to live is Christ and to die is gain* (Phil. 1:21). Aiming for physical immortality through science is wasteful.

- The sanctity of life: human life is sacred from conception to death and therefore abortion and euthanasia contravene God's moral law against killing.

- We have a moral obligation to feed all six billion of us. It is ethically immoral to starve people as a method of population control.

- There are no untouchables; everyone deserves food, medical care, and human rights.

These timeless principles make no sense to the humanists and naturalists of the West where women's rights to sexual freedom supercede the rights of the unborn. Neither do they apply in the East where Christians (such as the Mother Theresa) are left to care for the untouchables of Calcutta while cows, given divine status, are regarded with the dignity that rightly belongs to humans. In the other worldviews, such as Islam, social and political equality are but faraway dreams; the slavery of women is lauded, while the poor are exploited.

No, we are image bearers, tainted by sin but still marked with that divine imprint that comes to stand out in those who find their hope in Jesus Christ.

In Christ, I am...

While all humans are created in God's image and loved by Him, believers in Christ experience the rebirth guaranteeing eternal life in God's presence—salvation. Many Christians think of salvation as all in the future after they die. They don't fully understand the significance of the deliverance that is theirs here and now. They don't see themselves the way God sees them. They suffer from poor self-image and consequently live defeated lives, often in bondage to both emotional and physical afflictions. Neil Anderson, founder of Freedom in Christ Ministries and author of several books helping believers discover who they really are in Christ, exposes the tactic of Satan in keeping Christians feeling defeated:

> *And the crux of my interaction with people has been to expose the insidious reality of Satan's relentless assault of deception on the Christian's mind. He knows that if he can keep you from understanding who you are in Christ, he can keep you from experiencing the maturity and freedom which is your inheritance as a child of God.*[68]

Let's look in more detail what it means to be in Christ, because ultimately, our hope for health and immortality must lie here.

We have already discovered what we inherited from Adam—spiritual death or separation from God, subjection to the physical laws of decay in the cosmos, selfishness and strife in relationships, and emotional and physical sickness leading to ultimate death. Accompanying this inheritance are such negative emotions as fear, anxiety, selfishness, shame, guilt, and rejection, all of which we know lead to ill-health. In this fallen state, a human's spirit is dead toward God, crowded out by the intellect and emotions of the soul, which, in turn, are in subjection to "the god of this age," Satan.

Figure 9.1 illustrates fallen humanity. The central spirit of man is dead toward God. The soul—mind, will and emotions—are strongly influenced from the outside in and smother the inner spirit of man.

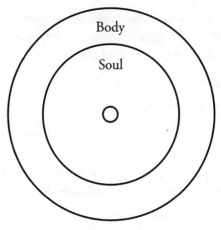

Figure 9.1
Fallen humanity

But if you are a Christian, you are no longer identified with the first Adam but rather with the "last Adam," Jesus. This identification occurs through faith and at the moment of rebirth, or regeneration, your dead spirit is made alive and becomes indwelt by the Spirit of Jesus, or the Holy Spirit. *The Spirit himself testifies with our spirit that we are God's children* (Rom. 8:16). And because we have that spiritual life of Jesus in us at the moment of our conversion, we inherit all of Christ's attributes—innocence, eternal life, citizenship in heaven, rulership. *Now if we are children, then we are heirs—heirs of God and co-heirs with Christ* (Rom. 8:17).

> *And just as we have borne the likeness of the earthly man (Adam), so shall we bear the likeness of the man from heaven (Jesus)* (1 Cor. 15:49).

Wow! Do you see in those last two verses how great our inheritance is in Christ? We are heirs of God bearing the likeness of Jesus. In fact, Paul explains that an exchange takes place—Christ's life for our life: *I have been crucified with Christ and I no longer live, but Christ lives in me* (Gal. 2:20). Here's a sample of more Scriptures itemizing our immeasurable riches when Christ's life replaces our life.

I am a child of God (John 1:12).

I am Christ's friend (John 15:15).

I am a joint heir with Christ, sharing His inheritance with Him (Rom. 8:17).

I am a temple—a dwelling place—of God. His Spirit and His life dwell in me (1 Cor. 3:16; 6:19).

I am a new creation (2 Cor. 5:17).

I am a saint (Eph. 1:1; 1 Cor. 1:2; Phil. 1:1; Col. 1:2).

I am a citizen of heaven, seated in heaven right now (Phil. 3:20; Eph. 2:6).

How does this contribute to our theme of finding wholeness? Neil Anderson puts it this way:

The only identity equation that works in God's kingdom is you plus Christ equals wholeness and meaning.[69]

Why? Because the life-giving spirit of Jesus works from the inside out, as illustrated in Figure 9.2. The Holy Spirit imparts life to our spirit, which, in turn, illuminates our minds to understand ultimate reality, stirs our emotions in the worship and adoration of God, and activates our will over our bodies for executing the will of God.

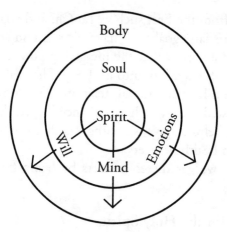

Figure 9.2
Regenerated humanity

Satan, however, influences us differently and this has profound implications on energy-based and mind-body healing systems. He has no direct access to our spirit, although in the unregenerate person it is crowded out by an expanded soul, but influences humans from the outside in, usually affecting the mind through the body although demons do have access to the mind directly. Herein lie problems with energy-based systems—they influence the soul and body directly, bypassing the spirit. Satan has no qualms about influencing the body and the mind, either negatively or positively, in order to keep the spirit inactivated. That is why energy-based systems work, and work so well in many cases. They keep the spirit from realizing its full destiny, and ultimately lead to the destruction of body and soul in separation from God. That's why in this work, strong warnings are issued to Christians to avoid alternate healing systems that are opposed to the Christian worldview, because they stand ultimately to harm our spirits. For the same reason, we advise strongly against physical exercise programs that encourage energy (spiritual) flow from outside in, as do those from the East such as Tai Chi and yoga.

The Christian's goal is to have his spirit so activated and full of the Holy Spirit that the life-giving power of Jesus permeates through his mind, into his body. That will lead to true wholeness and life! Emotional, relational, and physical health will be boosted. Self-worth is enhanced, gives hope, fosters inner peace, helps forgive, smooths relationships—all scientifically proven health boosters.

How do we get there? It starts by being filled with the Holy Spirit.

Be filled with the Holy Spirit

In the October 1999 issue of *National Geographic*, the writer of the article, "Science—Asking Infinite Questions," makes the observation that "the universe and life both seem to be self-organizing."[70] Rather than being "self-organizing" and breaking the second law of thermodynamics, the biblical worldview teaches that it is the Holy Spirit, the third person of the Trinity, that imparts organization and life. Early in the creation of the cosmos it was God's Spirit that brought order out of chaos:

> *Now the earth was formless and empty, darkness was over the surface of the deep, and the Spirit of God was hovering over the waters* (Gen. 1:2).

And it was God's Spirit that imparted God's life to human life:

> *The LORD God formed the man from the dust of the ground and breathed into his nostrils the breath of life, and the man became a living being* (Gen. 2:7).

And it was that same Holy Spirit that was poured out on the early Church on the day of Pentecost and He still empowers people today. In fact, the Apostle Paul admonishes us to *be filled with the Spirit* (Eph. 5:18). The more we are filled, the more God's "energy" will flow out through our soul and body, into our world.

The Holy Spirit's work is from the inside out and is three-fold—regeneration, sanctification, and empowerment.

- *Regeneration.* This is rebirth, or being "born again." The Holy Spirit starts by activating the intuitive in our spirit to recognize that God exists. He then convicts our conscience, leading to the recognition of sin that separates us from God, thus leading us to repentance. This then allows communion of our spirit with God, giving us direct access to God. Appendix A shows you how to be born again if you are not.

- *Sanctification.* The Holy Spirit, now working through the human spirit, has access to the soul—mind, will, and emotions. This enables us to understand God's Word, leading to a knowledge of the truth and allowing our emotions to grow fruit—love, joy, peace, patience, kindness, gentleness. Our will becomes increasingly conformed to God's will in obedience.

- *Empowerment.* The Holy Spirit from within the human spirit, through the soul, now activates the body into health, obedience and service. This promotes unity in the Church, empowers us to witness to the world around us, and gives us the gifts of the Holy Spirit to help others, including the gift of healing.

Although every Christian receives the Holy Spirit at the moment of rebirth, Nicky Gumbel in the well-known *Alpha Course,* likens it to the pilot light of a propane stove—we all have that tiny flame, but we need to turn on the gas for the full flame. He stresses that being filled with the Holy Spirit is not a onetime experience, but rather a continual filling. He shows that in the Greek, the tense of the verb used in Ephesians 5:18 is the present continuous tense.[71] In fact, Scripture teaches two kinds of filling which is not evident in our English translation. Dr. Brad Long beautifully teaches this in his weekend Dunamis Project Seminars.[72] Our English word "filled" is actually two different words in the Greek—*pletho* which is the repeated short-term filling for power and *pleroo* which is the onetime long-term filling for sanctification. The apostles were repeatedly filled for empowerment (*pletho*).

In the area of health and healing, we obviously need both the inner working the Spirit to permeate our entire being and bring life and health to our mind and body (for the healee). We also need the Spirit to activate spiritual gifts of healing and words of knowledge (in the healer) if we are to help other people heal.

How to be filled with the Spirit

Have you been baptized by the Holy Spirit? Do you need more of the Spirit in your life? Here are some steps you can take. You might want to have someone pray for you, but you can also pray on your own.

- Start with confession, asking God to forgive you for anything that might be a hindrance and asking Him to remove anything that might be a barrier such as fear or doubt. The biggest hindrance is a divided heart.

- Turn from any area of your life that you know is wrong.

- Ask God to fill you with His Spirit and equip you with His gifts. God will fill you to the extent that you open up to receive. Yield your will, emotions, and mind to the Holy Spirit. The more you yield, the more the Spirit will flow. The law of displacement works here—a glass filled with stones will hold less water than an empty one.

- Seek until you find, knock until the door is opened.

- Your emotional responses may vary. If you feel praises welling up from within, open your mouth and speak them, whether in a known language or an unknown language. Some people have very little emotional response, but later realize the significant change in their life and their devotion to God.

- Believe that what you have received is from God. Satan will try to convince you it's not real.

- Persevere. Being filled is much more than a one-time experience. Continually be filled.

Results of being filled

As you experience more of the fullness of the Holy Spirit, several things will be immediately evident:

- A deep assurance of being God's child;

- Scripture takes on a new and deeper meaning; the words come alive like never before followed by a greater desire to be obedient, not out of duty but out of gratitude;

- Prayer becomes deeper and more meaningful, and answers to prayer will be more common as you begin to pray according to God's will;

- A deeper emotional experience of joy and peace and deeper love for God and people;

- Worship will be more meaningful and more expressive;

- New boldness to share your faith;

- The recognition of spiritual gifts and passion and zeal for ministry in the areas of your giftedness;

- The recognition of God's plan and purpose for your life—your calling. Some may be called into a full-time ministry or missions. Some may change careers or directions, while others will recognize that they are to bloom where they are planted;

- A new sense of discernment and a recognition of erroneous worldviews.

So many Christians live defeated lives, never realizing these assets, because they seldom experience the fullness of the Spirit-filled life. They are content with their pilot light and neglect to turn on the gas for the full flame. Not only do they fail to reap the benefits of God's energy in their inner lives, their bodies are left subject to assault from without. As we will see, God cares about our bodies too.

My body—a temple of the Holy Spirit

Carl was a sincere Christian who loved God, spent time in prayer and Bible study and was active in church fellowship. In fact, he often took his turn leading services as a lay preacher. He loved visitation, challenging people in their faith and praying for them. He had one weakness however—food. When I took over his care at age fifty-four, he was already 50 percent overweight and had developed difficult high blood pressure and diabetes. Despite repeated counseling about the dangers of his excessive weight, he promptly went home and ignored my advice. Sadly, he went on to have several strokes which left him partially paralyzed and he now requires total care. Not only was his career short-tailed, so was his ministry in his church and community.

The Bible certainly stresses the need to nurture our inner lives, but does it also dictate that we should be concerned about our bodies? Is it important to be physically fit? Does it matter what or how we eat? And what about our sexuality or chemical addictions? Should we have regular medical check-ups or is that a sign of lack of faith? Should we be immunized?

Should we take nutritional supplements?

The Scripture has a lot to say about our bodies. It clearly teaches that our bodies are important and that we shouldn't neglect them. Wholeness implies a sound body as well as a healthy spirit and mind. Our bodies are our interface with the world—our speech, our demeanor, our service, and our witness are all expressed through bodily functions. Our calling and mission in life depend on our body for execution. So let's look at what Scripture says about the importance of the body.

In our tripartite human paradigm, we have seen that when we are filled with the Holy Spirit, our spirit is made alive thereby energizing the soul to godliness. Likewise, Scripture teaches that the Holy Spirit vitalizes our bodies:

> *And if the Spirit of him who raised Jesus from the dead is living in you, he who raised Christ from the dead will also give life to your mortal bodies through his Spirit, who lives in you* (Rom. 8:11).

In commenting on this verse, Watchman Nee, in *The Spiritual Man*, explains:

> What he (Paul) means is: you have the Holy Spirit indwelling you; therefore your mortal bodies should experience His life. This is the privilege shared by all who possess the indwelling Spirit. He does not wish any saint to miss this blessing through ignorance.[73]

Nee goes on to explain that the practical significance of this is that:

> ...the Holy Spirit will strengthen our earthly tents so that we can meet the requirements of God's work and walk in order that neither our life nor the kingdom of God will suffer through the weakness of the body.[74]

Another passage that emphasizes the inherent value of the

body is 1 Cor. 6:12-20. The subject is food and sexual immorality, both of which we will examine more closely later. Paul shows that we can't just do anything we want with our body because *the body is... for the Lord, and the Lord for the body* (1 Cor. 6:13).

The body is for the Lord

The first implication of, *the body is for the Lord,* is that we are not free to use our bodies for self-indulgent behavior. Whether it is the foods we eat, the drink we consume, or our sexual behavior, using them for personal gratification alone is not pleasing to God. We need to understand that this is not because God doesn't want us to enjoy life. On the contrary, He knows that these may be harmful to our bodies and wants to protect us from the consequences of overindulgence or misuse.

Secondly, *the body is for the Lord,* implies that it needs to be made available to God in service. As the interface with our world, our interactions with other people and our environment all depend on our bodily functions. In as much as we enslave it to self-indulgent behavior it is not available for service to co-labour with God in redeeming this broken world. Elsewhere Paul puts it this way:

> *Therefore, I urge you, brothers, in view of God's mercy, to offer your bodies as living sacrifices, holy and pleasing to God—this is your spiritual act of worship* (Rom. 12:1).

Part of our worship is to make our bodies available for God's ultimate purposes in the cosmos.

In essence, our bodies belong to God. *Do you not know that your bodies are members of Christ himself? You are not your own; you were bought at a price* (1 Cor. 6:15,19). They are entrusted to us to be maintained for God. Therefore, maintaining health and avoiding illness is of the utmost importance, and there are significant implications regarding the sanctity of life.

The Lord is for the body

The last part of verse 13 in 1 Corinthians 6—*the Lord is for the body*—is an incredibly wonderful statement, for God cares about our health and our bodies as much as He cares about our spirits and our souls. Here we see the reciprocal relationship between God and ourselves, strengthening what we alluded to when we explored worship—we serve God with our praise and God serves our needs with His sufficiency. The *body for the Lord* is using our bodies in expression of worship and *the Lord for the body* is God's meeting our need with His sufficiency. Those needs include our bodily, physical needs such as health, energy, and healing. Let's note here the full implications of this reciprocity, however. It is impossible to experience the *Lord for the body* if we use our body according to our wants and for our pleasure instead of presenting it entirely to the Lord. Yet were we to hand ourselves over completely to God, yielding our body parts as an instrument of righteousness and conducting ourselves in all matters according to God's order, He would surely endue us His life and power.

Secondly, *the Lord for the body* implies that He will help free us from the power of the flesh—those external bodily temptations that weaken us physically, emotionally, and spiritually. There may be such self-indulgent behaviors as greed, love of food, chemical addictions, or slavery to media such as television or the Internet. God, through His Spirit, empowers us daily to walk in obedience so that we can be free from the *power* of sin.

Thirdly, our bodily resurrection and glorification are guaranteed with a new, perfect body to spend eternity in God's presence. *By his power God raised the Lord from the dead, and he will raise us also* (1 Cor. 6:14). Paul reiterates this in his letter to the Philippians: *The Lord Jesus Christ... will transform our lowly bodies so that they will be like his glorious body* (Phil. 3:21).

All of these blessings are ours because of our union with Christ when we place our faith in Him. *But he who unites himself with the Lord is one with him in spirit* (1 Cor. 6:17). How we need to understand the full significance of this truth! God sees us not as individuals but in combination with Christ. It's like He has an image of us on one side of His computer screen and an image of Christ on the other. Then, with celestial computer graphics, He fuses the two images into one—all Christ's positive features get incorporated into our image. Now when God sees us, He also sees Christ in us.

The temple of the Holy Spirit

Finally, Paul ends his dissertation about the inherent value of the body by explaining that our body is a *temple,* or sanctuary, for the Holy Spirit. *Do you not know that your body is a temple of the Holy Spirit, who is in you, whom you have received from God?* (1 Cor. 6:19). In the Old Testament, before the Holy Spirit was poured out, God literally dwelt among His people in the portable tabernacle of early Jewish history and later in the permanent temple at Jerusalem. The area known as the Holy of Holies was off limits and here sat the Ark of the Covenant, so holy that it meant instant death for anyone trespassing or touching it. At the time of Jesus' death on the cross, the veil that separated the Holy of Holies was rent, signifying the end of that era. Because Christ's death on the cross satisfied God's need for justice (it made atonement), God could now rightly re-inhabit His people. Paul explains the end of the physical temple era and the inauguration of the new people-based temple this way:

> *Consequently, you are no longer foreigners and aliens, but fellow citizens with God's people and members of God's household, built on the foundation of the apostles and prophets, with Christ Jesus himself as the chief cornerstone.*

In him the whole building is joined together and rises to become a holy temple in the Lord. And in him you too are being built together to become a dwelling in which God lives by his Spirit (Eph 2:19-22).

Christians together, as the Church of Christ, are a temple and individually, our bodies are a temple. Paul uses both *you* plurally and singularly when he says, *You are a temple of the Holy Spirit.* In 1 Corinthians 3, the plural is used: *Don't you know that you* (plural) *yourselves are God's temple and that God's Spirit lives in you?* (1 Cor. 3:16).

The implication of being a sanctuary for God is imposing—whether as the corporate Church body or individual physical bodies. *If anyone destroys God's temple, God will destroy him; for God's temple is sacred, and you are that temple* (1 Cor. 3:17). God's earthly sanctuary needs the utmost care and maintenance to be healthy and strong. Any disregard for it is likely to be met with God's judgement.

All of this takes us back to our physical bodies and the responsibility we have to look after them and treat them well. *You are not your own; you were bought at a price. Therefore honor God with your body* (1 Cor. 6:20). To honour God with your body is to refrain from using it sinfully, to keep it fit through healthy habits and to make it available to positively influence our world for Christ. The Bible has some fairly explicit directions about how to do that. We want to explore these in the next chapter, and interestingly, we will find that medical science is confirming that many of these instructions are healthy.

9 | Living Well— by the Manual

> If you listen carefully to the voice of the LORD
> your God and do what is right in his eyes, if you
> pay attention to his commands and keep all his
> decrees, I will not bring on you any of the diseases
> I brought on the Egyptians, for I am the LORD,
> who heals you.
>
> God, 1500 BC, Exodus 15:26

During the time I served the mission hospital in Mkar in the early 80s, there were two diagnoses I became very adept at making—urethral strictures in men and ectopic pregnancies in women. Younger men presenting with difficulty voiding would, without further x-rays or investigations, be scheduled for urethral dilatation, a procedure in which instruments of increasing size were passed down the male urethra to stretch the strictured or narrowed area. This gave them relief for months to years, but they would invariably be back for repeat dilatations. Women with ectopic pregnancies presented so often that we taught the dictum, "any women of child-bearing age who presents with anemia (low blood), has an ectopic pregnancy until proven oth-erwise," to new doctors and medical students. An ectopic preg-nancy results when a fertilized egg starts growing somewhere outside the intended sanctum of the uterus, usually one of the fallopian tubes. At roughly six weeks of gestation, the growing pregnancy would rupture the tube, causing frank hemorrhage into the abdominal cavity. Again, without fancy tests such as ultrasounds, we simply documented the free blood in the abdomen with an abdominal tap using a simple needle and syringe and immediately sent to the OR for surgery. We saved many lives with this efficiency.

Both of these conditions resulted primarily from rampant, untreated gonorrhea, causing scarring of both the male urethra and the female fallopian tubes with consequent voiding diffi-culties in the men and infertility and ectopic pregnancies in the women. STDs (sexually transmitted diseases) are a direct consequence of failing to heed God's standard of sexual monogamy. Polygamy and sexual promiscuity result in wide-spread dissemination of gonorrhea and chlamydia. Today, even more deadly is the HIV virus being spread throughout Africa in similar fashion and throughout Western countries primari-ly through a gay lifestyle.

Years ago, as Moses was leading God's people out of Egypt, God spoke an incredible promise to the new nation:

> *If you listen carefully to the voice of the LORD your God and do what is right in his eyes, if you pay attention to his commands and keep all his decrees, I will not bring on you any of the diseases I brought on the Egyptians, for I am the LORD, who heals you* (Exod. 15:26).

An obedient lifestyle promotes health.

As we look at what our "Owner's Manual" says about the various aspects of healthy living, we will maintain a balanced par-adigm of science and spirituality as outlined in Part I.

Unbalancing them will cause us to veer into scientism on one hand or spiritualism on the other. We face areas today in which Scripture is silent specifically, although often explicit principally.

"SIX DAYS YOU SHALL LABOUR"

Donald and Judy were not poor, although they lived modestly in a their small farm home. They had some major financial commitments however, from a previously failed business in another province, and they had two kids in college. Don loved working his small mixed farm—they moved to P.E.I. to get away from the rat-race of the big city. Their income was meager most years, depending on the price of potatoes and beef. It was not enough to pay off his debts and helps his kids through college. So he applied for a job in the local potato processing plant and was able to get several night shifts a week. He was a conscientious worker and was soon in demand. Before long, he worked forty to fifty hours in addition to his regular farm work, including most weekends. Even though he was a committed Christian, there was now rarely time for church. He lacked sleep and became irritable. No longer did he take time for his quiet time. His dentist complained about his receding gums because he rarely took the time to floss his teeth. His relationship with Judy suffered—there was rarely time to talk and Don rarely had interest or energy for intimacy. Don brought home every cold or flu virus that hit the plant, and because he was already prone to allergies, he suffered all the worse, often ending with sinusitis or bronchitis. He spent several days sick in bed with most of these respiratory infections, only causing his workload to intensify after he recuperated.

What was supposed to be a quiet pastoral lifestyle had become as stressful and fast-paced as any urban executive might experience. In our materialistic society, no matter where you live, it's easy to become victimized by the clock, work schedules, financial commitments, parenting commitments, and even church commitments. The principle of Sabbath rest found in the Ten Commandments is still as valid and needed today as it was for the Israelites on their trek to the Promised Land. God knew our limits and we would be wise to heed His advice: *Six days you shall labor and do all your work, but the seventh day is a Sabbath to the LORD your God* (Exod. 20:9,10).

The concept of Sabbath rest, as the other Old Testament laws, has a practical, physical component as well as a spiritual application. These laws, particularly the Levitical Law sometimes called *The Book of the Law,* were given to God's chosen people, the Jewish nation, as a demonstration of their distinctiveness—they were a people separate from other nations, set apart for God's purposes of redeeming humankind. By keeping the Law, they physically demonstrated to other nations their distinctiveness. Meanwhile, spiritually, these laws pointed toward total reliance on God—the fact that they were unclean and needed God's cleansing and forgiveness.

Today, God's people are distinct because of the indwelling Holy Spirit which we receive through faith in Jesus, and we no longer need observance of the Old Testament Law to make us distinctive. Because Jesus kept God's Law perfectly, we say He "fulfilled the Law," satisfying its legal requirement. When we are in Christ, that legal requirement is satisfied for us as well, and we are excused from the Old Testament sacrifice system and the various laws about cleanness—we are clean in Christ. God's Law is now "written on our hearts" and inwardly we want to be distinct and separate—to live by godly standards. God spoke of that day through Jeremiah: *I will put my law in their minds and write it on their hearts* (Jer. 31:33).

Although legally we are excused from outwardly keeping the Law, inwardly the spiritual principles it teaches are timeless. These we don't want to miss. Likewise, God's Moral Law, particularly the Ten Commandments, is perpetual for all peoples.

Sabbath rest

God established a seven-day cycle in the early days of Judaism upon which our Gregorian calendars are based. The instructions were clear to Moses on Mt. Sinai—work for six days and set the seventh day aside for rest and worship. The consequences of disobedience were extreme:

> *Observe the Sabbath, because it is holy to you. Anyone who desecrates it must be put to death; whoever does any work on that day must be cut off from his people. For six days, work is to be done, but the seventh day is a Sabbath of rest, holy to the LORD. Whoever does any work on the Sabbath day must be put to death. The Israelites are to observe the Sabbath, celebrating it for the generations to come as a lasting covenant. It will be a sign between me and the Israelites forever, for in six days the LORD made the heavens and the earth, and on the seventh day he abstained from work and rested* (Exod. 31:14-17).

By the time Jesus arrived on the scene, the Pharisees had added many man-made rules to Sabbath observance—specific distances for travel, specific loads to carry, etc. Jesus seemed to go out of His way to demonstrate that they had lost the spirit of the Law, even though they rigorously kept the letter of it. For example, many of His healings were done on the Sabbath, demonstrating that acts of kindness and mercy were okay. In fact, they were a demonstration of the spiritual significance of Sabbath which is the concept of restoration, or re-creation. He declared, *The Sabbath was made for man, not man for the Sabbath* (Mark 2:27).

The early Christian church moved worship from the Jewish Sabbath (Saturday) to Sunday because it was the day Christ arose and the day when the Holy Spirit was poured out. Before the industrialization of the Western world, it was easy for Christians to observe a day of rest—farmers did only essential work such as milking and feeding the animals and merchants in villages and towns closed their shops. But with industrialization came factories that kept their lines going twenty-four hours a day, seven days a week. The move to Sunday shopping followed with Sunday-morning flea markets and brunches in every city, all competing for Sunday-morning worshipers. And even though most people only have a five-day workweek, they still fill their lives, running their kids to umpteen activities each week, trying to finish the housework, furthering their education, pursuing a sport, and on and on. The kids' hockey tournament or the parents' curling bonspiel is as likely to be on Sunday as on Saturday. So in it all, a day set aside for worship and rest has been lost by many, if not the majority, in our industrialized world. The information age hasn't helped with on-line everything twenty-four hours a day. Many spend hours upon hours surfing aimlessly. No wonder we are a stressed people with many on the verge of burnout. God knew all along that we were not designed for that kind of relentless running.

The principle of Sabbath rest and worship needs to be rediscovered if we are going to fulfill our destiny and maintain emotional and physical health. It may not be Sunday for everyone because of work schedules, but we do need a day to fill our spiritual tanks. It needs to be a day of true *re-creation*, not a lazy day on the couch in front of the TV watching sports. Perhaps the best illustration of the need for "Sabbath" rest is the story of two woodsmen.

Two woodsmen were working side-by-side felling trees. One worked feverishly without a break. The other took regular breaks throughout the day. At day's end, the latter had cut many more cords of lumber than the former. Exhausted and stunned, the first man asked, "How can it be that you cut more wood than me and yet you took all those breaks?"

The second replied, "Didn't you notice that when I rested I sat and sharpened my axe?"

Sabbath re-creation is sharpening the axe—the process of self-renewal. We need regular renewing in all four of our human dimensions—physical, mental, social, and spiritual.

Physically we need to be renewed through a balance of rest and proper exercise. Excessive activity and work, burning the candle at both ends without rest and proper sleep leads to stress and burnout, both of which lead to disease susceptibility. Plan your work for six days so you can take a complete break from it one day a week—discipline your mind to avoid even thinking about your workplace that day. Balance physical rest with exercise, especially if your work is sedentary and primarily cerebral in nature. This helps alleviate stress, while promoting bodily health. As we will see below, exercise can be combined with spiritual renewal by listening to music or teaching, or by praying, reading, or meditating while exercising.

Mentally we need to renew our minds by exercising it through reading, study, maybe writing, and possibly very select electronic media. Read and view wholesome, Kingdom building material—don't waste time reading trashy fiction or watching pointless movies. There is lots of good Christian literature available today, including fiction, that will help renew your mind rather than fill it with ungodliness. We need to keep our minds from being influenced by the culture as we are admonished in Romans: *Do not conform any longer to the pattern of this world, but be transformed by the renewing of your mind* (Rom. 12:2). Our mind renewal is to transform us into Christ-like distinctiveness. Likewise, in Philippians we are encouraged to think about positive things:

> *...whatever is true, whatever is noble, whatever is right, whatever is pure, whatever is lovely, whatever is admirable—if anything is excellent or praiseworthy—think about such things* (Phil. 4:8).

Remember the premise, "use it or lose it." In the area of the mind, one of the best preventions for dementia is to keep exercising your mind into elderhood.

Socially our relationships need to be strengthened and restored if they are strained. Sabbath re-creation in this area involves forgiveness, empathic communication, and creative co-operation. It means being so secure in who you are in Christ you don't need to look to other people to meet your needs—rather, you can give unconditionally. Scripture calls this *agape* love and it was most clearly demonstrated by Christ when He willingly went to the cross for us.

Spiritually Sabbath restoration obviously involves taking time for corporate and personal worship, reading and meditating on Scripture, and prayer. Above all, it involves an understanding of the spiritual principle at the root of Sabbath—stopping our own striving to rest in God. That timeless principle is expressed this way by the writer to the Hebrews:

> *There remains, then, a Sabbath-rest for the people of God; for anyone who enters God's rest also rests from his own work, just as God did from his. Let us, therefore, make every effort to enter that rest* (Heb. 4:9-11).

It signifies that we, as humans, are unable in our own strength to usher in the true new age, the Kingdom of God. We can't restore what was lost in the Fall in our own strength—neither through science or religiosity. Rather, God has accomplished it in Christ through grace, and we need to *rest* in Him, allowing God to bring it to completion in and through us. Practically, this means that Sabbath is not just stopping your regular work, it is a matter of knowing in your heart, and living out the reality, that the abundant life is not the result of our labors or effort or cleverness. It rests solely on the work of Christ. Thus, any activity that contributes to building the Kingdom of God is keeping Sabbath. Any activity that attempts to accomplish it by human means is breaking the Sabbath.

Here are some practical considerations for keeping the Sabbath:

- Make Saturday night, Sunday morning or mid-week worship a priority—schedule it regularly.

- Consider whether two full-time incomes are really necessary. Many two-income families are so tired by the weekend there is no energy for spiritual things.

- Fill the Sabbath with Kingdom-building activities—acts of mercy and kindness, sharing your faith, building your family.

- Young people should prayerfully consider their careers and work, particularly how it will relate to their faith—the opportunity to worship, the proximity of a healthy Church family.

"PHYSICAL TRAINING IS OF SOME VALUE"

The Apostle Paul, in writing to young Timothy, appreciated that there is some value in physical fitness, although he recognized that spiritual health was of the utmost importance. *Train yourself to be godly,* he said. *For physical training is of some value, but godliness has value for all things, holding promise for both the present life and the life to come* (1 Tim. 4:8).

Today we know from science that being physically fit "is of some value." In fact, becoming even moderately fit will dramatically reduce your risk of heart disease, as evidenced by a major study on 72,500 middle-aged women which showed that walking briskly for thirty minutes a day cut the risk of heart attack up to 40 percent.[75] The famous Framingham Heart Study clearly showed that a sedentary lifestyle is a risk factor for heart disease. Dr. Kenneth Cooper of the Cooper Institute for Aerobic Research, sometimes known as the "Father of Aerobics," says that the evidence relating fitness to better health is unquestionable:

> *Plenty of preventive medicine and fitness professionals,*
> *including myself, will tell you that getting in shape will give*
> *you more energy, better health and greater protection against*
> *various diseases. It's incontrovertible.*[76]

The health risks of inactivity include high blood pressure, obesity, adult-onset diabetes, osteoporosis, depression, stroke and colon cancer. The benefits of regular exercise include better posture and balance, stronger muscles and bones, conditioned heart and lungs, improved circulation, more energy, improved emotional health, less chronic pain, and the prospects for continued independent living in later life. Thirty minutes of exercise likely releases as many endorphins—naturally produced morphine substances known to give a "runner's high"—as does a course of acupuncture at much less cost and without the spiritual risk. Physical inactivity is clearly a phenomenon of the last century—our forebears got lots of exercise in their routine of daily living. Today most of us sit while we work, sit while we travel and sit during our leisure.

The secret to a physically healthy lifestyle is sensible, moderate exercise on a regular basis. Just like dieting, on-again off-again exercise may do more harm than good, and extreme exercise is more likely to cause musculoskeletal injuries particularly in midlife and beyond. As well, there is now some evidence that extreme exercise may cause harm through the release of free radicals, chemicals that can damages cells. Experts now recommend either thirty minutes four days a week or twenty minutes five days a week, with a combination of stretching, strengthening and aerobic endurance activities. Obviously, balance is important here—fitness can become an addiction or an idol causing you to neglect the other three quadrants, particularly the spiritual. It may also be so neglected that the physical quadrant shrinks, causing a "bumpy wheel" along life's road.

It's important to reiterate that our body is our interface with the world—in our tripartite human paradigm, it is the Holy Spirit through our bodies that allows us to fulfill our calling and mission in life. We have a spiritual responsibility to look after our "temple," and just as we learned that smoking is harmful to that temple, we now know that inactivity is harmful.

In the pursuit of fitness and the human need for spirituality, yoga and Tai Chi and the other martial arts are becoming increasingly popular among fitness buffs in the West. A strong word of warning: these activities do promote Eastern/New Age spirituality and stand diametrically opposed to the Christian worldview. Christians should avoid them. Rather, we can easily combine Christian spirituality with exercise by praying, singing, meditating, or reading while we work out. Try prayer walking—praying for your neighbours and their families as you briskly walk down your street. A particularly good resource for combining fitness with spirituality is *Faith-based Fitness* by Dr. Kenneth Cooper. It outlines a complete fitness plan for all ages and levels of fitness.

"FOOD DOES NOT BRING US NEAR TO GOD"

We only need to sit in a mall for thirty minutes to realize that obesity has reached epidemic proportions in our culture. Just count the overweight people as they pass. By contrast, in Nigeria I operated one day a week for various conditions and rarely did we encounter more than one centimeter of adipose tissue on the way in. I was shocked upon returning to Canada when I assisted on my Canadian patients. We routinely had to make our way through five to ten centimeters of it, often resulting in much larger incisions than would otherwise be required as well as much more difficult surgery. I realized that I had forgotten what fat looked like!

Epidemiologists know that North Americans are becoming

heavier all the time. *Maclean's* magazine, in January 1999, ran a cover story entitled "Canada's Obesity Epidemic," citing that about half of all adult Canadians are overweight or obese. Likewise, *Time* magazine, in its November 1999 issue on trends for the 21st century, showed that in 1975, 25 percent of women were overweight, compared to 47 percent in 1999. The author projected that by 2025 about 75 percent of people would be overweight.

From scientific studies, we know that obesity is a major risk factor for disease and early death. A 1972 article in National Geographic depicted some of the world's oldest people—not one of them was obese! Diabetes, heart disease, high blood pressure, gallstones, arthritis, respiratory problems, some cancers, and depression are all much more common in the overweight. We also know from epidemiology (comparing the various diets from different cultures around the world with disease prevalence) that certain foods do contribute to health while others promote disease. For example, the Nigerians of central Nigeria eat a very high-fibre diet, low in fat and high in carbohydrates. In five years I saw only one heart attack (in a visiting American) and rarely did we see gallstones. On the other hand, we saw numerous cases of volvulus (twist) of the colon due to the large volumes of stool they collected in their bowels.

Scientists grounded in the worldview of naturalism believe we're genetically programmed to become fatter due to our evolutionary heritage. Michael Lemonick explains:

> The trouble... is that our best intentions about weight control go up against several million years of human evolution. Our hunter-gatherer ancestors literally didn't know where their next meal was coming from. So evolution favored those who craved energy-rich, fatty foods—and whose metabolism stored excess calories against times of famine. Love handles, potbellies, and thick thighs are all part of Mother Nature's grand design.[77]

Mother Nature's grand design? Or was it Satan's temptation of Eve with food in Genesis 3?

> *"You will not surely die," the serpent said to the woman.*
> *"For God knows that when you eat of it your eyes will be*
> *opened, and you will be like God, knowing good and evil"*
> (Gen. 3:4,5).

Believers with a biblical worldview will recognize God as
the designer and question the theory cited above. Maybe love
of food, both quantity and type, is evidence of misdirected
spiritual hunger. Jesus put it this way:

> *So do not worry, saying, "What shall we eat?" or "What*
> *shall we drink?" or "What shall we wear?" For the pagans*
> *run after all these things, and your heavenly Father knows*
> *that you need them. But seek first his kingdom and his right-*
> *eousness, and all these things will be given to you as well*
> (Matt. 6:31-33).

Scripturally, Jesus' view that spiritual passion should precede
passion for food is supported in both Old and New
Testaments.

> *But food does not bring us near to God* (1 Cor. 8:8).

> *Therefore do not let anyone judge you by what you eat or*
> *drink...since... you have been raised with Christ, set your*
> *hearts on things above, where Christ is seated at the right*
> *hand of God. Set your minds on things above, not on earth-*
> *ly things* (Col. 2:16; 3:1,2).

> *Listen, my son, and be wise, and keep your heart on the right*
> *path. Do not join those who drink too much wine or gorge*
> *themselves on meat, for drunkards and gluttons become poor,*
> *and drowsiness clothes them in rags* (Prov. 23:19-21).

> *Do not be carried away by all kinds of strange teachings.*
> *It is good for our hearts to be strengthened by grace, not by*

ceremonial foods, which are of no value to those who eat them (Heb. 13:9).

Far more is said about the need for spiritual hunger than preoccupation with physical food. Nor is there a great deal of emphasis in the New Testament about types of foods to be eaten or avoided. This is in sharp contrast to the Old Testament Law where the Jewish rules about *kosher* (clean and unclean) foods are very prominent. New Testament writers make it clear that we are no longer in bondage to those food rules. In fact, Jesus made that clear Himself and Mark recorded it clearly: *In saying this, Jesus declared all foods "clean"* (Mark 7:19). Later, the Apostle Peter had a vision at Cornelius' home with the same message—the Old Testament laws of distinctiveness for Jews have been replaced by a new order, the indwelt Holy Spirit (Acts 10). Likewise, Paul in his letter to Timothy, issues rather strong warnings about an undue emphasis about "new food rules" in the end times.

> *The Spirit clearly says that in later times some will abandon the faith and follow deceiving spirits and things taught by demons...They forbid people to marry and order them to abstain from certain foods, which God created to be received with thanksgiving by those who believe and who know the truth. For everything God created is good, and nothing is to be rejected if it is received with thanksgiving, because it is consecrated by the word of God and prayer* (1 Tim. 4:1, 3-5).

We do live in a day when many diets are being promoted by various practitioners for various conditions. The discerning Christian should be careful lest the focus on food overshadows her devotion and love for God. In our Spiritual Life Cycle paradigm, our needs are ultimately met from the inside out by being filled with the Holy Spirit, Who in turn prompts us to the proper worship of God. Outside-in temptations, such as food, are subordinated through the Spirit's control of our will, mind and emotions. It is now a question of obedience since we know from science that too much or improper food leads to physical illness. And we know we are to look after our "temple" and that if *anyone destroys God's temple, God will destroy him* (1 Cor. 3:17).

Balancing spirituality and science

Our goal is to strike a proper balance between science and spirituality in the area of nutrition. Obviously we can err both ways—living recklessly at fast food outlets or obsession with counting calories. Remember, one of Satan's temptations for Jesus was to disregard the natural law of gravity and jump off the temple. *Jesus answered him, "It is also written: `Do not put the Lord your God to the test'"* (Matt. 4:7). Here are some guidelines.

- Avoid making food an idol—your hope for immortality lies in Christ, not your food or your vitamin.

- Maintain or achieve an ideal body weight through spiritual principles of loving God more than food, as mentioned above, and a balanced exercise program.

- View overeating as sin just as you would consider smoking or sexual immorality sinful. God cares far more about how much we eat than what we eat.

- Choose foods based on proven science. Canada's Food Guide[78] is an excellent starting point. We know that five to ten servings of fresh fruit and vegetables, particularly coloured ones, are health promoting, as are whole grains and fish. Balance nutrition and enjoyment. God has given us smell and taste in order to enjoy our food.

- Moderation is the key—avoid bondage. An ascetic lifestyle is not promoted in New Testament Christianity.

- Modify your diet into a therapeutic diet[79] if you have high cholesterol or heart disease, a strong family history of them, or other risk factors that predispose you to these illnesses.

- Modify your diet into a therapeutic diet[80] if you are a postmenopausal woman or if osteoporosis is a risk factor due to family history, particularly if you want to avoid estrogen replacement or if you already have osteoporosis.

- Avoid known carcinogens such as burnt meat.

- Make meal times spiritual "Sabbath" moments—times of restoration in all four human spheres. Earnestly pray for God to bless your food and to bless your relationships and your mind.

- Teach your children healthy eating—don't encourage the "eat all or else" model of our parents—it encourages overeating. A child will not starve in the presence of good food.

- Rediscover fasting, a spiritual discipline that stimulates our spiritual sphere, while temporally relegating our physical sphere into subservience.

What about pesticides and genetic modification?

A word about artificial fertilizer, pesticides and genetically modified foods. With the use of fertilizer and pesticides, worldwide food production exceeds present needs—excesses are fed to animals, stock-piled or dumped. At the time of this writing, part of the P.E.I. potato crop is being spread on the fields due to excess and a small corner of a field infected by a potato wart. However, most agricultural experts estimate that with a global ban on pesticides and fertilizers, production would fall to approximately 50 percent of present production, leading to a shortage of food for the present population let alone the growing world population. The potential for widespread crop failures would exist. Could more land be placed into production? Yes, but not without further risk to deforestation and global warming. Mass starvation would probably result, similar to the Irish potato famine of 1845 when late blight destroyed the crop, causing the death of 750,000 and forcing hundreds of thousands more to flee Ireland for other counties. Present organic farmers can succeed because neighbouring farmers help reduce widespread disease infestation, similar to why parents who don't immunize their children are unlikely to see polio in their kids— the rest of the kids in the neighbourhood are probably immune. A worldwide ban on polio immunization would inevitably be followed by polio epidemics.

What does the Christian worldview say about this? Clearly our responsibility is stewardship, what some call the "Cultural Commission." Our mandate is rulership, clearly spelled out in Genesis:

> *Then God said, "Let us make man in our image, in our likeness, and let them rule over the fish of the sea and the birds of the air, over the livestock, over all the earth, and over all the creatures that move along the ground"* (Gen. 1:26).

That involves feeding the masses while protecting the environment. Science and technology are servants to help fulfill that mandate, not tools for greed or human exploitation or the destruction of the environment. The answer is combining the best science with truly biblical morals and ethics. A global ban on pesticides and fertilizers at this time would make food unaffordable for the poor. Clearly Christ and historic Christianity have stood for care of the poor—*sell your possessions and give to the poor* (Luke 12:33). Given the choice between organically grown food and chemically supported food that are of equal appearance and price, we would undoubtedly pick the organic. But we must balance safety against the need to feed the world.

Similarly, while there are great risks in both agricultural science and medicine in the area of genetic engineering, this science may offer better solutions for pest control than chemical pesticides. Most of the genetic research in agricultural science is to produce pest-resistant crops. Obviously, this research needs to be driven by biblical ethics and herein lies the problem—corporations in which the bottom line is greed rather than the best for humanity and the environment. Christians need to stand together to demand testing to ensure the safety of these foods.

What about vitamins and supplements?

The vitamin and supplement industry is booming with multi-billion dollar sales. Many CAM practitioners encourage their use, pointing to the poor quality of today's food supply due to food processing and depletion of nutrients in the soil. Likewise, the antioxidant revolution is promising improved longevity with the prevention of cancer, cataracts and heart disease by wiping up the body's free radicals through regular use of antioxidants.

How do you know if you need to take supplements? Did God make a mistake in our design and in His provision for food? Is our food supply really that bad? Does the Bible speak about this? What does the best science say?

The Bible is silent on this topic as vitamins were not discovered until the scientific revolution. We can assume that God didn't make a mistake and, as He is Jehovah-Jireh, our provision, the food supply He designed for us should provide all we need. Some, such as Dr. Kenneth Cooper, author of *Antioxidant Revolution*, counter that modern changes in living have led to the damage done by free radicals and that we therefore benefit from daily antioxidants.[81]

A common source of information for consumers about the pros and cons of supplementation is marketing material. I have listened to numerous cassettes from network marketers, each espousing their line of products as the solution to human illness. One suggested intestinal parasites are the number-one problem, while another suggested it was copper and other trace mineral deficiencies that are the real culprits in the developed world.

In our quest for wholeness in this area then, we must marry biblical principles of God's sufficiency and His desire that our hope is in Him, with the best science, in determining a personal prevention plan.

In general, a well-balanced diet using Canada's Food Guide, with between five and ten servings of fruit and vegetables, will not lead to vitamin or mineral deficiencies. Exceptions are young children who may not eat a balanced diet, pregnant women whose needs for folic acid and iron exceed the general population's, postmenopausal women who need more calcium and vitamin D, and alcoholics and the elderly who may not absorb some vitamins. In an article entitled, "Supplements: fact and fiction," Dr. Jeejeebhoy, a professor of medicine at the University of Toronto, summarizes what science has proven so far through double-blind studies:[82]

- Vitamin D and calcium in postmenopausal women;

- Folic acid supplements in young women of child-bearing age to prevent birth defects such as spina bifida;

- Fish oil and possibly folic acid in older persons to prevent heart attacks;

- Multivitamins in the elderly to improve their immunity and reduce infections such as pneumonia.

Studies are still ongoing to evaluate the routine use of antioxidants. One of the most recent studies on Vitamin E was the HOPE study, published January 20, 2000 in the New England Journal of Medicine. This is the largest study looking at the effects of antioxidants in the prevention of cardiac disease. The researchers were disappointed that there was no effect on cardiac death compared to placebo, but there was improvement in cancer prevention, particularly prostate cancer. Other studies are ongoing to evaluate this, as well as the effects of selenium on the prevention of prostate cancer.

Here are some additional guidelines to keep in mind as you consider the use of supplements for yourself or your family.

- Supplements are multi-billion industry—promotional material is not always the most reliable source of information and is likely driven by push for sales.

- If little is good, more is not always better. Too much can be harmful, particularly some vitamins such as Vitamin A.

- Supplements may become an idol if your hope for health and longevity is placed on them.

- Many CAM practitioners mix supplementation with New Age healing techniques.

- Tailor your needs; men and women, for example, have differing needs.

- Use your genetic imprint (family history) in combination with the best science to determine which vitamins may be helpful in preventing disease. Discuss your supplement use with your primary health-care provider.

"MARRIAGE SHOULD BE HONOURED BY ALL"

The "New Morality," as it was dubbed, was fueled by the discovery of effective oral contraceptives in the 60s and a naturalistic worldview in which there is no God to set absolute standards. Earlier in the 20th century, Margaret Sanger wrote of how sexual restraint caused "injuries to health and dullness to the intellect." She maintained Christian ethics were "the cruel morality of self-denial" and promoted her own morality of sexual liberation whereby a person could find "inner peace and security and beauty."[83] Later, in the 1940s, Alfred Kinsey's books, *Sexual Behavior in the Human Male* and *Sexual Behavior in the Human Female*, attempted to liberate sex from morality by reducing sex to the sheer biological act of physical orgasm. He then claimed that all orgasms are morally equivalent—whether between married or unmarried persons, between people of the same or opposite sex, between adults or children, even between humans and animals.[84] In 1971, Dr. David Cooper, a British psychotherapist, authored a book entitled *The Death of the Family*, in which he emphasized the need to abolish the traditional family unit and to substitute new forms of human relationships.[85]

Where is sexuality headed in this century? The November 8, 1999 edition of *Time* magazine, dedicated to the future, asked the question: "Will we still need to have sex?" It stated:

> Having sex is too much fun for us to stop, but religious convictions aside, it will be more for recreation than for procreation. Many human beings, especially those who are rich, vain and ambitious, will be using test tubes—not just to get around infertility and the lack of suitable partner, but to clone themselves and tinker with their genes.[86]

Further tampering with God's reproductive design seems certain.

So are people happier being "liberated from biblical morality?" Are they healthier emotionally and physically through it? No. Evidence shows that couples maintaining a high level of Christian spirituality and lifetime monogamy are far happier and sexually fulfilled than any other demographic group. This proves that sexual intimacy, freed from the guilt of extramarital affairs, is far more satisfying.

Look at what have we reaped instead: fatherless homes, suicidal and promiscuous youth, an AIDS epidemic, prostitution, abortions on demand, to name just a few. Associated with these are mammoth social pathologies including school problems (such as violence and shootings), drug and alcohol abuse, welfare dependency, and crime.

Contrast the biblical norm for sexual morality which is heterosexual, lifetime monogamy:

Marriage should be honored by all, and the marriage bed kept pure, for God will judge the adulterer and all the sexually immoral (Heb. 13:4).

Do you not know that the wicked will not inherit the kingdom of God? Do not be deceived: Neither the sexually immoral nor idolaters nor adulterers nor male prostitutes nor homosexual offenders nor thieves nor the greedy nor drunkards nor slanderers nor swindlers will inherit the kingdom of God (1 Cor. 6:9,10).

Flee from sexual immorality (1 Cor. 6:18).

The acts of the sinful nature are obvious: sexual immorality, impurity and debauchery; idolatry and witchcraft; hatred, discord, jealousy, fits of rage, selfish ambition, dissensions, factions and envy; drunkenness, orgies, and the like. I warn you, as I did before, that those who live like this will not inherit the kingdom of God (Gal. 5:19-21).

Jesus Himself taught a high level of sexual morality:

You have heard that it was said, "Do not commit adultery." But I tell you that anyone who looks at a woman lustfully has already committed adultery with her in his heart. If your right eye causes you to sin, gouge it out and throw it away. It is better for you to lose one part of your body than for your whole body to be thrown into hell (Matt. 5:27-29).

Science has attested the clear relationship between health and lifestyle choices. In the HIV epidemic, medical scientists know exactly who are at risk and which sexual practices lead to infection. This clearly shows how individual moral choices determine the health of the entire society. What should we aim for?

- Teach our children abstinence until marriage.

- Teach our children to marry strong, Christian young persons.

- View homosexuality as God does—a sinful perversion of God's bodily design.

- Avoid all pornographic materials—men are drawn to magazines, the Internet, videos, and movies, while women prefer romantic novels and soap operas.

- Men should have an accountability partner to regularly meet and ask the tough questions in Appendix D.

- Pray together as couples, including during times of sexual intimacy.

The beauty of the reality of our Spiritual Life Cycle paradigm is that as you "draw near to God," He will "draw near to you" in the area of your sexuality. When your sufficiency is in Christ, you are suddenly able to give in the area of sexuality, rather than looking for what you can get.

The Greeks had several words for love and we have already seen how *agape* is the selfless, giving type of love typified by God's love for us. But as we allow God's *agape* love to flow through us to our mate, God also matures our eros love—romantic love from which we get our word "erotic." The result is that sexual arousal and orgasms become more acutely intensified the closer we are to God! Because sex is God's design, He made it for us to enjoy within the confines of His morality. Otherwise He could have designed us like most mammals—sexually receptive only during female estrus (heat) once in a long while.

God never prohibits anything that will not be harmful in the end. He provided rules for our own safety just as there are referees and rules in sports to keep players from hurting the opposing players with the intent of sidelining them. This truth flies directly against the pervasive non-Christian worldviews where Satan has blinded people into thinking that God is a stodgy killjoy who intends to restrict our fun.

Just a word on homosexuality, still an area of controversy within the Church. We need to love gay and lesbian people as Christ loved them and died for them. We need to welcome them into our churches and to lovingly help them to see that their homosexuality is part of the fallen state of humanity, not God's original design, and that there is restoration for them in Christ. We need to help them find wholeness.

"DO NOT GET DRUNK WITH WINE"

There is a clear correlation between such illnesses as lung cancer and liver cirrhosis with various addictions—tobacco, alcohol, or drugs. The connection of lung cancer and emphysema to cigarette use is irrefutable. Alcohol causes liver cirrhosis, brain damage, vitamin deficiencies, and car accidents, not to mention the families it destroys. The relation of intravenous drug use to Hepatitis C and AIDS is also well known, as well as its contribution to crime and violence.

The biblical standard is clear from Ephesians 5:18: *Do not get drunk on wine, which leads to debauchery.* Drunkenness is listed in Galatians 5 with the other acts of sinful nature. Addictions influence us from the outside in—physical (bodily) addictions influence our soul (emotions, will, mind) and drive the addiction cycle.

As we will see in Chapter 10, the addiction cycle is usually initiated because of a felt need or pain. Using our thirst metaphor from before, it causes us to be thirsty. For the addict, the perceived thirst is quenched by the drug of choice—it temporarily numbs the pain. Whether alcohol, heroin, nicotine, food, or work, all have the same effect. We forget our pain but shortly the effect wears off and we feel more pain. This then drives us back to our drug and the cycle is closed in a perpetual loop.

The second part of Ephesians 5:18 reveals the solution: be filled with the Spirit. By practicing the Spiritual Life Cycle, the Holy Spirit can heal the pain that drives the addiction cycle from the inside out. Drawing near to God will, in turn, allow God's strength to overcome the addiction. This is the basis of AA. Sadly, AA has lost the biblical roots with which it was founded and has substituted a "Higher Power" for Jehovah God of the Bible. The Church needs to redeem AA by developing truly Christian twelve step programs, such as Alcoholics Victorious (AV) or Overcomer's Anonymous (OA), and more closely relate these ministries to the church community. Similarly, the Church needs to offer more help to those with tobacco and drug addictions as well as food or gambling addictions.

Science has confirmed that the principles penned years ago by men inspired by the Holy Spirit are health promoting. Similarly, the principle of forgiveness toward those who have wounded us, as taught by Christ, is also healthy for body and soul. This is our next topic for exploration.

10 Healing Past Wounds

If you hold to my teaching, you are really my disciples. Then you will know the truth, and the truth will set you free.

Jesus Christ

One sport our family enjoys together is skiing. We got into it when our boys were young—we used to ski together but the boys are now far better than their parents, proof that the younger you are, the better you learn a new skill. As I write this we are spending a short winter vacation at Mont Tremblant, Quebec. Early in my skiing career, I had a collision with a tree resulting in the fracture of several ribs. It happened at Ski Wentworth, Nova Scotia, last run of the day. I hadn't been on this particular trail previously, but had been warned by my family about one icy spot. Thinking I had passed that spot safely, I decided to let loose a bit. However, there was another icy section and with too much speed, I couldn't negotiate the turn, got too close to the edge of the trail and caught my ski on a frozen piece of snow. I was headed straight for a large trunk of an unyielding spruce tree.

Fortunately, my head and neck were spared, but with the wind knocked out of me, I rolled in the snow, feeling the certain pain of cracked ribs. Before long, the ski patrol came by and I had a humiliating run down the hill on a toboggan. X-rays later confirmed the three fractured ribs and for several weeks, every time I breathed or rolled over in bed, I was reminded of the pain of my trauma. Friends now constantly torment me by reminding me to watch for trees when we announce a ski trip.

Skiing this weekend easily reminds me of the pain of my accident. In fact, fear sets in if the trail is too steep or if there are icy sections. I simply cannot enjoy a challenging trail—my muscles tighten and the fear of injury becomes disabling. Visions of an oncoming tree simply overwhelm me.

Similarly, emotional wounds which may have been inflicted years earlier can also be both emotionally or physically disabling, robbing us of joy and purpose in life as well as hindering our spiritual growth. It is a fact, confirmed by secular counselors and psychiatrists and Christian counselors, that emotional wounds are frequent contributors to our sense of well-being today.

We want to examine those emotional wounds now, and how they relate to our present health spiritually, emotionally, and physically. Then, using our Spiritual Life Cycle paradigm, we will examine ways in which we can be healed and set free. Obviously, an exhaustive look at inner healing is not possible here, but should you find this to be an area of need in your life, there are excellent resources available to get the help you need.

It should be noted before we proceed that, in both secular and Christian counseling circles, the pendulum has swung back and forth on the issue of past trauma and how it relates to the present. There are those who argue that the past needs to be forgotten, not remembered. There are others who dig deep into the past, sometimes coming up with stories that turn out to be fictional, causing a lot of family turmoil and pain in the process. Still others are critical of authors and counselors who do inner-healing work, somehow equating them with New Age and accusing them of liberalism or syncretism (the mixing of various faiths). I would strongly argue for an approach that is both biblical and practical, conservative and true to reality.

THE WOUNDS THAT FESTER

Joseph, in the book of Genesis, is a good illustration of a man with wounds in his past. As a teenage boy he was his father's favourite son—and spoiled at that—much to the disgust of his older brothers who hated him. After bragging about a dream in which he depicted his brothers bowing down to him, they plotted to get rid of him. First, they dumped him into a pit to die but later decided to sell him into slavery in Egypt. As a slave, he was wrongfully accused of raping his mistress and thrown into prison. There he languished for years. All this happened despite a love for God and an undisputable track record of obedience and respect for those in authority over him. When God finally did deliver him, he named his first born son Manasseh, saying, *It is because God has made me forget all my trouble and all my father's household* (Gen. 41:51).

Joseph's hurts were clearly inflicted by others. This is the most common kind of wounding we endure. But there are also wounds we bring onto ourselves by the choices we make.

Sources of wounding

The most frequently cited example of a wound inflicted by another is childhood sexual violation. Whether sexual molestation by a relative or frank rape by a stranger, the emotional wounds are frequently severe and deep. If it is an adult woman, it will affect her ability to trust her mate, and she is likely to have problems with sexual dysfunction in her relationship. We frequently see women who suffer with chronic pelvic pain or pain during intercourse, who have been sexually abused. The feeling of shame frequently coexists in these people.

There are, of course, innumerable other ways in which people may have wounded us. Alcoholism may have been present in one or two parents, resulting in an environment of physical abuse or neglect. It is not a secret in counseling circles that the adult children of alcoholics have major issues to work out in their own lives. The family of origin may have been religiously dysfunctional, with a strong emphasis on performance and legalism, leaving the children feeling inadequate and unloved. There may have been the loss of a parent, a sibling, or a close friend—even a pet. We may have been an unwanted pregnancy, rejected by either or both parents and maybe given up for adoption. We may have felt abandoned early in childhood, often the case in premature babies who have had trouble bonding with their mothers due to weeks or months in an incubator. Early hospitalization is often a particularly traumatic cause for feelings of abandonment and separation from parents.

As we will see later, people with these wounds often have a whole host of emotions and issues to deal with. Frequently there is resentment for the perpetrator, maybe even hatred or anger. Sometimes the victim is mad at God or society in general. In most cases, the individual tries to suppress his emotions and may not even be aware of why he is angry.

The self-inflicted wounds we endure have to do with choices we made in our remote or recent past, most of which we live to regret. An example of this may be a decision to abort an unwanted pregnancy. There may have been a choice to be unfaithful to a spouse, an act that can never be undone. There may be a criminal record due to financial misdealing. An episode of drunk driving may have led to injury or death in another family. Dabbling in pornography may have led to a constant flow of mental images leading to thoughts we cannot control. Falling into the temptation of gambling may have led to an addiction and financial ruin. Overeating may have caused us to hate our body image and led to anorexia or bulimia.

The bad choices we make are what the Bible calls *sin* and frequently result in the painful emotion of guilt. As in the case of wounds inflicted by others, many people try to suppress and ignore their guilt and pain, but it invariably comes back to haunt them, at either a subconscious level, a physical level, or in their interpersonal relationships.

How our past affects our present

Just as my long-ago ski accident affects my ability to enjoy skiing a steep trail today, emotional or physical trauma in our past will affect us today. Why is this so? The best answer is provided by Dr. Ed Smith in his teaching materials on *Theophostic Ministry.*[87] He contends, I think correctly, that remote emotional trauma causes us to believe a lie which we use to interpret subsequent situations. These lies begin to dictate our thinking and behavior, and, rather than the memory of the event itself, are the source of negative emotions. These lies can shut us down emotionally, relationally, and even spiritually. They affect our physical health as well.

How do those lies develop? They often develop as the result of a child's thinking and personal interpretation of what happened. Frequently this happens because a child, or maybe an adult, misinterprets an event because he is incapable of making a true interpretation of life. This may be due to immaturity or external values imposed on the individual through a significant person such as a parent, a teacher, or a coach. It may be a simple comment made by a significant other such as, "I wish you were never born," or "Can't you ever do anything right?" The media, such as television or music, may have imparted the lie. Sometimes these lies may be implanted through occultic or demonic means, particularly if the sexual abuse, for example, is part of Satanic ritual abuse or part of a generational curse. Drawing again from our skiing analogy, just as kids can learn to ski well in no time, so too children, at a very early age, quickly learn these lies, and they can be very difficult to unlearn.

Here is how such a lie becomes embedded. Say a young girl is physically molested by an older male relative. An adult would interpret this event as a clear sexual violation and might call the police and charge the man. She would understand that she is innocent. But a child interprets it wrongly, thinking she must be the cause and that she provoked or encouraged the man to violate her. Two lies are embedded into her childhood mind: sex is dirty and men can't be trusted. Attached to these lies are the negative emotions of shame and anger.

How do the lies and their attached emotions live out in the present situation? A conflict might arise in her present relationship over a sexual matter. Her mind connects the present conflict with the memory of the initial sexual violation. The two lies that were embedded as a result of the initial wounding, surface in the woman's mind—men can't be trusted and she feels sex is dirty. The emotional pain of the original wounding is now relived in the present, evoking all the same emotions of anger and guilt. Words are spoken and actions taken which don't reflect the reality of the present situation but the echo of the original wounding. Her spouse will not understand the logic of her argument or her angry demeanor. She feels unloved and used by a man whom she cannot trust. The conflict escalates. Before long there are physical manifestations that may eventually lead her to her doctor for help. Note that it is not the memory of the event that is causing the problem—it's the associated lies of an unhealthy view of sex and of men in general.

Going back to our tripartite human paradigm and our Spiritual Life Cycle, the lie is implanted and resides in the middle circle representing the soul. Here it is like a tape that plays over and over in our minds, telling us things like, "You're no good," or "You'll never amount to anything." Satan's strategy is to block the flow of God's Holy Spirit which will keep us spiritually immature and virtually useless in God's Kingdom service. This is illustrated in Figure 10-1. The lie believed will continue to give Satan legal ground for continued deception. Some authors call these lies "inner child" issues—unfinished business from childhood that reflects in the present.

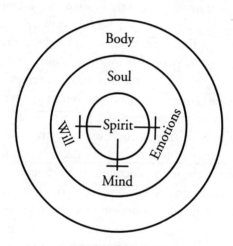

Figure 10-1
Believing the lie

It should also be noted in Figure 10-1 that the lie, which blocks the flow of God's Spirit, also hinders us in the area of obedience—lining up our will with God's will. This leads to recurring problems with sin leading to the sin-guilt-repentance cycle so much a part of the lives of defeated Christians. There are many testimonials of people who plateaued spiritually until the Holy Spirit revealed historical wounding and spoke truth to the lie which resulted. Then they started to blossom beautifully.

How many people out there subtly believe such lies? Although we can't be sure, Dr. Smith estimates that a significant portion of any local church congregation is hurting because of early suppressed wounds[88] and up to 50 percent of women have been the victim of some type of sexual violation.[89] As physicians, we too see unexplainable physical symptoms in a significant number of patients which we can often trace back to earlier emotional trauma.

Evidence of wounding

How do you know if you are a person with emotional baggage that may be affecting your health, your relationships, and God's call on your life? Of course, to a certain extent, we all carry some baggage—it is part of living in a broken world. None of our families are perfect, our parents weren't perfect, our teachers weren't perfect and our church leaders weren't perfect. Our genetic tree is littered with genes that may predispose us to certain personalities traits with their associated strengths and weaknesses. We may have genes which weaken our resistance to depression or anxiety disorder through biochemical mediators such as catecholamines, serotonin and endorphins. Combine certain personalities with a genetic predisposition to a weakened host response, add a traumatic life event or two, and you have fertile ground for emotional wounding which may manifest in one of the following ways:

- *Anxiety or panic disorders.* In her book *From Panic to Power,* Lucinda Bassett shares her story of how growing up in an alcoholic home, along with a family history of anxiety, led to her own problems with anxiety and agoraphobia. Crippled for years by fears, obsessive thinking, and numerous physical problems, she finally realized she needed help and healing. Not only did she find it for herself, she went on to found the Midwest Center for Stress and Anxiety and has helped countless others find help.[90]

- *Depression.* Although there is often a family history of depression, other factors are often triggers, such as lack of love, a loss, or unresolved anger.

- *Burnout.* Unresolved emotional baggage will often lead to burnout because the average person can only expend so much energy in suppressing either the guilt, shame, or anger resulting from previous wounds. It's like the tractor pull illustration in Chapter 4. Sooner or later the weight moves up on you and you either stall or spin out.

- *Spiritual stagnation.* Many people with unresolved issues reach a ceiling in their spiritual growth and maturity. They frequently get caught in a cycle of repeated sin, guilt and repentance, and as one author put it, "keep going around and around the mountain." They never find their calling and frequently come to church to get rather than to give.

- *String of broken relationships.* Many people with unresolved emotional issues are drawn like magnets to other people with similar problems. These relationships are fraught with problems—smothering and codependent on one hand, or distant and aloof on the other. Repeated marital failure is common in such people.

- *Uncontrolled anger.* Unbridled anger is frequently a sign of excessive mental energy directed inward to suppress unresolved issues, but bubbling over wildly when provoked, sometimes by relatively minor events.

- *Rebellion to authority.* People who have been hurt by an authority figure in their life, such as a parent, a teacher, or a coach, will frequently have major problems with submitting to authority in their adult life. A symptom of this in church-goers is church-hopping because of problems with submission to church leadership.

- *Addictions.* Shame or guilt frequently drives people to chemicals or behaviors to ease the pain. In the end though, these chemicals or behaviors frequently result in more guilt and shame requiring more ease—and so the cycle continues.

- *Dissociative disorder.* Previously called multiple personality disorder, this occurs in extreme cases of emotional trauma when the person develops coping skills that allow her to compartmentalize her mind. When the pain in one area becomes too great, they move to another compartment in their mind without any recollection of what happened in the first. These people are very resistant to treatment.

- *Recurring or chronic physical illness.* There are several ways in which unresolved emotional pain may affect our present physical health. We have already talked about the psychoneuroimmunology (PNI) pathway and how the neurotransmitters released from the brain affect our immune response to disease, thereby weakening us to such illness as infections and cancer. Some diseases are known to be directly associated with anxiety such as irritable bowel syndrome and eczema. Other diseases may result from chronically excessive levels of catecholamines (adrenalin) flowing through our body resulting in hypertension (high blood pressure) and heart disease. Another mechanism whereby emotional pain can cause physical sickness, particularly chronic pain or fatigue, is through what Dr. Ed Smith calls "physical memory."[91] This is the body's ability to remember the sights, sounds, smells and the pain associated with an historic event. By bringing the event to memory, these sensations may be relived. Sometimes, just the pain or fatigue are felt.

If you find yourself with any of these in your life, there is help. The lies associated with the memories of past trauma can be dispelled and you can experience freedom. But you need to persist. I trust the following section is just enough for you to see that there is hope for you.

FINDING HEALING

No doubt you have already looked for solutions to the pain in your life. Most people, by middle age, will have tried several coping strategies. You may identify with some of these.

- *Changing the environment.* Some people hope their problems will go away when they change spouses, jobs, churches, or move to a new community. Unfortunately, the problem being within, it follows them wherever they go.

- *Self-determination.* This is the "pull yourself up by the bootstraps" method. While self-effort and a strong will can a give temporary reprieve, they are also forerunners of burnout.

- *Self-help programs.* There are many good self-help programs available. Some may be more effective than others, and you might either have received help or been disappointed in the money you spent.

- *Intellectual change.* Getting more knowledge may make you an expert, but it doesn't always translate into changed living. Some have read every book on inner healing yet continue to live defeated lives.

- *Legalism.* This involves making rules for yourself which, in the end, will be impossible to keep without inducing more guilt and disappointment. Typically, people who have a view of God as being a demanding, harsh father do this to win His favour.

- *Busyness.* You might ease the pain through busyness, including lots of Christian service for good causes. By thinking that running will keep the pain at bay, you are preparing for the inevitable "tractor pull spin out."

- *Medication.* Antidepressants and anti-anxiety medications are tools that God allows us to use to ease our pain, but frequently, they postpone the need to deal with the root.

- *Digging up the past.* We will see that delving into your past is helpful, but most people don't know what to do when they get there, resulting in negative consequences and even more pain.

- *Counseling.* You may have tried secular or Christian counseling and still feel you have gotten nowhere. Or there may be improvement through improved coping skills. Frequently, however, the root lie may not have been dispelled.

- *Spiritual disciplines.* You may have cried out to God and committed yourself with renewed fervor to the disciplines of worship, prayer, and Bible-reading. You may have repented repeatedly of every known sin. And yet, the pain lingers.

- *Church-sponsored programs.* Some good Christian programs are available, such as *Lord, Heal My Hurts* by Kay Arthurs.[92] Many have been helped through these programs, although others may have missed the point.

While your situation may seem hopeless, I believe the Church is on the verge of truly being able to help people find their freedom in Christ. Jesus Himself said that He came *to proclaim freedom for the prisoners* (Luke 4:18). I don't believe that Jesus wants us to content ourselves with a weak gospel or to be a weakened church army full of wounded soldiers.

Keys to freedom

The key to total freedom is to dispel the lie that is at the root of damaged emotions or ill health. Ultimately, any method that really works will accomplish this. So let's look at the biblical solution to our pain.

The two keys that will unlock and dispel the lie for the vast majority of people are *forgiveness* and *repentance*. Wounds inflicted by others require you to forgive the offending person or persons, as well as to repent of the sin of unforgiveness. Self-inflicted wounds require you to repent of your sin.

Forgiveness

Humans were created to be in relationship with others. As image bearers of the triune God, we were designed to be intimately related to others in community, just as the Trinity is an intimate, eternal community of three. For that reason, God did not leave Adam alone but made *a helper suitable for him* (Gen. 2:18). Adam and Eve in Eden experienced the same kind of connection and intimacy as the Father had with the Son and both with the Holy Spirit.

Unfortunately, we already saw how the Fall caused a rift in Adam and Eve's perfect relationship. Now there would be strife in marriage, between parents and children, between neighbours, between co-workers, between countries, and so on. This strife is frequently a root of emotional pain, and is bad for your health as we have already mentioned. Consider frustrated statements like, "You make me sick" or "You're a pain in the neck." Although not always intended literally, they are, in fact, true statements. Sick relationships frequently are the forerunners of sick bodies. A ten-year University of Michigan study of 2754 adults in Tecumseh, Michigan, showed that people with the greatest number of healthy social contacts had one-half to one-fourth the mortality rate of those without supportive social networks.[93] John Bevere, in his book *The Bait of Satan*, shows that a spirit of offense resulting from unforgiveness is frequently the way Satan holds us in his trap of deceit.[94]

Jesus of course came to offer full salvation, including in the area of relationships. He taught the principles of "turning the other cheek" and "going the extra mile." He broke through the taboos of his day by talking to Samaritan women and prostitutes. And so, as followers of Jesus Christ, Paul gives us the mandate to *live at peace with everyone* (Rom. 12:18). Let's see how we can appropriate that now.

Here are some steps you can follow. Frequently, however, you will need the help of a counselor or pastor to successfully navigate through this process. It is best done within the context of loving, trusted community.

- *Pray for the Holy Spirit to reveal any memory that was painful.* You are looking for a memory picture in your past of a time when you were wounded by others. For some this may be obvious and going back to it will be easy. For others, where the memory was repressed, it may require some intense work by the Holy Spirit.

- *Revisit the emotions of the memory.* As you revisit the painful scene in your memory, the painful emotions that were associated with the event will be stirred. Feel them and either journal them or express them to a friend, counselor, or pastor. Invariably, there will be emotions directed toward the person or persons who inflicted the pain.

- *Repent of unforgiveness toward the perpetrator(s).* Invariably, you have been harbouring a spirit of offense and unforgiveness. This is wrong because we are told in Scripture to *love our enemies* (Matt. 5:44).

- *Forgive the perpetrator(s).* This is the hard part for many because it contravenes our sense of justice. Yet God did the same for us when we deserved punishment. This is the key that unlocks the rest of these steps.

- *Discern the lie that resulted from the offense.* Satan has undoubtedly implanted a lie which is the root of the lingering pain. Pray that the Holy Spirit will reveal this lie and He will. Journal, or express the lie to your counselor or pastor.

- *Allow Jesus, through His Spirit, to speak truth to the lies.* Only Christ can dispel the lies, because he is the ultimate Truth. Allow Him to speak truth into the lie, to dispel it once and for all.

- *Close the door on the lie.* Satan will invariably come back to re-instill the lie. Pray a daily spiritual warfare prayer that clothes you in the armour of Ephesians 6, such as the one in Appendix C.

- *Daily live from the inside out.* Go daily to God's fountain of living water and hold your empty glass high to be filled. Exercise the Spiritual Life Cycle.

A recent illustration of the power of forgiveness is that of Rev. Dale Lang from Tabor, Alberta. Days after his son was fatally shot at school, Rev. Lang was seen on public TV speaking words of forgiveness toward the boy that killed his son. Subsequently, he took his message of forgiveness on the road, addressing both secular and Christian crowds about his experiences. While grief and loss were real for Rev. Lang, the power of forgiveness helped ease the pain and shortened the grieving. This loss is not likely to cause intense emotional pain in later life.

Repentance

When a wound is self-inflicted through the bad choices we made, and guilt and poor self-esteem are the emotional results, we need to repent. We have already seen that the bad choices we make are what the Bible calls sin. We have also seen that the answer to sin is the righteousness that is ours through faith in Jesus Christ. However, many people don't avail themselves of God's forgiving grace and they wallow in guilt, shame, and low self-esteem.

Worldly attempts at dealing with low self-esteem often involve building self-esteem through self acceptance and positive self-talk. Biblically, though, the answer is to recognize that we are, in fact, unworthy, and that we are sinful and deserve to be punished. Here are the steps to take:

- *Ask God for insight.* In locating roots and associated lies, we need the Holy Spirit's help to uncover suppressed or dissociated areas of our lives. This may be difficult to do on your own, and you may need a skilled counselor or pastor to help you.

- *Bring the sin(s) to mind.* Blanket prayers like, "Lord, forgive all my sins" won't rid you of a lie that is rooted in a particular sin. Rather, focus on the particular sin or wrong attitude in which the lie is rooted.

- *Recognize the sin as rebellion and which gave Satan legal access to your mind.* Rebellion is an open door to the devil's work and lies in your life.[95]

- *Confess the sin.* As the sin, or wrong attitude, is brought to mind, admit to God that you were wrong and ask Him to forgive you through Jesus. Recognize that it is Christ's righteousness that you receive through faith in Him. It is nothing you do yourself to deserve it—it is a free gift.

- *Confess to others involved.* It is crucial when you have wronged someone to ask for their forgiveness. If the person is deceased, write a letter expressing your regret and ask them for forgiveness. Then burn it as an act of appropriating their forgiveness.

- *Confess to a friend.* James instructs: *confess your sins to each other and pray for each other so that you may be healed* (Jas. 5:16). Confessing to others will help with prayer support and will help you get rid of the associated lie by breaking the veil of secrecy.

- *Dispel the lie.* The most common lie associated with guilt is one of unworthiness—that we lack worth in God's eyes. Allow God to fill you with His Holy Spirit so that you can experience His unconditional love. You are His child. He is your loving Father. You are a person of worth.

- *Dispel the father of lies.* Jesus instructed us to pray, *Deliver us from the evil one* (Matt. 6:13), and James tells us to *resist the devil* (Jas. 4:7). Satan will invariably attempt to regain the legal foothold he has just lost. Close the door mentioned above.

- *Daily live from the inside out.* Go daily to God's fountain of living water and hold your empty glass high to be filled. Exercise the Spiritual Life Cycle.

Repentance is the key to breaking the legal hold Satan has on you when he convinces you of the lie that you are unworthy before God. An excellent resource for help in this area is James MacDonald's book, *I Really Want to Change... So, Help me God.*[96]

One of the saddest things I see in family practice, is mature adults retiring into their senior years still carrying their unresolved emotional baggage. Rather than enjoying the "golden years" and aging with grace, they are torn by unresolved family relationships. As we will see in the next chapter, this critically impacts issues of eldercare and peaceful aging.

11 | Aging with Grace

The days of our years are threescore years and ten;
and if by reason of strength they be fourscore years.

Moses

Both my wife, Cathy, and I are the youngest of large families. Our children arrived late because we struggled with infertility. Consequently, we are now in our mid-forties with teenage children. But we also have aged mothers—both in their mid-eighties, both of whom have lost their independence because of dementia. We are what is sometimes called the "sandwich generation," people sandwiched between the needs of aging parents and at-home children. Presently, we are the primary caregivers for my mother-in-law. My mother was cared for by my sister for seven years, with respite two or three days a week from the other children. Fourteen months ago it was decided at a family meeting that she would need nursing home care, and she is now a resident in a nursing home close to our home.

255

Like our moms, the needs of the elderly are going to increase. Average life expectancy is extending, now to about 80, interestingly enough back to where it was in Moses' day (Ps. 90:10) Through the advances of science and healthier living, it is likely to extend further, at least in developed countries. Along with that, the oldest baby boomers will start reaching retirement and elderhood soon. With diminished birthrates, we are seeing what is called the "greying" of society—a larger proportion of society being elderly. So governments and institutions that care for the elderly will need to prepare for the increased needs of the elderly.

Similarly, it behooves the Church to consider its future role in the care of the elderly. Children with aging parents need to consider their responsibilities toward their elders. And as we age ourselves, we must consider how we want to be cared for, and be willing to discuss that with our own children. And Scripture does have something to say about that.

And above all, as Christians, we want to age gracefully, enjoying our retirement but using our remaining days on earth to the best advantage possible, particularly in the spiritual realm. Our contribution to the physical realm may be limited, although we can still invest in the lives of our offspring, particularly spiritually. And we can pray, impacting the spiritual realm in positive ways. Some will be fit enough to continue some type of ministry. I recently met an elderly retired pastor, in his 80s, who has a ministry marrying couples in a little chapel in the mall in his city. Many are common-law couples who recognize their need before God to rectify their living arrangement and want a truly Christian wedding. It still gives him joy to do this.

So let's begin our journey by looking at what happens when we age. An in-depth examination of aging is beyond the scope of this book, so we hope to highlight the areas most impacted by a Christian worldview. For a more detailed look, I would suggest *As Parents Age* by Joseph Ilardo.[97]

WHAT HAPPENS WHEN WE AGE

They are called the "Golden Years." For many they can be years of intense joy, but for others they may be years of intense pain as bodies wear out. Arthritis can hamper mobility. Memory loss may hinder active social involvement. Heart disease can be restricting causing chest pain or shortness of breath. What is encouraging is that work with the elderly is revealing that much can be done to improve the quality of life among them.

The scientific term for aging is *senescence*, obviously where we get the old, now outdated word *senile* from. Senescence happens at a cellular level, and involves virtually all our cells. They are bigger than young cells, excrete proteins at a different rate and after 50 to 100 divisions, no longer divide. They do this because structures at the tips of their chromosomes called *telomeres*, lose short segments with each division. Once the telomeres are used up, the cell no longer divides. Scientists are vigorously researching for ways to restore the telomeres in order to make our cells immortal, thereby stopping the aging process.

There are two parallel processes involved in aging. *Primary aging* includes the aspects of aging which inevitable and over which a person has no control. They are genetically based, which as Christians we believe are the result of the Fall, as we saw in Chapter 1. One of the most significant changes that occurs during primary aging is the decline in levels of something gerontologists call *trophic factors,* hormone and hormone like substances produced by the body. These decreases result in the frailty so characteristic of the elderly—decline in skin thickness, in bone mass and in the number and strength of muscle fibers. Primary aging also involves a decline in the acuity of all the senses, vision and hearing having the most consequential effects. But decreases in the sense of touch leads to slowed reflexes and balance and gait problems. Food loses its taste for many seniors, and the result of a decrease in their body's ability to respond to flavors and to discriminate among them. The ability of the brain to process information slows, leading to slowed reflexes, and slower conversation.

Secondary aging refers to changes that occur in the elderly as the result of lifestyle, disease or trauma. As we have already seen, a person's health in old age is directly and dramatically influenced by the diet, exercise patterns, and the use of tobacco and alcohol throughout life. A person's occupation influences his aging—years ago dairy farmers invariably developed severe osteoarthritis of their hands from milking by hand. Rarely seen now because of milking machines, what I see now is worn out knees from getting up and down from putting on the milkers. People with sedentary jobs and an inactive lifestyle develop loss of lung capacity and weakness of the heart muscle. Cholesterol build-ups in arteries cause obstruction which leads to strokes, heart attacks and circulatory problems in the lower limbs. Loss of brain cells causes memory deficits so well documented in Alzheimer's disease.

And there are the emotional effects of aging. Aging is evidence of our own mortality, not an easily acceptable fact for some. Where the young are more passionate in their emotions, seniors often have fewer strong loves or hates. Where the young live in anticipation, the elderly live in memory. Loss of relationships and productivity lead to a loss of a sense of the future. Loss of physical attractiveness may affect their self-esteem. They lose authority, power and status which rob them of their sense of purpose. There are also positive emotional changes. They include deeper understanding and insight, increased compassion, an affirmation of one's life, and concern for the welfare of future generations. Erik Erikson, a psychoanalyst who has written extensively about aging, has made this observation:

One of the characteristics of the well-adjusted elderly person is ... "generativity," a deep concern about the welfare of the next generation. Rather than being absorbed in one's own emotional, financial, and physical needs, high-functioning seniors focus on sharing the wisdom acquired during their lives. They dedicate themselves to helping in what ways possible to make the world a better place for the next generation.[98]

Now there are things we can do to hasten the process, and things we can do to slow it. We have already examined these in Chapter 9, Living well—by the manual. David put it this way in one of his psalms:

Whoever of you loves life and desires to see many good days, keep your tongue from evil and your lips from speaking lies. Turn from evil and do good; seek peace and pursue it (Ps. 34:12).

Besides a holy, biblical lifestyle, the secret that I have seen from my practice is the "use it or lose it" principle.

Use it or lose it

In the area of mobility and fitness, maintaining an active life style is crucial. Muscles that you don't use will get smaller (atrophy) and become weaker. That's why it's so hard for someone who has been bedridden for a few weeks to get walking again. Some elderly patients in my practice have such wasted thigh muscles that they can hardly get up from a chair without rocking back and forth to get enough momentum to get up. They have no underlying condition that causes this other than disuse (the rocking syndrome). Similarly joints that aren't put through their full range of motion regularly will get stiff. The tissues around the joint tighten and the cartilage in the joint starts to deteriorate. Before long, the joint is stiff and painful, and hinders mobility. So it is crucial that seniors exercise daily. Walking is great exercise but I would also strongly recommend some stretching exercise, along with light weights to keep the muscles toned up. Then the walking or biking is a great aerobic exercise.

The same way, the best protection against memory loss, along with adequate antioxidants and prevention of mini-strokes, is using it. Exercising the brain is vital. So stay active with reading, thinking, praying, writing, continuing a ministry, doing crosswords, etc. Maintain as many active relationships as possible and visit frequently to maintain acquaintances. I would encourage healthy retirees to give some of their elder years in Christian service, whether missionary service abroad, or locally. This appears to be biblical. Timothy is admonished by Paul that

> widow(s should be) *known for* (their) *good deeds, such as bringing up children, showing hospitality, washing the feet of the saints, helping those in trouble and devoting* (themselves) *to all kinds of good deeds* (1 Tim. 5:9,10).

Now the emphasis here is on female widows, probably because elderly men continued to work, but certainly in our culture, that would apply to men as well. Really, there is no retirement in the Kingdom of God. I hear seniors in churches everywhere say that they had their day in ministry or service, and that now it's time for the next generation. It is unbiblical to sideline yourself because of seniority. Rather, be a mentor for younger people and share your wisdom of the years.

So I would particularly challenge our older Christian seniors to maintain very active prayer ministries. It seems that the older women in Ephesus did that. *The widow... puts her hope in God and continues night and day to pray and to ask God for help* (1 Tim. 5:5). Lay visitation teams might keep updated prayer lists for them, and encourage them to pray the list many times daily. Bedridden seniors could have prayer lists posted in large letters on their ceiling as to help to keep them focused. Similarly worship is important, and we should make every effort to keep our elders involved in worship. Most nursing homes are good to provide worship services in house, and that is to be encouraged and supported. Again visitation teams and parish healthcare workers can support and help in that important area.

PLANNING FOR ELDERCARE

It is a fact of life that as we age, despite the best medical and spiritual care, some of us will lose our independence because of degenerative diseases. That of course raises the issues of eldercare. In Nigeria during my years in medical missions, there was no such thing as a nursing home, as I suspect in most developing countries, where the care is given by the extended family. That was probably the case in Ephesus as well, because Paul admonishes Timothy about the care of the elderly who have offspring:

> *But if a widow has children or grandchildren, these should learn first of all to put their religion into practice by caring for their own family and so repaying their parents and grandparents, for this is pleasing to God... If anyone does not provide for his relatives, and especially for his immediate family, he has denied the faith and is worse than an unbeliever* (1 Tim. 5:4,8).

Paul's language here is very strong. Now in our culture, we have more of a focus on the nuclear family (parents and children) than in other cultures. It's often said that when you marry someone in African, or Latin American culture, you marry their relatives, because often it may mean that a widowed mother-in-law moves in with you for good. Although the cultural milieu behind Scripture may change, or vary from culture to culture, the underlying message does not, and that is that children and grandchildren need to take responsibility for their aging parents or grandparents.

Now in family practice I see it all. There are some children who are ready to sacrifice for their parents—they may remodel their homes into a "granny flat" or one of the couple may give up their job to look after a parent. Or if they do require nursing care, they are there daily for a visit, or to feed them. On the other hand, I see some very financially able children who place their parent in a nursing home and are seldom seen again, until they come to claim their inheritance.

If there are elderly in the church with no family or offspring, or they are estranged, the responsibility is laid on the church to care for them. In Ephesus they had a "*list of widows*" for whom the church provided: *Give proper recognition to those widows who are really in need* (1 Tim. 5:3). Culturally, we often assume that people today are cared for by their government pension cheque, but obviously the church still has a special responsibility here. The underlying message of Scripture never changes, despite cultural differences.

Your own eldercare

Depending on your age, your own requirements as a senior may seem far into the distant future, and thinking about care needs later in life seems utterly objectionable. However, far better to discuss your care needs with your family when fit, mentally and physically. You may assume your children will have you in their home, but they may be thinking differently. Many a son or daughter recalls hastily said phrases in passing such as, "Don't ever put me in a nursing home" or "I'd never want to live with my children." Sometimes, given little thought and blurted out, they become the modus operandi when care decisions are being made later in life, possibly after dementia has set in, and we can't really find what the senior's thoughts are now. Or those comments can invoke deep guilt if care requirements do require institutional care because of the nature of the condition. So the advice I give to people in my practice is, at the age of retirement, to have a meeting for the purpose of discussing their wishes with all their offspring.

Here are some considerations as you plan your meeting. If you are beyond retirement, have it sooner rather than later.

- Make sure there are no unresolved issues between you and your children. This is crucial. If there have been perceived wrongs which haven't been forgiven, it is not wise to move ahead. Make every effort to be fully reconciled. Reassure them of your unconditional love and if you have wronged them confess before God and apologize to them, asking for forgiveness. Far better to go into elderhood with healthy family relationships. Don't leave any children or children-in-laws out.

- Children may be resistant to discuss these care issues because of their own unresolved issues regarding aging and death. Reassure them that you are at peace about aging and death, and have no fears. If they are still uneasy give them time.

- As you outline your wishes, make contingency plans for "what if" scenarios. For example, "I would like to live in my own home with Home Support as long as possible, but if I need 24 hour supervision, then I would like to live in a Community Care facility," and name the institution.

- This is also a good time to write a health care directive, sometimes called a Living Will (see below). Discuss it with your family and appoint a proxy decision maker for when you are no longer able.

- Keep written notes of your meeting because memories are all volatile no matter what the age. Give your kids a copy for their own records.

• Revisit your care needs about every five years if you continue to be healthy, sooner if care appears more imminent.

If you are a widow or widower, or a couple, without children or relatives, meet with the church leadership to review what role the church can play in your care. If your church has a Parish Nurse, involve her in your meeting.

Your parent's eldercare

Many current baby boomers have elderly parents approaching their loss of independence. Many of that generation were not proactive enough to plan a family meeting when they were fit. It can be a very difficult time for families when no previous plans were made. Particularly in dysfunctional families, there are strong feelings of guilt, unresolved issues of the past can resurface and elder abuse may occur.

As you approach decisions, here are some guidelines:

• Review the scriptural injunction for children to take responsibility for their parents. The way to apply those Scriptures is to genuinely consider their best interests. Sometimes the best is professional care. However, family care can go along way in compensating for that.

• Try to find out your parent's wishes, if their mental health allows.

• Get a handle on your parent's financial resources. This may impact the type of care they can afford.

• Have a family meeting with all children, and their spouses present. Volatile families with unresolved issues may need an unbiased third party to act as chairperson. This may be a pastor, physician, therapist or other mutually acceptable person. All ideas may be discussed. Use an easel to record pros and cons of various options. Don't rush.

This can become a great time of reconciliation between siblings and their spouses.

• When a decision is reached, there needs to be family unity and solidarity in cooperating to make it happen. If a son or daughter wishes to care for the parent in their own home, but needs respite, others should cooperate with that plan and help however possible.

Health Care Directives

Most jurisdictions now have legislation which allow seniors, or persons of any age over the age of majority, to write down their wishes for end-of-life care. Where medical science has given us the ability to support life through such means of ventilators (artificial respirators), cardiac pacemakers, intravenous fluids, drugs to keep the blood pressure up and drugs to help the kidneys get rid of excessive fluids, it is not everyone's wishes to apply this technology, if they have had a full life, particularly if they have an irreversible condition. Likewise, resuscitation through CPR can bring back those with a sudden cardiac arrest, but if there has been any delay there may be a chance of brain damage.

A health care directive, or the so-called Living Will, is a legal document written by anyone over the age of majority who are still capable of making health care decisions and understanding the consequences of that decision. In it you state your wishes regarding such issues as resuscitation (CPR), the use of life support such as ventilators, intravenous fluids or emergency surgery. You also appoint a proxy decision maker to help guide the decision making process should you become unable to make the decisions yourself. The document is signed, witnessed and dated, and is only applied once you are no longer able to consent to such measures due to loss of mental capacity.

Some Christians may wonder if it is morally right to withhold any treatment that may somehow extend life. We already saw how much of science's drive to extend life at all cost is driven by the naturalistic worldview which considers that this life is all there is. So death is always an enemy. Not so for the Christian who sees it as a stepping stone to a better life hereafter. So while we don't condone the taking of life through such means as euthanasia, or mercy killing, we don't have a moral obligation to use every available means to artificially extend it in every case. Thus, the Christian Medical and Dental Society of Canada has the following in their policy statement on euthanasia:

> If medical treatment is no longer effective and is merely prolonging the process of dying, it is appropriate to withhold or terminate that treatment.

Here are some guidelines as you prayerfully consider writing your own health care directive:

- Decide whether you want to be resuscitate from sudden cardiac arrest through CPR (mouth to mouth and chest compressions, as well as electrical shock).

- Decide whether you want to be placed on a ventilator (usually a tube in your throat which is connected to a machine to pump air into your lungs).

- Decide whether you want intravenous fluids (usually involves repeatedly having needles inserted into your veins).

- Decide whether you would want to be fed through a nasogastric tube (a tube through your nose into your stomach for feeding).

- Decide whether you would want emergency surgery for conditions such as a ruptured aneurysm.

- Decide whether you would want extensive blood tests (usually means having blood taken from the veins in your arms).

- Decide if you would prefer to be cared for at home, or a nursing home, versus a hospital.

- Write your wishes, appoint a proxy decision maker, most often the eldest child and call a family meeting to discuss what you have written.

- Use this time as a testimony of your assurance of eternal life. If you are not sure, review the steps to finding peace with God in Appendix A.

A written health care directive makes decision making for your loved ones much easier and I would strongly encourage you to do this, and discuss it with your family doctor and your pastor as well as your family. So often family members are torn because they don't know the wishes of their loved one. It will help them in their loss, as we will see next as we learn to face our losses with dignity.

12 | Facing Loss with Dignity

It is appointed unto men once to die.

Writer to Hebrews, AD 60

For to me, to live is Christ and to die is gain.

Apostle Paul

O n this side of the Christ's second coming we are going to continue to age and remain mortal— the historic Christian position. So we do need to prepare ourselves for the inevitable losses we will all experience, sooner or later. Death is a fact of the human experience. Some will experience lifelong illness or disability. If you are a married woman, there is a good chance you will become widowed, or if a man, you will likely face the loss of productivity and usefulness in your occupation as you reach elderhood. Most will lose parents. Some may lose children or grandchildren. The cycle of life really is a series of losses— adolescence the loss of childhood, middle age the loss of youth, elderhood the loss of productivity. But the key for the

Christian is that each loss has its gain:

> *And we know that in all things God works for the good of those who love him, who have been called according to his purpose. What, then, shall we say in response to this? If God is for us, who can be against us? Who shall separate us from the love of Christ? Shall trouble or hardship or persecution or famine or nakedness or danger or sword? No, in all these things we are more than conquerors through him who loved us. For I am convinced that neither death nor life, neither angels nor demons, neither the present nor the future, nor any powers, neither height nor depth, nor anything else in all creation, will be able to separate us from the love of God that is in Christ Jesus our Lord* (Rom. 8:28,31,35,37-39).

These well-known verses from Romans 8 are cherished by believers around the world as they face disappointment and loss. They apply to those that have died for their faith, whether in missionary service, or as martyrs; to those that have kept their testimonies despite lifelong disabilities, such as Joni Eareckson Tada; to those that have given up financial wealth for obedience to Christ. Charles Stanley, in his book *The Blessings of Brokenness*, shows how God sometimes allows us to go through loss to bring us to a place of brokenness from which we can be placed on a path of greater blessing:

> In choosing to be fashioned by God, we inevitably must choose to yield to brokenness and to allow God to remake us and renew us as he desires—even if that means suffering pain, hardship, and trials.[99]

John Bevere shares a similar message and calls these trials "wilderness experiences."[100] He demonstrates how most great men and women, used by God to fulfill a major calling in their lives, experienced wilderness times as preparation for service.

Examples are the lives of Joseph, Moses, and Paul. Christ Himself spent forty days in the wilderness as preparation for His ministry. So we too, as God places His hand upon us, may be called to wilderness times to prepare us for the greater things God has in store.

Let's begin this part of our journey by defining loss.

UNDERSTANDING LOSSES

In order to know what loss is, we must identify what our needs and longings are. Several authors in the field of sociology have done that, Maslow being one. He describes our needs using a pyramid in which the most basic needs are at the bottom and the deepest spiritual needs are at the top (see Figure 12-1). At the bottom are our physiological needs—food, water, shelter, sexuality. Above that are the needs of safety and security, losses people experience in war zones. Next are the relational needs of belonging and feeling accepted and loved. As we rise further up the pyramid we see the more intangible needs such as self-esteem and recognition, and the mind's need to know and grow and learn. Then, near the top, are our needs for beauty, often expressed in the arts or the appreciation of nature. Finally, the top need is the realization of who we are and why we are here. Maslow pointed out that these needs are additive—without the basic needs at the bottom met, the higher needs were unlikely to be met. I beg to differ. People who know God can lose virtually everything and still remain "self-actualized," keeping their faith in God and remaining secure in Him.

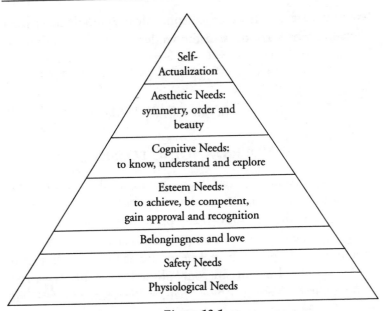

Figure 12.1
Maslow's Hierarchy of Human Needs

Now if you are a student of the Bible, you will immediately recognize that Adam and Eve had all of the needs pointed to by Maslow met in the Garden of Eden. From the most basic need of food, through safety, love, esteem, and beauty—they had it all. They certainly knew their Creator intimately as well as their purpose for being. Adam and Eve introduced loss to the human race when they turned their backs on God. That's where the pain began as we saw in Chapter 1.

Most simply stated then, loss is the pain associated with the deprivation of any of our human needs or longings. It may be a need that was never gained, or gained once but then lost. For example, a girl may never have fallen in love and remained single, never enjoying the intimacy of marriage, while a widow once knew it, but lost it. Singleness is a loss for both.

Since we still live in a world very affected by the Fall, we will experience losses throughout our cycle of life. Here are some possibilities you can identify with:

- Job loss either due to layoffs, injury or retirement. Drought or pests may cause crop failures and hunger. A tornado may ravish your home. As a single mom without the ability to work, social assistance may not cover your basic needs;

- Depending on where we live, we may lose our safety due to war, crime, or ethnic hatred. Safety on the roads may be challenged by drunk drivers or inexperienced drivers. We may be sexually violated resulting in the loss of virginity;

- Loss of a spouse due to death or divorce, a parent or a sibling due to death. Family or loved ones may move away. Estrangement may cause separation, possibly worse than death. A son or daughter may be called to missions in a faraway land. A child may be prodigal with no information of his or her origins. An adopted child may not be able to find her birth mother;

- Project failures, litigation for incompetency, decline in business clientele may all be losses in the esteem category. Or loss of a body part such as a breast or a limb;

- Dementia from stroke or Alzheimer disease leads to loss of mental functioning;

- Loss of vision or hearing affects us in the aesthetic segment of Maslow's triangle. The loss of a limb may prevent our expression in music or art;

- Turning one's back on God and worshiping idols is a loss in the spiritual pinnacle. Deception is another loss.

One of the scriptural metaphors we already used to describe

our longings and losses is that of *thirsting for water*. Recall that, in his conversation with the woman at the well in John 4:13 and 14, Jesus said:

> *Everyone who drinks this water will be thirsty again, but whoever drinks the water I give him will never thirst. Indeed, the water I give him will become in him a spring of water welling up to eternal life.*

Similarly, the Old Testament prophet Jeremiah spoke during a time when God's people were slipping far away from Him:

> *My people have committed two sins: They have forsaken me, the spring of living water, and have dug their own cisterns, broken cisterns that cannot hold water.*

We saw that there were three principles in these "water" passages:

1. *People are thirsty—we have unmet longings.* We were designed to enjoy the abundance Adam and Eve had in the Garden and we rightfully long for what was lost in the Fall. It's okay to be thirsty but it does matters what we do with our thirst.

2. *People move in wrong directions in response to their thirst.* Rather than turning to God through Jesus Christ, people refuse to trust God to look after their thirst and develop wrong strategies to find the life they desire.

3. *Only God will fully satisfy the deepest thirst and longings in our hearts.* His provision is through faith in Jesus Christ.

In the area of health, we are thirsty because we are mortal and suffer because of sickness. Strained relationships add to our burden of ills and deep emotional wants leave us depressed and discouraged.

Picture a glass of water deep within your being, representing your thirst. Maybe you had a happy childhood and started life happily married. You know God and have a personal relationship with Him through Jesus Christ. An education and a decent job, the prospect of purchasing your own home, and your glass is pretty full—may seem like you are on top of the world with your glass overflowing.

But then your father whom you have admired and has been your source of inspiration suddenly dies of a heart attack—a good bit of water is suddenly spilled from your glass. Perhaps for the first time in your life you are actually thirsty. But before your glass has a chance to be refilled, your boss starts to be critical of your work and the workplace becomes very stressful—more water out of your glass. You are overjoyed when your wife conceives your first born and it seems like your thirst is being quenched—your glass is filling. But suddenly she miscarries and you are at an all-time low. Now it seems you are on empty. Where do you turn? Suddenly relief of the resulting pain becomes a priority. Where you turn is critical. What many of us do is develop self-protective strategies that may be harmful and spiritually dangerous. Some turn to alcohol, gambling, or pornography. Others turn to their work for relief, spending more time in the office hoping the pain at home will go away. Some throw themselves into church work, thinking more service to God will help them feel better. Still others pursue their sport, spending all their free time on the golf course. What we really need to do is turn to God in the midst of our pain.

Turning to God in our losses

In his book *Inside Out*, Dr. Larry Crabb divides our human longings into three categories—crucial, critical, and casual.[101] They correspond to our tripartite human paradigm and Maslow's pyramid as outlined in Table 12.1.

Tripartite Human	Crabb	Maslow
Spirit	*Crucial—* Communion with God	Self-actualization
Soul	*Critical—* strong relationships	Belongingness & love, Esteem
Body	*Casual—* bodily comfort, pleasant circum- stances	Physiological & safety

Table 12.1

As mentioned earlier, Maslow proposed a bottom-up approach to satisfying needs, starting at the bottom of his pyramid with self-actualization at the top only happening if all other needs are met. In our tripartite human paradigm, that would be equivalent to an *outside-in* fulfilment of needs. Larry Crabb, on the other hand, as we have already seen this in our Spiritual Life Cycle paradigm, argues an *inside-out* change to satisfy thirst. We start with a deep longing for God who then fills our spirit with His Spirit. Then we have the added joy of relationship which grows in the caring Community of the King. Finally, God's Spirit permeates into our physical realm, bringing total satisfaction—partly now, but completely when the Kingdom comes.

Why do we belabour this? Because if you approach life from the outside in, losses in the sphere of the body or the soul will be major blows to your happiness and thirst. If, on the other hand, you are being filled from the inside out, your glass will be kept full despite losses that inevitably come your way. Even people in the harshest conditions, such as Corrie

Ten Boom in a Nazi concentration camp or Joseph in prison, can maintain their communion with God. It is then that your losses are turned into gain, as taught in Romans 8, and the very weapon that you take from the enemy's hand becomes a weapon you use against him in furthering God's Kingdom. In God's eternal perspective, that is far more important than your immediate comfort. This was my experience in Africa— people with very little in the way of outward comforts, when empowered by the Spirit from within, were some of the happiest people I have ever met.

Be aware of well-meaning Christian teachers who subtly teach an outside-in approach, beginning with physical comfort which is supposedly followed by changed lives. That is any easy gospel to preach amidst the wealth of North America but doesn't make sense to many of our brothers and sisters in Africa, Latin America, South America, and Asia. People with our wealth-based theology find it very difficult to face loss. They take a very demanding stance toward God, insisting that physical comfort is their right. Although I agree we need to exercise faith strongly in prayer (many of us don't exercise enough faith), and we do have rights as children of the King, and the King does desire abundance, somewhere we may cross a line insisting on our "rights" as heirs of things being reserved until the Kingdom comes. There needs to be a balance of "Kingdom now" versus "Kingdom future." What's far more important to God than the comfort of the soldiers who have yet to take the land, is that the land be taken—the advancement of the Kingdom, pushing back the darkness as passionately sought in the Lord's Prayer: *Your Kingdom come.* But if you are a soldier in the prime of life, feeling defeated by losses or pain, you need to be made whole so you can resume the battle your Lord calls you to. You need to get on your personal path to wholeness and it begins with transformation from the inside out.

When God does not heal now

There will be some reading these pages who have been trusting in God for healing and have followed every step they know from popular books and teachings on healing. You have exercised faith—strongly, even claimed your healing in your thoughts and have spoken it publicly. You have prayed the Scriptures that promise healing and affirmed them for yourself. You called the elders of your church for anointing and you have repented of all past sins of omission and commission. You have gone to people with whom relationships needed mending and made them right. You have been delivered from demonic oppression and have broken ancestral curses. You have associated only with positive people who have spoken healing words to you. You have attended healing crusades, been prayed over by those who have the spiritual gift of healing, and may have been slain in the spirit.

And yet, that pain, that fatigue, that colostomy, that weakness, the chemotherapy reminds you that your body is not whole and the talk of wholeness and God being our healer is nauseating to you. In the midst of your disappointment, your biggest question will continue to be the one in our opening chapter: "Why am I still sick and why hasn't God intervened to heal me?"

Some well-meaning people may have an easy answer by telling you it is God's will that everyone be healed and it's only because of your lack of faith that it hasn't happened. Let's look at why God doesn't always heal now. An excellent resource here is a book by Larry Keefauver, *When God Doesn't Heal Now.*[102]

You ARE healed—in Christ

The right answer of course is that you have been healed—in eternity. The correct question to ask is, "When will my healing be manifest in my body?"

God either heals in created time and space or in eternity. It is a principle of the cosmos that transactions in the spiritual realm will always precede those in the natural realm. The timing of natural-realm transactions varies greatly. For God, created time as we know it, is irrelevant. His perspective is eternal.

Here are some guidelines to help you wait for your healing:

- ***You are healed if you have trusted Christ as Saviour.*** The spiritual transaction has been accomplished. The natural transaction will be partly manifest in time and space, but completely in eternity. Salvation (*sozo*) includes spiritual, emotional, relational, and physical healing and will be fully manifest in eternity.

- ***Continue to "walk by faith."*** Believe that the God of the cosmos who created space and time, will, in His own time, fulfill in the natural realm the spiritual transaction already accomplished. Believe that truth with all your will, mind, and emotions.

- ***Yield the timing to God's sovereign will.*** Don't compromise your faith in God, your healer.

- ***Watch for "faith in faith" dangers.*** Faith in faith happens when you take your eyes off God as your healer and concentrate on worldly mind-over-matter techniques.

- ***Watch for diminished trust and increased trying.*** Out of desperation you may be tempted to try treatments that are either scientifically unproven or spiritually dangerous.

- ***Allow God to build character as you wait.*** His purpose is eternal and He is preparing you to reign. Some call it "training for reigning."

- ***God will never allow you to be tried beyond what you can endure.*** He will give you the grace to endure. Call on God for the provision of grace in your life

- *Don't allow the illness to hinder your testimony.* Powerfully use your present state to testify about your reliance on God, no matter what, just as Job of old.

- *Beware of being sidelined.* Don't give Satan a victory by being sidelined out of the Kingdom battle. Continue to exert your authority in Christ in prayer and, unless you are absolutely bedridden, get out to minister as God enables you. Some great men and women of God had major physical hurdles to overcome. Charles Spurgeon for example, suffered extreme pain from gout but never allowed it to hinder one of the most impressive preaching ministries in all of Christendom.

There will be some whose illness is "unto death." Although the final enemy, death is not the enemy for you that it is for the naturalist.

DEATH—FRIEND OR FOE?

We have seen how, for the secular humanist, death is the final defeat of life as he knows it. We have seen how scientism's hope for immortality lies in medical advances, particularly now in genetic engineering and turning off our "aging gene." Death is an enemy to be avoided at all cost. And costly it is. A considerable portion of our health-care costs are incurred in the last few months of our lives. New genetics won't come cheaply either. Moreover, if everyone does live so much longer (or forever), how would we feed everyone? Seems to me this is the equivalent of people of a much earlier age (see Genesis 11) who wanted to be gods by building the tower of Babel. As I recall, God ably thwarted that plan.

So what is the Christian view of death and mortality? For the Apostle Paul it was friend rather than foe: *For to me, to live is Christ and to die is gain* (Phil. 1:21). For him it was simple—

while he lived he would serve Christ with gusto and joy, and at his death he could rejoice in his inheritance. The Christian has a hope for the future—death is not the final blow but an entrance into a place of peace and beauty for eternity.

Death—the doorway to heaven

Scripture clearly teaches that upon death, the believer is ushered into a place of bliss. Jesus told the thief on the cross, *I tell you the truth, today you will be with me in paradise* (Luke 23:43). *Paradise* is a word of oriental origin which implies a garden or pleasure ground. It is synonymous with the *third heaven* which Paul talks about in 2 Corinthians:

> *I know a man in Christ who fourteen years ago was caught up to the third heaven. Whether it was in the body or out of the body I do not know—God knows. And I know that this man—whether in the body or apart from the body I do not know, but God knows—was caught up to paradise. He heard inexpressible things, things that man is not permitted to tell* (2 Cor. 12:2-4).

The *third heaven* is the place beyond the immediate heaven of the earth's atmosphere and beyond the further heaven of outer space and the cosmos, into the presence of God Himself. Christ is said to have passed *through the heavens* (Heb. 4:14), and to have *ascended higher than all the heavens* (Eph. 4:10).

All the descriptions of heaven are peaceful, beautiful. It is a place of worship and song and endless joy. Paul described it as being *at home with the Lord* (2 Cor. 5:8). Before the resurrection when Christ returns, we will be disembodied—*away from the body* (2 Cor. 5:8). Heaven involves an inheritance:

> *Praise be to the God and Father of our Lord Jesus Christ! In his great mercy he has given us new birth into a living hope through the resurrection of Jesus Christ from the dead, and into an inheritance that can never perish, spoil or fade—*

kept in heaven for you, who through faith are shielded by God's power until the coming of the salvation that is ready to be revealed in the last time (1 Pet. 1:3-5).

As God's sons and daughters, we share our inheritance with Christ—*now if we are children, then we are heirs—heirs of God and co-heirs with Christ* (Rom. 8:17) and *we will also reign with him* (2 Tim. 2:12).

Finally our thirsting will cease; we will be completely quenched! Heaven is the complete restoration of all we lost in the Fall so our longings can cease. And God looks forward to having us home: *Precious in the sight of the LORD is the death of his saints* (Ps. 116:15).

We should be very clear that Scripture nowhere supports the notion of reincarnation, the belief that our souls come back in another body or the body of an animal. There is no basis for the "former life therapies" that some intuitive healers are doing. Likewise, the Bible clearly prohibits communicating with the dead.

Scripture does not teach universalism, that all people, regardless of faith, will spend eternity together in a place of bliss. Much to the contrary, the Bible teaches about a literal Hell prepared for Satan and his followers where there will be endless *weeping and gnashing of teeth* (Matt. 8:12). Heaven is reserved for believers who have trusted in Jesus as their Saviour. Jesus Himself said, *I am the way and the truth and the life. No one comes to the Father except through me* (John 14:6).

Toward a Christian view of death

How does the Christian view of death and the afterlife translate into practical terms for ourselves or our loved ones? Obviously it means death is not the end and not the final enemy to be avoided at all cost. The Christian ready to go home should be given all available means of comfort, but we should not unnecessarily prolong their journey. Life is sacred and we may not kill through euthanasia as we already saw. But neither do we need to unnecessarily prolong life artificially when someone is ready to meet their Maker. We already looked at the value of writing a health-care directive in the last chapter.

Obviously there are many people who fear death because they are unsure of their faith or about the existence of God and the afterlife. Others may have avoided thinking about spiritual things until a health crisis occurs and it finally hits them that they might die. There may be some believers who lack assurance. Here are some steps that may help:

- *Face your fears.* It's okay to think about your ultimate mortality. Denial is worse.

- *Make your peace with God.* If you are unsure, accept Christ as Saviour and follow the steps in Appendix A.

- *Get help.* If you are still not at peace, get help from a trusted pastor, Christian counselor, or friend. Have them help you find Scripture passages on assurance of salvation.

- *Journal the date you settled the issue.* Writing it down in a personal journal will help defeat the lies of Satan who will invariably try to tell you that you are not good enough for God.

- *Make a public testimony.* Tell everyone who visits you of your assurance and readiness to die. Declaring publically what you decide privately is powerful reinforcement and holds you accountable.

- *Daily put on your spiritual armour.* You are still in a battle and require the spiritual armour of Ephesians 6. Pray the prayer in Appendix C.

- *Be a worshiper.* Listen to praise music daily and worship with God's people every chance you get. Have someone wheel you to church in a wheelchair if necessary, but unless it's absolutely impossible, be there.

How to prepare for death

You can make your own death easier on loved ones, and a loved one's death easier on yourself and the rest of the family, by preparing for death with the following steps.

- *Lay a firm spiritual foundation.* Recognise that your thirst will only ever be satisfied by God—not family, not friends, not achievements, not belongings. Make sure you and your loved ones are at peace with God. Do this now! Tomorrow may be too late.

- *Resolve family conflicts.* Unresolved relational conflicts in the family will hinder grief and lead to guilt. Christianity is the only worldview that is truly conciliatory. Jesus was the greatest teacher on reconciliation there ever was. You must ask for and give forgiveness. Even if the other person won't forgive you, you must forgive him or her.

- *Make sure your will and financial matters are in order.* Clearly communicate this with the executor of your will.

- *Write a health-care directive.* This will involve appointing a proxy decision maker.

- *Plan your funeral.* Plan your funeral to be a celebration of a life lived at God's fountain of living water.

GRIEVING YOUR LOSS

We will all face death and the loss of people dear to us, as well as other losses such as the death of pets or friends that move away. Grief is the ability of our soul (will, mind and emotions) to deal with loss. Often an emotional roller coaster, it usually involves denial and disbelief initially, followed by anger and a sense of unfairness, an attempt to bargain with God, depression and hopelessness, and finally acceptance and healing. Frequently there is associated guilt with feelings such as, "If I had only done this, he wouldn't have died." Many people experience anger toward God. Grief is an important part of growing emotionally.

Here are some ways to facilitate your grief or ways to help someone close to you grieve:

- *Face your pain.* For many, denial is the first emotion. Sometimes the loss is not obvious because it has become emotionally suppressed out of your immediate memory. It may be in the remote past.

- *Allow yourself to grieve.* It is okay to grieve, even as a strong believer. The Bible clearly instructs us to *mourn with those who mourn* (Rom. 12:15). Jesus Himself is said to be *a man of sorrows, and acquainted with grief* (Isa. 53:3 KJV).

- *Ventilate your feelings.* Share your emotions, even your anger, with someone you trust or someone who has been there. Let the tears flow.

- *Ventilate your feelings toward God.* God can handle your anger.

- *Forgive.* If you find yourself blaming another person for the loss, forgive them. This may be the hardest, especially if your loved one was murdered or hit by a drunk driver, or you have been sexually violated, but it is crucial.

- *Exercise your Spiritual Life Cycle.* Many people withdraw from God; do the opposite. Allow this trial to draw you closer to Him. Pray, read Scripture, worship with God's people, and listen to music.

- *Attend a Grief Support Group.* If there is no group in your area or church, you might want to encourage your pastor to start one. *GriefShare*[103] is an excellent video-based resource that is easy to implement within a church fellowship.

People who find themselves in dysfunctional families are often prevented from the normal grief process because the three unspoken rules of these families—don't feel, don't trust, don't talk—hinder the acknowledgement of pain and loss. They are either ridiculed or ignored, and emotions become suppressed resulting in chronic anxiety, tension, anger, resentment, guilt, depression and many physical symptoms such as fatigue and chronic pain. If you have not finished your grief of a loss in your earlier years, you may need to go back to the grieving process. This will involve some of the steps shared in Chapter 10.

From the cradle to the grave, life is a journey. I join the writer to the Hebrews in his encouragement to us all.

> *Therefore, since we are surrounded by such a great cloud of witnesses, let us throw off everything that hinders and the sin that so easily entangles, and let us run with perseverance the race marked out for us. Let us fix our eyes on Jesus, the author and perfecter of our faith, who for the joy set before him endured the cross, scorning its shame, and sat down at the right hand of the throne of God. Consider him who endured such opposition from sinful men, so that you will not grow weary and lose heart* (Heb. 12:1-3).

May you keep your eyes on Jesus, this and every day.

Epilogue

Then the angel showed me the river of the water of life, as clear as crystal, flowing from the throne of God and of the Lamb down the middle of the great street of the city. On each side of the river stood the tree of life, bearing twelve crops of fruit, yielding its fruit every month. And the leaves of the tree are for the healing of the nations. No longer will there be any curse (Rev. 22:1-3).

Blessed are those who wash their robes, that they may have the right to the tree of life and may go through the gates into the city. Outside are the dogs, those who practice magic arts, the sexually immoral, the murderers, the idolaters and everyone who loves and practices falsehood (Rev. 22:14,15).

The Spirit and the bride say, "Come!" And let him who hears say, "Come!" Whoever is thirsty, let him come; and whoever wishes, let him take the free gift of the water of life (Rev. 22:17).

When life is lived in the foothills of the *river of the water of life*, our thirst will be forever quenched. While it may seem that we remain parched and dehydrated, we are, in fact, dripping with the abundance of the Father's love and blessing. With such saturation we need not seek after the god of scientism or the New Age hope for self-discovery or reincarnation.

Friends, do not grow weary in waiting for your inheritance. Live life to the fullest at God's fountain regardless of your external circumstances. In Christ there are no good days and bad days—only days of enduring grace. Fulfill your calling as a mighty warrior in God's army, called to advance God's Kingdom, until *the times will have reached their fulfillment—to bring all things in heaven and on earth together under one head, even Christ* (Eph. 2:10).

Burn passionately for the living God. Be happy when you can and joyful the rest of the time.

God bless you.

Appendix A

FINDING PEACE WITH GOD

It is my heart's prayer that you experience peace with God. While God planned for us to have peace and abundant life, most people spend a lifetime searching for it but never find it. The Bible teaches that we are separated from God because of sin or disobedience, causing a chasm between a Holy God and sinful humankind. *For all have sinned and fall short of the glory of God* (Rom. 3:23). *For the wages of sin is death, but the gift of God is eternal life in Christ Jesus our Lord* (Rom. 6:23).

Over the years, humans have tried to bridge that gap through good works, religion, philosophy, or morality. But none of these can span the great divide; they are but human attempts to reach an Almighty God. Others try to find fulfilment and peace in possessions, money, achievements, careers, sports, food, alcohol, drugs, sex, or fun living. These too leave countless individuals empty, as the shipwrecked lives of many celebrities are a testimony to.

> *But your iniquities have separated you from your God; your sins have hidden his face from you, so that he will not hear* (Isa. 59:2).

The Bible teaches that Jesus Christ is the only answer to this problem. Jesus said, "*I am the way and the truth and the life. No one comes to the Father except through me*" (John 14:6). He died on the cross and rose from the grave, paying the penalty for our sin and bridging the gap between God and humankind. In order to allow Him to be the bridge between God and us, we need to trust Christ and receive Him as our Saviour by personal invitation.

> *But God demonstrates his own love for us in this: While we were still sinners, Christ died for us* (Rom. 5:8).

> *That if you confess with your mouth, "Jesus is Lord," and believe in your heart that God raised him from the dead, you will be saved* (Rom. 10:9).

Is there any reason why you cannot receive Jesus Christ right now if you haven't already done so? Admit that you are a sinner and need forgiveness. Be willing to turn from your sins. Believe that Jesus Christ died for you on the cross and rose from the grave. Through prayer, invite Jesus Christ to come in and be your personal Saviour and friend.

> *Dear Lord Jesus,*
>
> *I know that I am a sinner and need your forgiveness. I believe that you died for my sins. I want to turn from my sins. I now invite you to come into my heart and life. I want to trust you as Savior and follow you as Lord, in the fellowship of your Church. Amen.*

The Bible says in John 1:12, *Yet to all who received him, to those who believed in his name, he gave the right to become children of God.* As children, we are also heirs, heirs of abundant life everlasting.

As a new believer, it is important that you deepen your relationship with God by reading God's Word, praying, and worshiping with other believers in a Bible-believing church. As Christ's representative in a needy world, demonstrate your new life by your love and concern for others.

God bless you as you start your new life.

	Spiritual	**Natural**
Biblical ethics	Spiritual gift of healing	Insulin
Non-biblical ethics	Former life therapy	Abortion

Figure B.1

Appendix B

ASSESSING HEALING ARTS

It is theoretically possible to place any healing art or act in one of four quadrants as in the illustration on the left. In the two quadrants on the right are those healing acts or arts that are scientifically plausible and verifiable. On the left are those in the extra-dimensional realm, for which no scientific explanation exists. In the upper two quadrants are those healing acts that adhere to biblical ethics, while those in the bottom two quadrants do not. By this, we point to whether the practice is supported or prohibited scripturally. For example, both sorcery and divination (clairvoyance) are prohibited and fall in the left lower quadrant of our grid.

Placing any given healing in one of these quadrants is obviously subjective and will be determined to a great extent by a person's worldview. Also, new scientific information may be forthcoming which may move a treatment from the left quadrants (spiritual) into the right (natural). To illustrate, we will use four examples with which most people with a Christian worldview will agree.

In the right upper corner we might place the alleviation of suffering of a diabetic through the use of insulin. In the right lower quadrant is the use of scientific medicine to terminate a pregnancy. In the left lower quadrant is a medical intuitive doing former life therapy. Finally, in the left upper quadrant is the spiritual gift of healing administered through the laying on of hands and anointing with oil.

As Christians, we need to choose healing arts and acts that are clearly in the upper half of our illustration, beginning in the left upper quadrant and avoiding those in the lower half. It is also paramount that the Church recovers its role in healing in both upper quadrants—spiritual healing and the use of science to alleviate suffering. The Church needs to educate people about the spiritual dangers of all healing arts in the lower half of our diagram, both those within scientific medicine and those in the spiritual realm.

To help readers choose their healers wisely, the following table was prepared using the four quadrants as a guide, and the references as listed in the endnotes.[104] [105] The *Reader's Digest Encyclopedia of Healing Therapies* is quite detailed, has a good scientific critique of each therapy, and will allow you to evaluate any other healing art not listed below. The Internet Web page hosted by Dr. Stephen Barett, www.quackwatch.com, is a good resource for a scientific evaluation of healing methods, but he holds a naturalistic worldview that would deny the power of Christian prayer. The following table is also posted and will be updated on our own Web page at www.wholenessfc.com.

Healing Art	Founder	Religion or Worldview	Diagnostic Validation	Therapeutic Validation	Medical Dangers	Spiritual Dangers	Use it?
Acupuncture	China, 3000 BC	Eastern/Taoism	n/a	Works by releasing endorphins.	Safe, rare infection. Often used by physiotherapists.	Classical acupuncture based on Taoism and pantheism. Meridians and qi not proven. Avoid acupuncture by a practitioner of TCM.	Use safer alternative.
Applied kinesiology (not to be confused w kinesiology)	George Goodheart, chiropractor	Vitalism, "energy based"	No	n/a	Misdiagnosis	Energy medicine	No
Aromatherapy (aromatic oils, essential oils)	Modern use: René-Maurice Gattefosse, France	Ancient Middle Eastern, including Bible (Ex. 30:22-25) anointing oil also used for healing	n/a	—	Some smells may aggravate asthma or allergies.	Some practitioners may have pantheistic view of inherent energies in plants, or mix other CAM therapies.	Yes, watch for mixers.

Healing Art	Founder	Religion or Worldview	Diagnostic Validation	Therapeutic Validation	Medical Dangers	Spiritual Dangers	Use it?
Ayurveda	India, 2500 BC	Hinduism, pantheism	Exam for imbalance of *doshas* not validated.	—	Misdiagnosis	Controlling *prana* is energy medicine. System of healing is based on Hinduism.	No
Biofeedback		Science, 1940's	n/a	—	No	Some therapists using biofeedback may rely on meditation practices of the East, or guided imagery.	Yes, but watch for mixers.
Chelation (EDTA treatment)	US Navy, 1940's	Science	n/a	Proven treatment for heavy metal poisoning but not for heart disease.	New lower dose EDTA treatment is no more toxic than placebo. Effective scientifically based treatment is available for blocked arteries.	No	No

Healing Art	Founder	Religion or Worldview	Diagnostic Validation	Therapeutic Validation	Medical Dangers	Spiritual Dangers	Use it?
Chiropractic	D.D. Palmer	Most of modern chiropractic is scientifically based.	— / n/a	—	Modern chiropractic treatment is gentler with minimal risk of injury.	Some chiropractors are "mixers" and integrate other spiritually harmful treatments.	Yes, watch for mixers.
Colonic therapy	Egypt, China, India	Hinduism (part of Ayurveda), TCM (Trad. Chinese Med.)	n/a	No. Toxins said to be removed not validated.	Infection	Pantheistic roots. Is sometimes combined with other CAM therapies.	No
Craniosacral therapy	John Upledger, osteopath	n/a	No	No	No	No	No
Herbalism	Ancient	Multiple cultures & religions	n/a	Some herbs are being studied with double blind studies.	Some herbs are toxic or addictive.	Some herbalists are pantheistic. Some integrate psychic healing. Watch for "mixers."	Depends on the herb.

Healing Art	Founder	Religion or Worldview	Diagnostic Validation	Therapeutic Validation	Medical Dangers	Spiritual Dangers	Use it?
Homeopathy	Samual Hahnemann	Vitalism, "energy based"	n/a	No scientific explanation for its effects but WHO considers it valid.	Medicines are so dilute they are safe.	"Potentization" is energy based medicine.	No
Hydrotherapy	Ancient Greece	Multiple cultures and religions	n/a	Sitz baths, cool mist steam, warm soaks used by MD's. Pool therapy by physio's.	No	Some spas may integrate other spiritually harmful therapies. Some natural springs thought to have latent healing power.	Yes, watch for mixers.
Hypnotherapy	Franz Mesmer	Ancient Egypt, Greece, Africa. Mesmer believed in vitalism.	Some medical intuitives do a reading while in a trance.	Moderate success with addictions, particularly food or cigarettes.	None	Opening the mind to external control, possibly to the demonic realm.	No, rely on the Holy Spirit.
Iridology	Ignatz von Peczely	Ancient Mesopotamia	No. Disproven in a 1988 study.	n/a	Misdiagnosis	Akin to palm reading.	No

Healing Art	Founder	Religion or Worldview	Diagnostic Validation	Therapeutic Validation	Medical Dangers	Spiritual Dangers	Use it?
Magnetic Therapy (electromagnetic fields) EMF	Franz Mesmer	Strong EMFs based on science.	n/a	Strong EMFs proven to heal fractures but not the weak EMFs of magnets.	None	No	Strong EMFs to heal fractures.
Massage	Ancient cultures	Modern massage based on anatomy and science.	n/a	—	No	No, but some practitioners and spas may mix other spiritually dangerous therapies.	Yes
Naturopathy	John Scheel, Claude Bernard, Benedict Lust	Naturopathy is several healing arts: Nutrition Herbalism Homeopathy TCM Hydrotherapy Manipulation.	Diagnostic validation is limited.	Several components are valid.	As per individual arts.	Those of homeopathy which is based on vitalism, and TCM based on Taoism. Naturopaths are "mixers" by definition.	Some

Healing Art	Founder	Religion or Worldview	Diagnostic Validation	Therapeutic Validation	Medical Dangers	Spiritual Dangers	Use it?
Osteopathy	Andrew Taylor	Modern osteopathy based on science	Many osteopaths use similar methods to diagnose as MDs.	—	Small risk of injury from manipulation.	None, unless the practitioner is a mixer.	Yes
Qigong		TCM	n/a	No	No	Based on TCM, qi and meridians, therefore energy based.	No
Reflexology	William Fitzgerald, Eunice Ingham	Eastern (China), Egypt Vitalism, energy based	n/a	No, although foot massage is relaxing.	No	Energy based	No
Reiki	Mikao Usui	Tibetan Buddhism, Vitalism	No	No	No	Uses "channeling." Energy based. Sometimes used for "absent healing."	No
Shiatsu		Japanese, but origins in TCM	No	Similar to acupuncture	No	Based on TCM and Taoism, therefore energy based.	No

Healing Art	Founder	Religion or Worldview	Diagnostic Validation	Therapeutic Validation	Medical Dangers	Spiritual Dangers	Use it?
T'ai Chi		Taoism	n/a	The exercises themselves are healthy.	No	Based on Taoism	No, use safe alternative.
Therapeutic touch	Deloris Krieger	Vitalism	No. Uses "centering" for intuitive diagnosis	No	No	Energy based.	No
Visualization (Guided imagery)		Multiple cultures and religions	n/a	Athletes frequently visualize their victory.	No	Often used in New Age Medicine to contact the spirit world.	No. Meditate on God's Word.
Yoga		India, Hinduism	n/a	The exercises themselves are healthy	No	Based on Hinduism.	No, use safe alternative.

Appendix C

These prayers are for your personal use. They may be photocopied so that you can put them in your prayer journal, or you can print them from our web page at www.wholenessfc.com.

PRAYER FOR PERSONAL HEALING

My loving Father, I thank You that You are the Great Physician. You say in Your Word, *I am the LORD that healeth thee,* and that Jesus *was pierced for our transgressions* and *crushed for our iniquities* and that *the punishment that brought us peace was upon him* and that *by his wounds we are healed.*

I praise You that it is Your desire that all be made whole. I thank You that You are so personal, so loving and that You care about all my needs. You desire to heal me spiritually, emotionally, as well as physically. I praise You for Your mighty power. I thank You that You are sovereign, all-knowing, and present here with me through Your Holy Spirit.

Father, I thank You that all my needs are met through faith in Jesus Christ. I accept Your provision for my wholeness through faith in Him. I repent of my sins and accept Christ as my Saviour. Jesus, You are the source of Living Water provided through Your death and resurrection. I repent and ask Your forgiveness for the times I turn to other sources for water, for digging my own wells. I thank you that when I drink deeply from Your well of Living Water, I will not hunger or thirst but will be satisfied with true wholeness. Teach me, O LORD, to drink only from Your well.

God, I thank You for the outpoured Holy Spirit who fills my inner being with Your Life. I hold up my cup to be filled with more of Your Spirit. Holy Spirit, come and fill me. Pour out Your power in my inner being so that I will be transformed from the inside out into the likeness of Jesus. Renew my mind and fill it with positive thoughts. Bring to mind any sins that require confession or relationships that require reconciliation. Transform my emotions with the growth of Your fruit—love, joy, peace, patience, kindness, goodness, gentleness, and self-control. Empower my will to be obedient to Your leading. And may Your power flow through my body for strength, energy, acts of worship, acts of service, and healing. I give You my body as a living sacrifice. Help me to use the gifts of the Spirit with which You empower me.

I now thank You that greater are You in me than Satan and all his demons in the world. They are defeated foes, and I break any power or curse that the enemy has over my life or my body in the mighty name of

Jesus. I dispel the lies he has implanted in my mind
and replace them with Your truth. I put on the armour
to ward off any fiery darts of the enemy.

Lord, I pray for wholeness in my relationships. I
forgive_____ for the pain he/she caused me. I
release him/her and pray Your richest blessing on
his/her life. Forgive me for the unforgiveness I have
harboured against him/her.

Now God, thank You for this time of prayer and
may Your peace flood my soul with the joy of the
Lord. In the mighty name of Jesus. Amen.

RELAXATION & MEDITATION PRAYER

(For this prayer, find a quiet comfortable place where you
can relax and experience complete solitude—allow the Holy
Spirit to speak to you).

My loving Father in Heaven, I thank You that in
the stillness of this hour, I can relax in Your presence
and meditate on Your Word and love for me. I recognize that the only way I can come into Your presence
is through Jesus, and I now place my trust and faith in
Him. Jesus, thank You for dying for me and taking my
guilt upon Yourself so that I can come into the Father's
presence, washed as white as snow. For,

> *Though (my) sins are like scarlet,*
> *they shall be as white as snow;*
> *though they are red as crimson,*
> *they shall be like wool.*

I long for Your presence passionately, Lord. I thirst
for You and for Your Living Water to refresh my
parched lips.

As the deer pants for streams of water,
so my soul pants for you, O God.
My soul thirsts for God, for the living God.
When can I go and meet with God?

Jesus, thank You that You at that source of Living Water, because You said, *Whoever drinks the water* (You) *give ... will never thirst* (but that it would) *become in him a spring of water welling up to eternal life.* I hold up my glass, Jesus, for you to fill to overflowing, and I drink deeply from it, taking it deep into my inner being.

I now still myself in Your Presence, Lord, for Your Word says, *Be still, and know that I am God.* Still my mind—may it be full of Your thoughts. Still my body—relax my tensions, ease my pains. I give You my *body as a living sacrifice, holy and acceptable to You, as my spiritual act of worship.* Holy Spirit, come now and fill me, flow out through me and I yield my body as a willing vessel to be an instrument of righteousness.

Lord, my hope is in You, and I will find refuge and shelter in You from the harsh world around me, because,

> *He who dwells in the shelter of the Most High*
> *will rest in the shadow of the Almighty.*
> *I will say of the LORD, "He is my refuge and my fortress,*
> *my God, in whom I trust."*

God, *keep me as the apple of your eye; hide me in the shadow of your wings,* just as a chick under her mother's wing. Cover me with Your feathers and protect me from the storms around me.

Lord, I now meditate on Your Word, for it *is a lamp to my feet and a light for my path.* It is truth that will never let me down, and that I can count on. I dispel the lies of Satan with *the sword of the Spirit, which is the word of God.* Lord, fill me with Your truth now; may I *be transformed by the renewing of* (my) *mind.*

Lord, I now look to You for strength because *even youths grow tired and weary, and young men stumble and fall.* So I place my hope in You for

> *Those who hope in the LORD*
> *will renew their strength.*
> *They will soar on wings like eagles;*
> *they will run and not grow weary,*
> *they will walk and not be faint.*

God, I now bask in Your presence and I thank You for Your love and peace. I thank You for the beauty of Your creation and the joy of serving You. You are an awesome God. I worship You. Amen.

WARFARE PRAYER

(As you put on each piece of spiritual armour, use your arms and picture in your mind the act of putting them on).

Lord, You tell us that our *struggle is not against flesh and blood, but against the rulers, against the authorities, against the powers of this dark world and against the spiritual forces of evil in the heavenly realms.* Therefore, in this time of prayer, *I put on the full armor of God,* so that I *may be able to stand* my *ground* against the dark spiritual realm that opposes You and Your followers in every way. I pray for Your protection in this time of prayer.

I put on the *belt of truth*—Jesus, You *are the way and the truth and the life.* I put on the *breastplate of righteousness*—Jesus, You made me righteous by taking my guilt upon Yourself. I put the shoes of the *gospel of peace* on my feet—may I carry the Good News wherever I go. I hold up the *shield of faith* to *extinguish all the flaming arrows of the evil one.* I put on my *helmet of salvation* and wield the *sword of the Spirit, which is the Word of God.*

(Confess any area of sin that may have given Satan a foothold in your life or your family line.)

And now, I take my stand against Satan and his followers. Satan, I command you, in the name of the Lord Jesus Christ, to leave my presence with all your demons, and I bring the blood of the Lord Jesus Christ between us. You are a defeated foe and you have no legal right in my life because I am Christ's. I break any curse against me and my family, and I break any curse that my parents, grandparents or great-grandparents have brought into my family tree.

Lord God, I thank You that *though we live in the world, we do not wage war as the world does and that the weapons we fight with are not the weapons of the world.* Rather, You empower us with *divine power to demolish strongholds.* I therefore exert that authority to *demolish arguments and every pretension that sets itself up against the knowledge of God, and* I *take captive every thought to make it obedient to Christ.*

Lord Jesus, I thank You that You *disarmed* the demonic realm and *made a public spectacle of them, triumphing over them by the cross.* I stand in that victory as my life is hid in Yours by my faith. In Jesus' name. Amen.

PRAYER FOR THE CHURCH
TO BE HEALING FOR THE NATIONS

Lord, I thank You that You have chosen the Church, the Body of Christ, to be the agent through which You wish to advance Your Kingdom on earth. Lord Jesus, You are our Commander-in-Chief, and I pledge You my allegiance and promise to obey Your marching orders.

Jesus, You have told us to make disciples of all nations. I pledge my support to that cause, both near and far. I pray Your blessing and empowerment on all those who labor in Your vineyard where the harvest is ripe.

God, You have said I am a co-labourer with You, an agent of reconciliation and an ambassador for Christ. Help me, oh God, to fulfil Your calling on my life. Help me to use my gifts mightily in Your Kingdom service. Let me *throw off everything that hinders and the sin that so easily entangles,* and let me *run with perseverance the race marked out for me.*

And Lord, may Your Church be the agent of healing to a hurting and broken world. Jesus, You sent Your followers to preach and to heal. May we do likewise. May my church, and the churches in my community and around the globe, be safe communities where the wounded can experience Your healing and Your wholeness. May we seek to actively set the captives free. May we lead the way in caring for the hurting—the young and the elderly, for as You say, *religion that* (You) *accept as pure and faultless is this: to look after orphans and widows in their distress.*

Pour out Your Spirit upon Your Church, oh Lord. In this final hour we need more than ever to be a holy people, set apart for You. Keep us from watered-down Christianity or intermingling with false religions. May we discern the enemy's tactic to infiltrate the Church with New Age thinking and the false hope of salvation through science, particularly in the area of health and healing. Help us to stand against any healing method or theory that is contrary to Your Word.

I pray this in the name of Jesus. Amen.

Appendix D

ACCOUNTABILITY QUESTIONS FOR MEN

The following are sample questions for men who meet together regularly in order maintain mutual accountability in the areas of family, spiritual disciplines, sexuality, finances, abuse of power, and calling.[106]

1. Have you been with a woman this week in such as way that was inappropriate or could have looked to others that you were using poor judgement?

2. Have you been completely above reproach in all your financial dealings this week?

3. Have you exposed yourself to any explicit material this week?

4. Have you spent time daily in prayer and in the Scriptures this week?

5. Have you fulfilled the mandate of your calling this week?

6. Are you misusing your power?

7. Have you taken time off to be with your family this week?

8. Have you just lied to me?

Endnotes

[1] John Fuller, *Fever! The Hunt for the New Killer Virus* (Grand Rapids: Zondervan Publishing House, 1974), p. 1.

[2] Frank Press, *Science and Creationism: A View from the National Academy of Sciences* (Washington: National Academy Press, 1984).

[3] Randolph Nesse and George Williams, *Why We Get Sick* (New York: Vintage Books, 1994), p. 236.

[4] Leonard Hayflick, *How and Why We Age* (New York: Ballantine Books, 1994), p. 229.

[5] Michael Lemonick, "Edwin Hubble," *Time* Magazine, 29 March 1999, p. 90.

[6] James Trefil, *The Dark Side of the Universe* (New York: Macmillan Publishing Co., 1988), p. 52.

[7] Trefil, p. 41.

[8] Trefil, p. 42.

[9] The Apostle Paul confirms this biblical view of man when he says, *May your whole spirit, soul and body be kept blameless at the coming of our Lord Jesus Christ* (1 Thess. 5:23).

[10] Hugh Ross, *Beyond the Cosmos* (Colorado Springs: NavPress, 1996), p. 196.

[11] Ross, p. 196.

[12] Paul Kurtz, *Humanist Manifesto 2000* (Amherst, N.Y.: Prometheus Books, 1999), p. 26.

[13] Hugh Ross, *The Fingerprint of God* (Orange, CA: Promise Publishing Co., 1991), p. 124.

[14] Trefil, p. 55.

[15] Ross, *The Fingerprint of God,* pp. 121-127. Some of these are the gravitational coupling constant, the strong nuclear force coupling constant, the weak nuclear force coupling constant, the electromagnetic coupling constant, the ratio of protons to electrons, the expansion rate of the universe, the age of the universe, the entropy level of the universe, and the velocity of light.

[16] Ross, p. 138.

[17] George Otis Jr., *The Twilight Labyrinth* (Grand Rapids: Baker Book House Co., 1997), p. 12.

[18] George Otis Jr., *Transformations* Video (Global Net Productions, 1999).

[19] Michael Lemonick, "Are the Bible's Stories True?" *Time* Magazine, 18 December 1995, pp. 43, 44.

[20] Lemonick, *Time,* p. 44.

[21] Lemonick, *Time,* p. 43.

[22] Donald Bierle, *Surprised by Faith* (Lynwood, WA: Emerald Books, 1992), p. 40.

[23] Bierle, p. 40.

[24] Nicky Gumbel, *Questions of Life* (Colorado Springs: David C. Cook Publishing Co., 1993), p. 25.

[25] Gumbel, p. 26.

[26] C.S. Lewis, *Mere Christianity* (London: Fount, 1952), p. 42.

[27] Nicky Cruz, *The Magnificent Three* (Old Tappan, NJ: Fleming H. Revell Co., 1976), from the cover jacket.

[28] Ross, *Beyond the Cosmos,* Chapter 3: Science breaks through to new realms.

[29] Barbara Powell, *Good Relationships are Good Medicine* (1987).

[30] John Bevere, *The Bait of Satan* (Lake Mary: Creation House, 1994), back cover. This book is an excellent resource for dealing with a spirit of offence.

[31] Nicky Gumbel, *Searching Issues* (Colorado Springs: David C. Cook Publishing Co., 1994), pp. 90, 91.

[32] Charles Colson & Nancy Pearcey, *How Now Shall We Live?* (Wheaton: Tyndale House Publishers, Inc., 1999), p. 248.

[33] Stephen Hawking, *A Brief History in Time* (New York: Bantam Books, 1988).

[34] Colson, p. 249.

[35] C. Norman Shealy, *Miracles do Happen* (Rockport, MA: Element Books, Inc., 1995), p. 33.

[36] Shealy, p. 34.

[37] Shealy, p. 35.

[38] Caroline Myss & C. Norman Shealy, *The Creation of Health* (New York: Three Rivers Press, 1988).

[39] Larry Dossey, *Reinventing Medicine* (San Francisco: HarperCollins, 1999), p. 119.

[40] Shealy, p. 30.

[41] Dossey, p. 10.

[42] Myss & Shealy, p. 88.

[43] Dossey, p. 11.

[44] John Ankerberg and John Weldon, *Can You Trust Your Doctor?* (Brentwood: Wolgemuth & Hyatt, Publishers, Inc., 1991), p. 243.

[45] Uma Silbey, *The Complete Crystal Guidebook* (New York: Bantam, 1987), p. 1.

[46] Machaelle Small Wright, *The Perelandra Garden Workbook: A Complete Guide to Gardening with Nature Intelligences* (U.K.: Perelandra Ltd., 1987).

[47] Ankerberg & Weldon, p. 257.

[48] Andrew Weil, *Health and Healing* (Boston: Houghton Mifflin Co., 1983), p. 37.

[49] Charles Colson and Nancy Pearcey, *How Now Shall We Live?* (Wheaton: Tyndale House Publishers, Inc., 1999), p. xiv.

[50] Elliott Dacher, *Psychoneuroimmunology: The new mind/body healing program* (New York: Paragon House, 1991), p. 20.

[51] Larry Crabb, *Connecting* (Nashville: Word Publishing, 1997), pp. xi, xii.

[52] Leo Galland, *The Four Pillars of Healing* (New York: Random House, 1997), p. 87.

[53] Galland, p. 88.

[54] Crabb, p. xii.

[55] Harold Koenig, *The Healing Power of Faith* (New York: Simon & Schuster, 1999), p. 296.

[56] Many churches have a long way to go in mobilizing lay people to visit the sick at home and shut-in's in nursing homes. Another way churches can provide compassionate care for the elderly and ill is through a concept known as Parish Nursing. Here a nurse works as part of the pastoral staff offering nursing care, counselling, prayer, and teaching.

[57] George Otis Jr., *Transformations* (Global Net Productions, 1999).

[58] Michael Lemonick, "Doctors' Deadly Mistakes," *Time* Magazine, 13 December 1999, p. 40.

[59] Joel Wallach & Ma Lan, *Dead Doctors Don't Lie* (Franklin: Legacy Communications Group, 1999).

[60] Lynne McTaggart, *What Doctors Don't Tell You* (New York: Avon Books, Inc., 1996).

[61] Nesamoni Lysander, *First Choice for the Next Millennium* (Belleville: Essence Publishing, 1998), p. 316.

[62] Marilyn Ferguson, *The Aquarian Conspiracy*, p. 257.

[63] Charles Hobbs, *The New Time Power* (Salt Lake City: The Charles R. Hobbs Corp., 1991).

[64] Stephen Covey, *The 7 Habits of Highly Effective People* (New York: Simon & Schuster, 1989), p. 109.

[65] Statistics Canada: Clark, "Religious Observance, Marriage and Family," op. cit., pp. 2-4; *The Daily*, 15 September, 1998, pp. 1-3.

[66] Colson & Pearcey, p. 312.

[67] Colson & Pearcey, p. 129.

[68] Neil Anderson, *Victory over the Darkness* (Ventura: Regal Books, 1990), p. 10.

[69] Anderson, p. 21.

[70] *National Geographic,* Oct. 1999, p. 5.

[71] Nicky Gumbel, *Questions of Life,* p. 163.

[72] Brad Long, *The Dunamis Project* (Presbyterian & Reformed Renewal Ministries International, 1991).

[73] Watchman Nee, *The Spiritual Man* (New York: Christian Fellowship Publishers, Inc., 1968), Vol. III, p. 142.

[74] Nee, p. 143.

[75] *Time* Magazine, Sept. 6, 1999.

[76] Kenneth Cooper, *Faith-based Fitness* (Nashville: Thomas Nelson Publishers, 1995), p. 15.

[77] *Time* Magazine, 8 November 1999, p. 54.

[78] See our Web page **www.wholenessfc.com** for links to Canada's Food Guide.

[79] If you have strong risk factors for heart disease or stroke, such as high blood pressure, high cholesterol, or a strong family history, you should be on a fat-reduced diet which restricts fat to between 20 and 30 percent of your total calories, and include fish oils. Equally important is to maintain an ideal body weight and to exercise regularly. You can download a lipid-lowering diet from our Web page at **www.wholenessfc.com**.

[80] Postmenopausal women may want to consider a diet high in phytoestrogens in order to help menopausal symptoms, as well as increased calcium to protect against osteoporosis.

[81] Kenneth Copper, *Antioxidant Revolution* (Nashville: Thomas Nelson Inc., 1994).

[82] Khursheed Jeejeebhoy, "Supplements: Fact and Fiction," *The Medical Post,* 13 February 2001, p. 15.

[83] Colson & Pearcey, p. 238.

[84] Colson & Pearcey, p. 239.

[85] *Focus on the Family Newsletter,* January 2000, p. 1.

[86] *Time* Magazine, 8 November 1999, p. 66.

[87] Ed Smith, *Beyond Tolerable Recovery* (Campbellsville: Family Care Publishing, 1996), p. 31.

[88] Smith, p. 24.

[89] Smith, p. 25.

[90] Lucinda Bassett, *From Panic to Power* (New York: HarperCollins, 1995), pp. xiii - xix.

[91] Smith, p. 48.

[92] Kay Arthurs, *Lord, Heal my Hurts* (Oregon: Multinomah Books, 1989).

[93] Barbara Powell, *Good Relationships are Good Medicine* (1987), p. 6.

[94] John Bevere, *The Bait of Satan* (Orlando: Creation House, 1994).

[95] An excellent resource here is John Bevere, *The Devil's Door* (Orlando: Creation House, 1996).

[96] James MacDonald, *I Really Want to Change... So, Help Me God* (Chicago: Moody Press, 2000).

[97] Joseph Ilardo, *As Parents Age: A psychological and practical guide* (Acton: VanderWyk & Burnham, 1998).

[98] Ilardo, p. 17.

[99] Charles Stanley, *The Blessings of Brokenness* (Grand Rapids: Zondervan, 1997), p. 14.

[100] John Bevere, *Victory in the Wilderness* (Apopka: Messenger Press, 1992).

[101] Larry Crabb, *Inside Out* (Colorado Springs: NavPress, 1988), p. 87.

[102] Larry Keefauver, *When God Doesn't Heal Now* (Nashville: Thomas Nelson Publishers, 2000).

[103] For information on how go get GriefShare, check our Web page at **www.wholenessfc.com**

[104] Anne Woodham & David Peters, *Reader's Digest Encyclopedia of Healing Therapies* (Montreal: Reader's Digest Assoc., 1988).

[105] Isadore Rosenfeld, *Dr. Rosenfeld's Guide to Alternative Medicine* (New York: Ballantine Books, 1996).

[106] I am indebted to Chuck Swindoll for these sample questions. John Maxwell has published similar questions.

For additional resources,
or to order more copies of this book:

E-mail: info@wholenessfc.com
Phone: (902) 658-2000
Fax: (902) 658-2594

For • *additional health information* • *suggested reading lists*
and • *links to reliable health Web sites*, visit our Web page at:

www.wholenessfc.com

We would also love to hear your **stories of miraculous healing**.
If you have a medically confirmed miracle to share and consent to having it published on our Web page or in a future
book, please e-mail, fax or mail to:

Wholeness Family Clinic
P.O. Box 90
Crapaud, PEI
C0A 1J0 Canada

• Please indicate if you would like us to use your real name or
a pseudonym (pen name).